No Victory, No Peace

No Victory, No Peace

ANGELO M. CODEVILLA

THE CLAREMONT INSTITUTE
FOR THE STUDY OF STATESMANSHIP AND POLITICAL PHILOSOPHY

ROWMAN & LITTLEFIELD PUBLISHERS, INC.
Lanham • Boulder • New York • Toronto • Oxford

ROWMAN & LITTLEFIELD PUBLISHERS, INC.

Published in the United States of America
by Rowman & Littlefield Publishers, Inc.
A wholly owned subsidiary of The Rowman & Littlefield Publishing Group, Inc.
4501 Forbes Boulevard, Suite 200, Lanham, Maryland 20706
www.rowmanlittlefield.com

PO Box 317
Oxford
OX2 9RU, UK

British Library Cataloguing in Publication Information Available
Library of Congress Cataloging-in-Publication Data

Codevilla, Angelo, 1943–
    No victory, no peace / Angelo M. Codevilla.
        p. cm.
    Includes index.
    ISBN 0-7425-5002-8 (hardcover : alk. paper) -- ISBN 0-7425-5003-6 (pbk. : alk.
paper)
        1. War on Terrorism, 2001– 2. Terrorism—Government policy—United States.
3. Iraq War, 2003. 4. United States—Foreign relations—2001– 5. United States—
Military policy. I. Title.

E902.C64 2005
973.931—dc22   2005011512

Printed in the United States of America
⊖™ The paper used in this publication meets the minimum requirements of American
National Standard for Information Sciences—Permanence of Paper for Printed Library
Materials, ANSI/NISO Z39.48-1992.

Table of Contents

Author's Preface

"What is to be our war?" Archidamus, King of Sparta

This book is a collection of my essays on the war that burst upon America on September 11, 2001. Written primarily for the *Claremont Review of Books*, they are a critical history of the United States government's handling of the War on Terror, as well as explanations of important aspects of warfare, particularly strategic intelligence. The book ends with my own views of how the War on Terror could produce the peace that America wants, as well as an assessment of the war's most important result—its effect on America.

I began these essays in the fall of 2001 because it seemed to me that the George W. Bush team's failure to formulate a plan for victory was contrary to the principles of warfare. Its collective mind was muddled. After the murder of some 3,000 Americans, it would surely do something. But what? Against whom? To what end? All too soon it was clear that the team had no idea, or too many ideas, and that the result would be incompetence.

Intentionally, this book is being published *after* the American election of 2004. Nominally, the War on Terror was the election's primary issue. In fact, while both candidates vied to project strength, neither the Democrat John Kerry nor the Republican George W. Bush specified a plan to end the terrorism that had bloodied Americans since the 1970s. Necessarily, my critique focused on the one who had been responsible for what the government did and did not do. If this book had been published before November 2004, readers might have misunderstood it as a partisan indictment of President Bush. But no. Competence and incompetence are nonpartisan.

In 2004 the Democrats, backed by the media and reflecting the views of the Central Intelligence Agency, the State Department, much of academe, as well as the sometime views of George W. Bush, argued that America's War on Terror should consist of killing terrorists and destroying al-Qaeda. This is nonsense. Those who pull triggers and carry bombs often die in the act. And killing those who have acted and survived does not necessarily diminish the supply of people who might act in the future. Moreover, to think that a war can be won simply by killing enemy soldiers is intellectually bankrupt. The notion that eliminating al-Qaeda will end terrorism presupposes that terrorism begins and ends with one private organization. Even those who say this do not believe it.

But George W. Bush, backed by Norman Podhoretz and many bright, sincere publicists, believes that the way to eliminate terrorism is to transform the Middle East from a place of tyranny, exploitation, unproductiveness, ignorance and fanaticism into one of liberal democracy, equal rights for women, and capitalist economics. No doubt. The administration's problem however is the same as that of the proverbial mice who decided to deal with the stealthy house cat by putting a bell around its neck. They could not answer the question: "Who will bell the cat?"

How, indeed, does one government transform the alien culture of a whole region on the other side of the globe? Destroying enemy governments is easy. Destroying enemy regimes is hard, but quite doable. Building viable new governments in foreign lands is extraordinarily difficult, and building wholly new regimes near impossible. Native regimes may change cultures over generations, but the notion that foreigners who cannot even speak the language can do it in a few years is a pipe dream. Is anything sillier than the notion that American secularists can convince Muslims about what true Islam commands? Armed forces can do a few things well, others barely, and some not at all.

In short, neither before nor since September 11 have either the Democrats or the Republicans discussed realistically what the U.S. armed forces can and cannot do to rid America of terrorism from the Middle East. This book is intended to be useful regardless of who leads the U.S. government.

From the beginning I asked: Why the collective incompetence? What is the proper way to make America safe from acts such as those of September 11? As a professor of international affairs, I addressed these questions while explaining some of the principles of warfare, the keys to victory, and hence to peace.

These essays, while written in response to particular events, were meant to be read as well years after the events they described. Every chapter is labeled with the date it was published.[1] The reader is to judge the worth of the principles and of how I apply them, in part by measuring them—as well as the thoughts of the Bush team and of its other critics—against events.

By the summer of 2004, having fought terrorism with blood and treasure abroad for nearly three years, and having changed for the worse how Americans live at home, the U.S. government found that enemies were becoming more numerous. More Third World recruits were willing to take up arms against an America which they were bloodying and whose best punches they could survive. In Pakistan, Iraq, and Saudi Arabia they were "demonstratively" beheading Americans, and the U.S. government could do nothing to stop them. At the same time, America had become the object of hate and contempt among perhaps the majority of human beings on the globe. Neutrals were becoming opponents, and friends were tending toward neutrality. Spain and the Philippines, which had once contributed troops to the U.S. effort, were seeking separate deals with the terrorists. Such things happen to losers of wars, not to winners. In war, the only alternative to an A is an F. There was no doubt that the war had been conducted incompetently.

I observed that the Bush team's incompetence was due to its habit of pursuing mutually incompatible courses of action based on mutually contradictory premises. Its very highly credentialed principals seemed to be strangers to the dictionary meaning of the word "strategy"—the art of tailoring the means at hand to produce the ends desired, and conversely, to choose ends within the grasp of one's means.

Intellectually, the members of the Bush team were far from being starry-eyed progressives. Few shared the early to mid-twentieth century view of "the community of nations" as a source of legitimacy, or believed in collective security. They saw themselves as hard-nosed patriots ready to do whatever was necessary to secure America. This

---

1. *The exhange at the end of Chapter II has been edited for brevity, and slightly different versions of Appendices A and B appeared in the* American Spectator. *Only part of Chapter VIII was published in the* Claremont Review of Books.

was both their strength and their weakness, because it justified in their minds the president's penchant to advocate incompatible courses of action. That is why the team ended up often following the progressive doctrines embedded in the old bureaucracies of the CIA and the Department of State while at the same time pursuing nationalist ends and using words that provoked those bureaucracies and their constituencies into bitter opposition.

Sincerely ready to "change everything" for the sake of ridding America of terror, in fact the Bush team tried daily to change long-standing U.S. foreign policy as little as possible. Perhaps most important, eager as they were to fight terror, many, including President Bush, believed that terrorism had become a permanent part of the modern world. This war, in other words, could not aim at an end. Properly speaking, then, it was not a war at all—just as John Kerry his opponent said. Never mind that President Bush maintained adamantly that it was a war, that "this war will not be endless," and that he was apparently comfortable with the contradiction.

Contradiction and incompetence are two words for the same phenomenon. Nevertheless, the Bush team's incompetence was tempered by its members' commitment to America's national interest. Stumble and err as it did, the Bush team had nothing against doing the right things. It was not incorrigible in principle. Waiting in the wings of American politics, however, was an incorrigible incompetence based very much on principle.

The Democratic Party and its allies in the media, academe, and the State/CIA bureaucracies did not suffer from the kind of confusion that afflicted the Bush team. This is not the place for a full discussion of the modern Democratic Party's view of America's role in the world. Suffice it to note that it is dominated by a peculiar version of progressivism, forged from the communist-influenced Wallaceite movement of the 1940s, by Senator J. W. Fulbright in the 1950s and the works of William Appleman Williams in the 1960s. Its protagonists' successful movement to defeat the U.S. in Vietnam marginalized and eventually even influenced intellectually such stalwarts of the old Democratic foreign policy Establishment as Zbigniev Brzezinski and Joseph Nye. Democrats such as Dean Acheson and Henry Jackson would be strangers to it—as Joseph Lieberman certainly is. This new Establishment conquered the minds of the party's base to the extent that the personal views of Democratic officeholders became of secondary importance.

The principals in the new Establishment made their careers trying to diminish and restrain U.S. power, which—unlike the early twentieth century Progressives—they described as the source of much that is wrong in the world. The new Democratic Establishment was anti-anticommunist, and became anti-anti-Muslim. Once soft on Communist regimes, they became soft on Arab regimes. In short, this Establishment is in favor of almost anything that is anti-American. Its tolerance for the majority of Americans is of the intolerant kind.

George McGovern, who led the successful turning of the Democratic Party between 1968 and 1972, began his political activity in the massive 1948 Wallaceite march to protest U.S. opposition to the Soviet conquest of Eastern Europe. Since the Vietnam War, the McGovernite intellectual guiding lights of the party, Anthony Lake, Morton Halperin, and Noam Chomsky led the party to blame what they consider America's nefarious role in the world on faults in the American people, chiefly its morality. The party's *de facto* intellectual leader on foreign affairs in 2004, Michael Moore, had been fired by the leftist *Mother Jones* magazine for killing mild criticism of Communist totalitarianism in Nicaragua. In 2004 Moore regaled Europeans with tales of the criminal stupidity of Americans. Thus do today's Democrats seek abroad support for their struggles at home.

Although these elites are very much for involving America in the world's troubles, they oppose doing so on behalf of America's own national interest, as defined by Americans. Like Williams and Moore, they want America to serve the cause of "the revolution." Less strident versions of the same thing would have America serving a multilateral agenda set cooperatively with "the Europeans" (the proper kind, of course) or the UN.

Like the original Wilsonians and, emphatically, unlike most contemporary Republicans, the Democratic leftist elites are allergic on principle to the notion of a peculiar American national interest. Instinctively, today's Progressives, unlike most of the original ones, recoil from the language, symbols, and heroes of American patriotism. Almost as a matter of principle, they also exclude consideration of the relationship between ends and means. Conducting a war on behalf of a country whose grandeur one does not have at heart, whose mores one finds repugnant, makes for a kind of incompetence more surely disastrous than any confusion.

This war, like all wars, put much more at stake than the country's international relations. By the general elections of 2004, America's major parties had come to represent quite incompatible notions of how Americans ought to live at home as well. Hence the defeat of President Bush's party on "the war" would have opened the possibility of "regime change" in America itself. Changes in the regime are a natural, almost unavoidable consequence of defeat in any war. Defeat in Vietnam was the catalyst for the social revolution of the 1970s, even though in the 1970s the forces for regime change were a small minority of the Democratic Party. In 2004 they *were* the party. On the other hand, the victory of a Republican majority simply empowered George W. Bush, in the name of patriotism, to pursue policies whose failures might well discredit patriotism's cause.

In sum, I have tried to explain how decisions (albeit often by default) to conduct a war without connecting operations to a plan for ending it all will inevitably result in failure. The failure to grasp that the only alternative to victory is defeat with all its costs, opens America to far more than terrorist acts. Ideas have consequences.

THE PROBLEM

The problem is that since the end of the nineteenth century, many prominent Americans have trained themselves not to understand that peace is the product of war. Hence it proved beyond the capacity of the Bush administration to ask, never mind answer, questions fundamental to any war: What peace do we want out of this "war on terror"? Who, precisely, stands in the way of this peace? What combination of operations will actually eliminate the obstacles to our peace? What, in this war, is victory? What is defeat? How do we avoid it?

Anyone who conducts a war must focus on how operations can produce peace. Thucydides teaches that the Peloponnesian War did not produce peace for the Spartan winners any more than for the Athenian losers, because neither Athenians nor Spartans had a vision of the peace that should have followed the war. Consequently, though their operations were more or less wise or foolish, their behavior more or less noble or corrupt, everything they did turned to waste or worse because none of it aimed at the only thing that makes sense of war, namely a worthy and sustainable peace. Their fight was worse than wasted. *To move successfully, one must understand the state of rest to which one must come. To tailor operations for a victory worthy of the name, one must understand the peace that victory is to produce, and what stands in its way*. This is as true in the twenty-first century AD as it was in the fifth century BC.

Progressive dogma, however, deemed war a relic of our less enlightened forebears, and allowed discussion only of how to end it forever. Since World War I, many have imagined military actions either as law enforcement, punitive, pedagogic ("teaching a lesson"), or final struggles for millennial conditions. Polite company even banished the concept of enemy. By the 1950s the Soviet Union had become merely the "adversary." By the 1960s it was a "competitor." And by the 1970s "containment" had become more about "cooperation" than "competition." The U.S. government declared war on disease, hunger, ignorance, poverty, drugs, intolerance, and inequality of the sexes, but not on any foreign enemy. No wonder U.S. forces have lacked intellectual guides for military operations.

Beginning in the 1930s, a peculiar branch of American Progressivism asserted that an America that failed to bring about the millennialist transformation of the world had no right to assert itself. It was especially wrong to oppose countries that these elites considered the agents of human progress. Until the 1980s, a host of American liberals were not shy about their belief that the Soviet Union, Communist China, or the Third World were worthier than America. Indeed, they believed that America itself would benefit from losing its confrontations with such countries. The proposition that defeat in Vietnam had brought America closer to the values it should have had was in fact the theme of President Jimmy Carter's first address on foreign affairs, at Notre Dame, in 1977. The address was written by Anthony Lake, a pillar of Democratic foreign policy from George McGovern to Jimmy Carter to Bill Clinton.

The interplay between American patriotism, progressivism, and the press of events is why, although American military action in the twentieth century was invariably successful, its results in terms of peace were mixed. American blood bought stalemate in Korea; defeat in Vietnam; contempt in Lebanon and Somalia and nothing but thin pretense in the Balkans.

By the turn of the twenty-first century, American troops were on guard over much of the globe. Their government, pulled in different directions by Progressivism, a sterile Realism, and the exigencies of the national interest, had defined no enemy, much less a strategy to defeat him, and even less any times or conditions when the troops might stand down. At most, an operation might be guided by an "exit strategy." This retromingent concept begged the question of what accomplishments would justify the intervention in the first place. The U.S. government's most sophisticated definition of peace was "stability" (something which is inherently impossible), or "democracy" (which was badly understood and utterly unenforceable). Worse, the troops were to accomplish the unlikely and the impossible by not making too many waves. General Omar Bradley first stated in 1951 what had become the general military policy of the United States: "to fight it out in general...without committing too great forces." Henry Kissinger's critique of what he called "policy without clear cut objectives"[2] is valid for all post-1945 military operations.

Once American leaders had banished the concept of victory, once means were no longer reasonably calculated to lead to ends, every soldier's death became merely "tragic." Beginning in Korea and culminating in Vietnam, America's leaders fought wars the cost of which could not be offset by the peace that would reasonably follow. War's burden became bearable only to America's Best and Brightest—whose families progressively bore less of the actual burdens of fighting wars.

Beginning in 1990, the U.S. government committed much blood and treasure to military action in the Middle East. Under President George H. W. Bush, and to a lesser extent under his successor Bill Clinton, these actions aimed at affirming a liberal democratic life that had never existed in the region. But the U.S. government hardly noticed that neither it nor any other entity on earth had the power to endow any people with the capacity to transmogrify into liberal democrats. Because the U.S. government had long since lost the habit of proportioning the things it actually did to the things it professed to desire, its demands ended up engendering hatred, while its incapacity to enforce them earned contempt.

Even though in 1990 the word "war" returned to good standing in the official lexicon, incompetence regarding the relationship between ends and means produced what Donald and Frederick Kagan, writing in 2000, called "a legacy of half measures."[3] In 2000, I concluded a book on contemporary U.S. foreign policy by noting that nothing earns a country the deadly combination of hate and contempt, more than the profession of grandiose ends coupled with means proportioned to

2. Henry Kissinger, Diplomacy (New York: Simon and Schuster, 1994), 486.
3. David Kagan and Frederick Kagan, While America Sleeps (New York: St. Martin's Press, 2000).

the smallness, ignorance, incompetence, if not corruption, of their authors. The makers of U.S. policy, I wrote, needed to learn some basic lessons. My final sentence was a prayer that God might let these lessons be taught gently.[4]

On September 11, 2001, it became cruelly clear that inconsequential war-making in the Middle East had brought an attack on America more deadly than that of December 7, 1941. President George W. Bush then declared that America was at "war" against "Terrorism"—an abstract noun rather than a real enemy.

Angelo M. Codevilla
Plymouth, California
November 2004

4. Angelo M. Codevilla, Between the Alps and a Hard Place (New York: Regnery, 2001).

1: This Book

No Victory, No Peace was written not as one book, but as
running accounts of events. These commentaries on various aspects
of American foreign policy have appeared with some modifications in
various magazines. This summary introduction compensates for the
difference between self-standing essays, and a book that treats a theme
systematically. I intended to illustrate principles such as the primordial importance of selecting the proper objective and of understanding
correctly against whom to direct fire. Nor did I shy from predicting the
consequences of the events and decisions I was describing. But the
very need to describe events as they happened meant that events—
more than thematic coherence—dictated how I organized each essay.

Hence this book begins with the present chapter, which organizes
as well as summarizes the principal points of the essays. Herein I also
flesh out some of the arguments with material that did not fit the
purpose of any given essay at the time it was written.

THE PROPER OBJECTIVE

The second chapter consists of "Magnificent, But Was It War?" which
appeared on the first anniversary of the Gulf War of 1990-1991. Against
the grain of opinion, I argued that because George Bush Sr. had
misidentified what stood in the way of peace, America had fought and
won a battle, but not a war. I argued that the Saddam Hussein regime,
like a cancer disturbed but uneradicated, would cause America greater
troubles in the future than it had in the past. Our failure to undo our

enemies would not allow us, or anyone who sided with us, to enjoy peace. In the magazine's July 1992 issue, Elliott Cohen and others defended George Bush's, Colin Powell's, and Brent Scowcroft's judgments. They had defined victory in terms of the achievement of the U.S. government's objectives; they were satisfied that the war had pushed events in the region in the proper direction. I replied that setting objectives other than the ones that rid you of your problems is the biggest mistake anyone can make in war.

The Bush team of 1990—not so different from that of 2001-2004—at first decided in effect to approve Saddam's invasion of Kuwait. Then, after British Prime Minister Margaret Thatcher had performed her famous "backbone transplant" on the U.S. President, the team took America to war. But against whom? To accomplish what? Would the half-million Americans sent to the Gulf War do America any good? The Bush team did not ask the fundamental questions: What in all this endangers America? Is it Iraq's invasion of Kuwait? Is it the possibility that Saddam might invade other countries? Is it that he might exercise the wrong kind of leadership in the Arab world? To what extent should we interfere in the internal affairs of the Gulf countries? Can we make sure that these countries respect the interests of the West by punishing their leaders when they transgress? If so, how? Do we have to overthrow them? Do we have to try to run their countries? What are we willing and able to do?

Without dealing with these questions, the Bush team settled on the objective of removing Saddam's army from Kuwait because—much as a dozen years later another version of that team would settle on ridding Iraq of Weapons of Mass Destruction—it was the objective which the team calculated would provoke the fewest objections from Europe, Moscow, United Nations headquarters, and the Arab world. Both Bush teams also wanted to avoid doing anything that would encourage Iraq's Shiite majority and the Kurds—the country's second largest ethnic group—from breaking away from the Sunni dominated central government. The Bush teams did not compare the costs of the course chosen with that of courses rejected.

As would happen a dozen years later, the course chosen in 1990 involved prolonging the presence of U.S. troops on Arab soil—without an offensive mission. I argued that this would not frighten America's enemies but strengthen them. And in fact the host of troubles for America and its few friends which have flowed from that presence have been the subject of debates ever since.

THE RIGHT ENEMY

The third chapter is "Victory," written in the weeks following September 11, 2001. Crowds dancing in the streets of Arab capitals as TV replayed the collapsing World Trade Center towers, recruits flocking to anti-American terrorism, Arab leaders safely giving America gratuitous advice, all this left no doubt that their cause had won a victory. In America, the barricades, the random searches, the mourning, the fear, the tumbling stock market, rising gasoline prices, and the consensus that safety would never return, left no doubt about who had been defeated. Losers have to change the way they live, winners are confident in theirs. Would the Bush administration try to reverse the roles, to make mourners of revelers, and revelers of mourners? Already by the end of September 2001 it was clear that Bush and his advisers would not even try.

They pointed not to Arab regimes, but to "the shadowy al-Qaeda" as the proximate cause of terrorist acts against America, as if a private organization, or any number of organizations, could freely organize worldwide mayhem from Arab police states without the complicity of those governments. "Victory," however, pointed out that offensive operations against Afghanistan and al-Qaeda, regardless of how successful, would not give America peace because it was not al-Qaeda, but rather several Arab regimes that embodied the notion that defying America was the path to success for the Arab world. "In life as in math" I wrote, one judges the importance of any factor by factoring it out. Factor out Afghanistan and al-Qaeda, and you still get terror. What, I asked, would bring peace if factored out? I argued that Arab regimes hostile to America foster terrorism even when they do not direct it. They are its *sine qua non*. "It's the Regime, Stupid!"

I made clear that "regime" means much more than "the government" and that undoing an enemy regime means the dramatic demise of the several thousand people who give a country its character at any given time. But those in the Bush administration who thought in terms of regimes were less concerned with the exemplary killing of enemy regimes than with building new, liberal democratic ones. I warned that this is near impossible, and that the attempt to do it is pregnant with trouble.

"Victory" disagreed with the Bush team's decision to attack Afghanistan's Taliban, because the source of anti-American terrorism lay not in the Taliban's tolerance of a base in Afghanistan (al-Qaeda)

for Arab terrorists, much less in the peculiarities of the Taliban's reli-
giosity. Rather, it consisted of the hate and contempt for America that
had become standard in the Arab world. The Taliban's demise would
merely dent Arab terrorism peripherally, and the American
government's involvement in the obscurities of Afghan politics to build
a liberal democratic way of life in Afghanistan—complete with equality for women—would turn out to be costly and irrelevant to America's
security.

It should have occurred to me at the time (but did not) that the
confusion between regime and government would also contribute to
misunderstanding terrorism itself. Already in 1993 the Clinton administration had adopted the CIA's view that terrorism was the work of
private individuals. This was prompted in part by a CIA that could not
find evidence that governments were ordering terrorism—lousy reasoning on the basis of lousy information. First, in places like Iraq and
Saudi Arabia, where there is little or no civil society outside the regime, the doings of government ministries and those of unofficial important persons should not be distinguished. Second, the CIA found
no evidence of government orders for terrorism because hiding such
evidence is the essence of indirect warfare, very much the standard
method of warfare in the Middle East. Third, looking for evidence of
connections between official government agencies and al-Qaeda, defined as a more or less corporate organization, amounts to putting on
blinders—this is particularly bad for an outfit like the CIA that has a
history of failing to see even the obvious.

What after all is al-Qaeda? And what *is* the evidence of its responsibility for 9/11 and anti-U.S. terrorism in general? For sure, it began
as a base, organized by Osama bin Laden and financed by Saudi money,
for Arabs fighting against the 1980s Soviet occupation of Afghanistan.
Some of these Arabs stayed in Afghanistan and became known as
"Afghan Arabs." They became a base for armed aid to Muslim causes
from Bosnia to Tajikistan. Though most of these Arabs remained in
Afghanistan, bin Laden moved his organization back to Saudi Arabia
in 1990; he was eventually expelled to Sudan in 1992. Before U.S.
diplomatic pressure forced him to move back to Afghanistan in 1996,
Saudi Arabia was arguably his chief target—because it hosted large
numbers of American troops in the aftermath of the Gulf War. According to an Iraqi intelligence document from that time, Iraqi intelligence
worked with bin Laden at least with regard to Saudi Arabia. Beginning in
the mid-1990s, U.S. intelligence received reports from Arab intelligence

sources imputing various acts of anti-U.S. terrorism to bin Laden. But, before the 1998 bombings of U.S. embassies in Africa, the U.S. press—reflecting American intelligence—scarcely mentioned al-Qaeda.

How U.S. intelligence attributed 9/11 to bin Laden is by no means self-evident. The evidence that bin Laden is the author of the attack does not amount to the "game, set, match" which CIA Director George Tenet declared to President Bush on September 12, 2001. A trial of bin Laden (which will never occur) would embarrass many U.S. officials. Most of the human intelligence that points to bin Laden and al-Qaeda comes from the intelligence services of Arab governments. The CIA is loath to discuss how the agendas of these governments affect the veracity of their reports. And in fact the direct evidence in U.S. hands points in a different direction.

Officially, the government maintains that the mastermind of 9/11 was one Khalid Shaik Mohammed, who fled to Afghanistan and al-Qaeda after the failure of his 1995 effort in the Philippines to plant bombs on ten American airliners. Captured in 2003, he is in U.S. custody. Also caught in the Philippine plot was his alleged nephew, one Ramzi Yousef, convicted and serving a life sentence as leader of the 1993 World Trade Center bombing.

Yes, Mohammed told his CIA interrogators exactly what they wanted to hear: that bin Laden had been the hands-on manager of 9/11. But in fact Mohammed and Yousef, all by themselves, had done similar things without bin Laden or his "base." Indisputably, before any contact with al-Qaeda they had the idea, the capacity, and the resources to attack the World Trade Center in 1993, and to use airliners as weapons in 1995. Moreover, for the first as well as for the second attack on the World Trade Center, Mohammed's funds came from another of his alleged nephews, Ali, alias Ammar al Baluchi. None of these people is the creature of bin Laden or the product of al-Qaeda. Yousef never met bin Laden, and Khalid did so only in 1996. Indeed, the government believes officially that neither Mohammed nor any of his associates were "members" of al-Qaeda (whatever that might mean) before 1996. Hence the relevance of this organization to 9/11 is by no means clear. *Factor out bin Laden, and 9/11 still happens.*

The U.S. government in fact officially believes that Mohammed and his closest collaborators are a real, extended family from Baluchistan. But if that were so the family ties would supersede and predate al-Qaeda. It is not easy to reconcile the imputation of such a key role to one family with the overarching role the government imputes simultaneously to al-Qaeda. Indeed, as we shall see, there is reason to believe that even the names of Mohammed, Yousef, and their alleged cousins as well as their acts are products of Iraqi intelligence.

As for bin Laden, there is more than a little reason to believe that his own relationship with Iraqi intelligence was deep. When Sudan kicked him out in 1996 on America's suggestion, the Sudanese government seized his assets. Bin Laden needed some $30 million annually to run al-Qaeda, and more to buy his way into the graces of the Taliban. The "fatwa" he issued little more than a year later, in February 1998, may provide a hint of how he got the money. This edict was largely in support of a country, Iraq, that had not concerned bin Laden before, and whose form of government was anathema to him. And the country that the "fatwa" blamed for Iraq's troubles was another to which bin Laden had paid scant attention: the U.S.A. Earlier, a memo from Iraqi intelligence to Saddam Hussein had recommended that Iraq make use of the Arab militants who had fought the Soviets in Afghanistan and now were stranded in Sudan. Iraq may or may not have paid bin Laden's bills. The American government does not know where his funds came from. Iraqi intelligence certainly infiltrated bin Laden's group, just as other Arab intelligence services did, and just as these services infiltrated all violent groups. But the point here is that there is a lack of evidence from disinterested sources for imputing America's troubles to al-Qaeda.

The practical meaning of al-Qaeda should have become clear when, *after* U.S. troops had deposed the organization's supposed enablers, the Taliban, destroyed its base and captured a substantial percentage of the "Afghan Arabs," the number of terrorist acts for which the perpetrators claimed credit on behalf of al-Qaeda increased geometrically. Unlike crab grass or the mythical Hydra, human organizations do not respond to severe cutbacks by instantly sprouting multiple new tentacles. So, by February 2004, the CIA accounted for this counterintuitive growth phenomenon as "the dissemination of al-Qaeda's destructive expertise" to a wider Sunni extremist movement—as if motivation depended on expertise!

A more reasonable explanation for the increase in the number of acts attributed to al-Qaeda is that those who wish to frighten America, learned that the mere repetition of the name al-Qaeda frightens America and American intelligence agencies don't know any better than to accept the claims at face value. In 2004, one Abu Musab al Zarqawi almost instantly replaced bin Laden as the name to which so many terrorists imputed their deeds. America's information-starved intelligence agencies designated him as the threat *du jour*, and continued to believe that terrorism was about discrete individuals and their followers. Nevertheless, for the U.S. government "terrorism" and "al-Qaeda" continued to be synonymous. Go figure.

In a nutshell, the al-Qaedas, bin Ladens, and Zarqawis are less the engines, the artificers, the *sine qua non* of terrorism, than they are its banners. Perhaps they are best understood as bullfighters' capes, waved by an increasingly vast movement of terrorist *banderilleros* and *picadores* dashing in and out from the safe haven of Arab regimes to bloody the unintelligent American bull.

The relevant question then becomes: what makes this movement possible; who is the enemy? The answer is the combination of anti-American regimes providing the indispensable country-sized bases, the real al-Qaedas, regimes that embody causes complete with propaganda machines and television stations, and America's own impotent intrusion into Middle Eastern affairs. Finally, there are the terrorists' own successes. So long as all these exist, recruits will flock to the banners of bin Laden and his ilk. Radical Islam no doubt contributes to terrorism (see Appendix B). But it is neither a necessary nor a sufficient condition.

Secular, successful anti-American terrorism predates the flowering of the Islamist movement. Anti-Americanism is not the origin of Islamism. Of the five regimes that were the sources of anti-American terror—Iraq, the Palestinian Authority, Syria, Iran and Saudi Arabia—the first three were bitter enemies of Islam. Hate and contempt for America had become the common denominator of secular *and* religious terrorism.

I wrote that intelligence could not safeguard America against terrorism because not even the finest intelligence can learn the plans of countless organizations and individuals who have easy choices among myriad targets. That is why a "Homeland Security" program as tight as Israel's would not give peace to Americans any more than it has given peace to Israelis.

Machiavelli, no bleeding heart liberal, wrote that attempts at securing a country against unknown enemies must alienate the regime from its natural friends. Hence my essay showed that the government has to choose between winning peace through war against foreign enemies of its choosing, or treating American citizens as potential enemies—which would be the opposite of peace.

War, Phony and Real

The fourth chapter consists of two "Victory Watch" essays written in February and May, 2002. In 2001 President Bush had declared war on terrorism and taken Afghanistan. But no one imagined that the victory in Afghanistan had defeated terror or avenged 9/11. There had to be something else to the war on terrorism. What would it be? Bush's instincts had always told him that somehow Iraq was the key. Slowly and deliberately, he prodded the Pentagon—whose leadership agreed with him—to develop plans for invading Iraq and deposing its regime. He did not seek the views of the State Department and CIA, which everyone knew were opposed. The push and pull of opposing presidential advisers, rather than any vision of peace, determined the president's actions and inactions in 2002. Nevertheless, the logic of war insisted, at first quietly, and then more incessantly that something decisive must be done.

The Bush team had invoked war, but aimed its military operations and diplomacy chiefly at minimizing the discomfort of "friendly" Arab governments. The outstanding event of the first half of 2002 was the Saudi regent Abdullah's diplomatic offensive. Working with State and the CIA, he convinced Bush that he could and would deliver the support of all Arab governments to track down terrorists. Then the war would be won by coordinated police measures. All Bush had to do to earn this cooperation was to interpose Americans between Israelis and Palestinians, to make sure that the Palestinians were treated fairly— as the Arabs would see it—while reassuring Israel. Here was something proffered as the key to the war. The CIA eagerly accepted the task of "working with" Palestinian security forces, while State set about seeing what additional cooperation the various Arab states had in mind.

That turned out to be just more pressure on the United States to exert influence on Israel. That is because even "friendly" governments, like those of Egypt and Saudi Arabia, were increasingly enthralled by the terror states of Iraq, Syria, and the Palestinian Authority, as well as by the Saudi Wahhabi movement. This made them accessories to the terrorist attacks on America.

And so during the first half of 2002 the media were full of stories of American troops chasing down small bands in the Philippines or capturing caves in Afghanistan. American intelligence, according to its model of al-Qaeda as the terrorist nerve center, supposed the caves to contain sophisticated command centers right out of James Bond movies.

Instead, they turned out to be cold, bare-rock hideouts from the anti-Soviet resistance of the 1980s. For the first time too, American troops mistakenly killed Afghan civilians.

These attacks, and the virtual occupation of the tribal areas on the border between Pakistan and Afghanistan, were aimed at capturing Osama bin Laden. No reliable source had seen him since September 11. I wrote that the quality and content of a video tape in which he arguably took credit for 9/11 suggested it was a fabrication. Most likely, I surmised, once it became clear that Americans and their allies would takeover Afghanistan and once bin Laden was captured he would become a liability to all who had ever worked with him. Dead and disappeared, he would confound the Americans forever. Hence, I bet that his associates had killed him and disposed of his body. Since then, video and audio tapes purportedly of bin Laden—but unverifiable—have been broadcast from time to time. No blindfolded journalist has been taken to his presence. No credible person claims to have seen him. In November 2004, Pakistan withdrew its troops from the area where he was believed to be hiding, having become convinced that he had never been there. Moreover the Pakistanis said that there was never any hard evidence of his presence anywhere since 2001. I find it noteworthy that the CIA, followed by the *New York Times*, takes the total lack of evidence concerning bin Laden's whereabouts as certain proof that he is alive somewhere in the border region. At the same time, both find the scarcity of evidence regarding chemical weapons in Iraq as proof that they did not exist. At any rate, my best guess that he died in November 2001 is based on no less fact—and more logic—than are claims that he is still alive.

The search for bin Laden amounted to a war intended to change U.S. foreign policy as little as possible, and of acts of war connected to outcomes by wish lists—the definition of a phony war. What other label fits a policy that kept hundreds of low level persons incommunicado at Guantanamo Bay, evidence of whose relationship with terror was usually weak and second-hand at best, while continuing to prop up the Saudi regime *cum* Wahhabism, financing Yasser Arafat's PLA, and sparing Saddam's and Syria's Baath regimes?

"Victory Watch" argued that the more one side ignores the seriousness of war, the less it is capable of pursuing its own version of peace, and the more it stimulates the enemy and disheartens one's own side. As 2002 reached its midpoint, the pressure to do something significant increased.

THE ALTERNATIVES

The Bush administration was of many minds about the nature of the War on Terror. Its decisions about the proper way of conducting it were something like the geometric resultant of different vectors. The fifth chapter is a set of comments on the first three articles of the series by persons each of whom, willy-nilly, expressed some of the elements that had gone into the administration's decisions. I added my reflections on each of the administration's decision vectors.

Reflecting explicitly the dovish wing of the Bush team, especially the intelligence agencies, and anticipating the themes of the Democrats' 2004 campaign, the Naval Post Graduate School's David Tucker argued that terrorism is not due to states, and hence that Homeland Security is the essence of what the War on Terror must be about. Contemptuously, he rejected my premise that victory for America must consist of reestablishing the peace Americans enjoyed before September 11. According to Tucker, such a peace is impossible. Like Bush's Department of Homeland Security, Tucker wrote that Americans must adapt, permanently, to living without the freedoms of yesteryear. The real danger is "extremist Americans" who interfere with this adaptation.

I replied that the record of American intelligence agencies in the Middle East is ignorance compounded by lack of the quality control commonly known as counterintelligence. The agencies' involvement in local politics is reminiscent of the sorcerer's apprentices. I noted as well that making enemies of domestic critics—undermining peace at home—is the inescapable consequence of not focusing war on well-identified enemies abroad. Besides, why should Americans give up freedoms to please the U.S. government any more than to please any set of Arabs?

The Naval War College's Mackubin Owens, following the Bush team's military members, prized military success without relating it to the war's outcome. Prudence, he argued, validated the Bush focus on Afghanistan and al-Qaeda rather than Iraq because operations against the former were easier to turn into successes.

I noted that it is possible to label "prudent" any action or lack thereof only retrospectively, according to the action's contribution to a worthy end. But since conquering Afghanistan and capturing much of al-Qaeda could not possibly have brought peace, labeling these operations prudent made no sense. Also, I pointed out that Owens mistakenly cited distance and climate as more favorable to *military operational* success in Afghanistan than in Iraq. The last time I looked, Afghanistan was not accessible by sea. Iraq was. In fact, not prudence but the Bush team's internal dynamics had determined the choice.

Norman Podhoretz reflected the view of those Bush advisers who thought that since peace comes from democracy, good anti-terrorist policy would have to include America's "benign and temporary imperialism" in the Middle East, aimed at changing its culture.

I replied that America's peace does not require that foreigners be like us in any way, that creating liberal democratic mentalities is beyond the capacity of any foreign power, and that America does not have the corps of colonial administrators who could even make a respectable stab at changing foreign cultures. The disaster of the 2003-2004 American viceroyalty in Iraq showed once again that imperialism of any kind is foreign to America.

Frank Gaffney shared my view that peace would mean the destruction of enemy regimes, beginning with Iraq. But Gaffney, like some Pentagon civilians, thought that Bush shared this view as well, though he had not yet shown it. Gaffney listed a set of means adequate to the undoing of regimes from Gaza to Damascus to Baghdad to Riyadh, and expressed hortatory confidence that the Bush team would adopt them.

I agreed with the list of means, but doubted that the Bush administration would adopt them *with the spirit necessary to make them work.* The reason, I wrote, was that the Bush team argued about discrete measures—often monosyllabically and focusing on how the decision would "look"—without understanding the end at which any and all measures should aim. In short, I doubted that the administration knew what it was doing.

William F. Buckley Jr. deprecated what he called my "gloom," praised what he called my advocacy of "strategic marksmanship" regarding Saddam Hussein, but thought that the time had passed for the Bush team's adoption of it. My reply amounted to "it's never too late." Time, I wrote, is not the problem, lack of understanding is.

TO IRAQ OR NOT TO IRAQ?

By late summer 2002 the only alternative anyone suggested for ending the War on Terror was invading Iraq. But how would this accomplish the objective? Many suggested it would not. The administration had so many answers that they amounted to no answer at all.

The sixth chapter consists of the "Victory Watch" essays written in early November 2002 and mid-February 2003, during the Bush team's tortured preparations for the invasion of Iraq. The president never resolved the contrast, indeed the conflict, between a war aimed, in his words, at bringing terrorists "to justice, one at a time" and one in which invading Iraq would be the centerpiece. The first might make sense if the CIA and FBI view were correct, that terrorism is the result of "loose networks" at odds with regimes. The second made sense only if regimes themselves are the enemy. President Bush never understood that pursuing both versions of the war simultaneously would produce the results of neither.

On September 12, 2001, Bush had accepted the CIA's judgment that intercepted conversations between Osama bin Laden's associates rejoicing in 9/11 proved that al-Qaeda was definitely the problem. In the same way, he later accepted the CIA's judgment that the case proving Saddam Hussein possessed Weapons of Mass Destruction in 2002-2003 was a "slam dunk." Initially Bush seems to have expressed reservations about both judgments. It is impossible to tell—indeed it is ultimately irrelevant—whether he first decided to follow the CIA on al-Qaeda, and later to follow his instincts and invade Iraq with the ostensible purpose of ridding Saddam's regime of WMDs, or whether he sought courses of action that were likely to minimize opposition. At any rate, the highly credentialed people in Bush's National Security Council apparently did not try to force clarity between what the intelligence agencies *knew*, what they *believed*, and what they *preferred to believe*.

I noted once again that the administration's deliberations had little to do with understanding the causes on behalf of which the terrorists had begun striking America. Only by understanding the causes that these terrorists were serving, *and who embodied those causes*, could the U.S. government set out to defeat them. History teaches that people risk their lives for causes they deem worthy, *and* that they believe have a reasonable chance of success. Consider communism: Between 1917 and 1991 the world was full of communists. Spontaneously, people filled the ranks of Communist parties. Even more people sympathized with communist projects. But when the Soviet Union disappeared, the communist cause ceased to exist. Once the sun had set, the sunflowers could no longer follow it.

The sun of terrorism is hate and contempt for America. It is embodied in regimes that radiate it, and is made possible by the U.S.

government's *peculiar combination of intrusiveness and fecklessness.* That fecklessness flows in no small part from the tortured deliberations of the Bush team.

CONFUSION AND POWER

The sixth chapter also includes my review of Bob Woodward's *Bush at War* (2002), a very well-sourced account of the vectors that the team's senior members brought to its deliberations, and of the shorthand ways in which they jumbled alternatives. The result, Woodward shows, amounts to an attempt to pursue contradictory approaches simultaneously. Woodward's *Plan of Attack*, published in 2004, long after these essays were written, further documents his view (and mine) that although Bush had in some sense decided to depose Iraq's Saddam Hussein, he never thought seriously about what might result and what he would have to do to make sure that Saddam's fall would be decisive in the War on Terror.

By the spring of 2003, the Bush team's irresolution, flowing from its internal divisions, had eroded support for any action against Iraq. Its indecision had decreased respect for Bush at home and stoked anti-Americanism abroad. I explained that President Bush's deference to Secretary of State Powell's request to ask ill-disposed Europeans and a hostile UN to support an invasion that he himself had not yet decided upon (at least publicly), while pretending that his decision to invade would depend on their support, amounted to begging for opposition. To what extent Secretary Powell was drumming up European and UN support for his own intramural opposition, we cannot know. Nor is it relevant, because President Bush himself declined to explain why (or when) he inclined to one side or the other of the battles within his team. His truism that terrorists are better fought away from America's shores neither explained why doing away with Saddam would strike a decisive blow against terror, nor did it refute the argument that undoing Saddam would detract from the War on Terror.

Bush said that as the top man he was not obliged to explain anything to anybody. Alas, those who choose not to explain to others often do so to avoid explaining to themselves. I pointed out, on the contrary, that leadership consists of articulating the problem, the plan for dealing with it, and each party's part in that plan.

The essays do explain that imagining—as President Bush did on October 21, 2002, following Secretary of State Powell's lead—that whatever problem Iraq posed consisted substantially of "Weapons of Mass Destruction" amounted to precisely the same confusion that had led the first Bush team a decade earlier to convince themselves that the problem was Iraq's occupation of Kuwait, thereby wasting the lives of hundreds of Americans plus those of countless Iraqis. Both Bush administrations feared explaining the glaring truth: that Saddam's real Weapon of Mass Destruction was his *political success*, the consequences of which America could not suffer, and which it must destroy by war. Explaining Saddam's political success would have required explaining the failures of a generation of American statesmen as well as the misjudgments of a generation of intelligence officers and scholars.

The intelligence on Iraq's chemical weapons, and on its projects to acquire nuclear and biological ones, had always been thin. Secretary of State Powell's dramatic presentation of it at the UN on February 5, 2003, made that clear to anyone who knew the intelligence business. There had been no direct, reliable reporting at all since 1998. After the UN inspectors' departure, information on the subject had come from Arab intelligence services. Until three days before the invasion, these services continued to assure the CIA that the weapons were there. The administration's decision to tell the world that its main concern with Iraq was its sure possession of WMDs, and that Iraq's connection to terrorism was less certain, was due not to the quality of information available, but to the balance of forces within the administration. At any rate, I wrote that hanging the legitimacy of the invasion on finding items easily transferred, hidden, taken apart, or destroyed, amounted to leading with America's political chin. If indeed Saddam had WMDs and intended to use them, a public, hesitant, year-long buildup to the invasion amounted to inviting him to use them.

The American people and the world asked: What does this invasion have to do with September 11? This was a good question that deserved a good answer. Some in and out of the Defense Department had an answer they thought good: Saddam's political success was a big part of the matrix of terrorism. On the other side, CIA and State (later echoed by the Democrats' 2004 campaign) thought the invasion would be irrelevant to fighting terrorism, at best. Bush agreed a bit with both sides of these contradictory views. So as the invasion came closer, the Bush team scrambled for more appealing rationalizations for something it was going to do but did not quite know why. In the end, the title of the operation turned out to be neither about WMDs nor about terrorism, but rather about "Iraqi Freedom." Humanitarianism too would backfire.

Finally, the essays explain how the multilayered confusion of ends necessarily would befoul the conduct of any U.S. military operations. American forces would sweep over Iraq, all right, but given misunderstanding about what the problem was, how could they fix it?

POWER, CONFUSED AND FRUSTRATED

The seventh chapter consists of the three "Victory Watch" essays written in late May, mid-August, and early November 2003. As the U.S. attack began on March 20, it became ever clearer that Saddam's regime had pre-empted the attack by going underground. Why, and with what strategic intentions American intelligence had not the slightest clue—just as thirteen years after the Gulf War it still had no idea what had been on Saddam's mind at the time. Once again, U.S intelligence was strategically blind and its blindness led to a strategically misinformed America. Clearly though, the defeat of Iraq's hapless armed forces would solve no U.S. problem. By the time that American forces secured Baghdad on April 9, the U.S. government once again was on the way to turning military victory into strategic defeat.

The Bush team failed to heed Machiavelli's common sense counsel—and indeed the American experience in Afghanistan—that the only way to conquer an enemy country is to arm one's clients within it and to help them work their will on the common enemy. The result of the administration's failure to decide among opposing Iraqi clients was that none governed, anarchy reigned, and the U.S. government was justly blamed for it.

State and CIA argued that it would be wrong to hand power in Iraq to a set of exiles. In fact State/C.I.A. argued thus to brake the momentum that the Defense Department had built up in favor of *its* favorite exiles—all anti-Baathists. State/C.I.A. had *its own* set of favorite exiles who they thought should run the country. All of them had at some time worked with Saddam. (By June 30, 2004, State/CIA's dominance of U.S. policy had become such that in fact the U.S. government handed power precisely to the CIA's favorite exiles in pursuit of its perennial objective, "Saddamism without Saddam.") Beginning in the summer of 2003, the vast State/CIA dominated Coalition Provisional Authority headed by Ambassador Paul Bremer replaced the Defense Department's small group under General Charles Garner. The CPA reversed the Pentagon's policy of not trying to run the country and of shunning anyone associated with Saddam or his Baath party. But this attempt to run the country directly through second-rank Baathists proved unacceptable to American public opinion. The CPA could not govern—it could only prevent Saddam's opponents from doing so. Thus protected, the body of the old regime began to bleed U.S. occupation troops.

The fact that Americans could protect Iraqis who chose to work with them even less than they could protect themselves made Americans contemptible. Being pro-American carried few rewards and in fact was dangerous. As for the corps of U.S. administrators, they were ignorant of the local language, and merely huddled in front of air conditioners behind "Green Zone" security screens. They were thus far from being teachers of democracy and anything but effective imperialists. The U.S. armed forces had destroyed a government, but American "Nation Builders" proved incapable of rooting out the old regime, never mind making a new one.

If "regime change" were to happen, either Americans would have to root out the regime's network among Sunni Arabs it did not know, or they would have to turn the country over to their local enemies, principally Shiite Arabs and Kurds. These would likely massacre their Sunni tormentors and break up Iraq. The Bush team however had advertised, long before the invasion, that it would not allow either of these to happen. Fearful of what was likely to happen if Iraqis were left to their own devices, the Bush team kept a tight leash on them. "Iraqi freedom?" The Americans would not allow it, yet. Thus by failing to choose one side, the Bush team made America resented by all.

Talk of Weapons of Mass Destruction, which the Bush team judged convenient before the invasion, became a bludgeon in the hands of its enemies, foreign and domestic. For reasons obviously associated with his decision not to fight the invasion but rather to strike at the Americans thereafter, Saddam Hussein somehow had rid his country of the things that the Americans had made into the *casus belli*. Since the WMDs were not there, Bush had been mistaken, period. It proved all too easy for his enemies to paint Bush's incompetence as fraud.

The Bush team's bigger error of judgment had been officially to disbelieve, or only to semi-believe, and certainly to misunderstand, the connection between the Iraqi regime—indeed any regime—and terrorism. Once the ploy of WMDs had backfired, few credited the Bush administration's divided, halfhearted attempts to link the invasion to the War on Terror by citing Iraq's links to terrorism.

The Bush team's behavior toward other states that foster terrorism also discredited its claims. After all, the evidence of Iraq's involvement in terrorism paled alongside the evidence of the Saudi, Syrian and Palestinian regimes' involvement. And yet the U.S. government took pains to support these regimes. Bush's National Security Adviser, Condolezza Rice, described the diplomacy surrounding the war as a model of coercive diplomacy. *Pace* the distinguished former chief academic officer of Stanford University, I showed that the Bush team's failure to exploit its battlefield victory to undo these regimes amounted to diplomatic malpractice.

And so, at the threshold of 2004, just about no one in America, certainly no one in the Bush administration, was satisfied with how the Iraq war had turned out. At one time or another, in one way or another, the president's policies had included or at least bowed toward each of the administration's factions, indeed toward just about all of America's political tendencies. And yet none of the operations were turning out as those who proposed them thought they would. That is because war does not consist of successful operations, any more than love consists of intercourse consummated. Like all meaningful human activities, war naturally consists of achieving certain ends. The minimum definition of the peace America sought by war was safety from terrorism.

The administration did not institute the Department of Homeland Security to help win a war. Rather, President Bush explained that terrorism is a permanent condition to which America and the entire world must adjust. Hence according to Homeland Security's founding document, September 11 was "a wake-up call," even a welcome one, about reality. Bush and his Department assume that enemies are ubiquitous and indistinguishable, and that they will remain so. Hence Homeland Security is all about giving the U.S. government powers and discretion not so much to end terrorism as to adapt America to its demands.

The greatest adaptation is in the relationship between the American people and its government. From the onset of modern terrorism in the 1960s the government's approach has been to mistrust the people.

Security would have to depend on professionals, and they would be more and more militarized. Every major federal agency, and many state and local ones as well, have paramilitary units. For their members, Special Weapons and Training teams are more exciting and safer than paintball wars. But together they have changed life in America without making it safer. That is because SWAT teams do not distinguish well between the citizens they are supposed to protect and enemies.

Underlying all the governmental insufficiencies regarding terrorism is the inability to identify enemies. This incapacity is deadly because terrorism, a variant of indirect warfare, is based precisely on confusing the identity of its perpetrators. This incapacity, however, exists primarily among persons with a certain kind of education, a certain kind of sophistication. I showed that, since Plato, men have known that a kind of simplicity akin to that of dogs is more conducive to survival.

THE REAL WAR, THE PERILOUS REGIME

The ease with which irregulars killed Americans and their collaborators in Iraq between the summer of 2003 and my writing in the fall of 2004 reminds us that no security measures can take the heart out of enemies in war. Only victory over their causes can do that. The premise of the eighth chapter is that once blood is spilled, any and all fights are potentially fights to the death—any and all wars are potentially total wars. And the more that one side looks like the loser, the more it is bloodied with impunity, and the greater the incentive for many to join its enemies, the bigger the war that the loser must fight. Nothing fails like failure. The basic fact about the war in Iraq after April 2003 is that, although several of the factions involved used terror tactics, it was not a fight between Americans and "terrorism," but mostly a fight between Iraqis against their own domestic enemies and for their own futures—with America caught in the middle.

For America, it once mattered hardly at all whether Sunnis ruled Shias or the other way around, or whether the Kurds were under the Arabs or on their own, or whether Iraq existed at all. Few if any of its inhabitants would have contributed to anti-American terror. But Saddam Hussein had made Iraq's Sunni based regime into one of the primary engines of anti-Americanism, and George W. Bush had made war on that regime with the avowed purpose of transforming Iraq into a liberal democracy and declaring that "terrorism" was the enemy.

And so while in one sense Americans in Iraq after 2003 were involved in quarrels meaningless to them and irrelevant to whether America would ever again be attacked by terrorists, in another sense they were in a fight that, if lost, would put America in dire straits because the loss would highlight America's incapacity to deal with terrorism. But what would constitute victory in Iraq? More important, what would it take to secure America against terror? And ultimately, what would Americans have to do to preserve their own regime?

Nearly all terrorism is what certain regimes want to happen or let happen. That is why the invasion of Iraq was potentially so important to winning the war. Saddam's political victory in the Gulf War had consisted of using enmity to America to transcend the many divides amongst Arabs, indeed Muslims, and of putting himself at the head of that enmity. The spreading sense throughout the Islamic world, among secularists and religious alike, that anti-American action was good as well as safe, and that opposing it was bad and dangerous, became a mortal threat to America. This deadly phenomenon took on a life of its own. America's war would have to consist of reversing that paradigm by destroying some Arab regimes in ways that would *decourager les autres.*

Precisely because America's intervention in Iraq was, as President Bush said, the central battle in the War on Terror, his mismanagement of it proved to be disastrous. The goal of a free, liberal and democratic Iraq was inherently contradictory and therefore impossible to achieve. The body of the Baath regime among the Sunni population was left intact and the resentment engendered by their loss of power was unabated, even increased. Americans dallied even as their reconstruction projects were sabotaged and Iraqis of various stripes fought Americans and one another. The Americans' ill informed searches for their tormentors understandably became more violent, less discriminate, and more outrageous to the local population. Ignorant, indecorous, futile attempts to gather intelligence from prisoners about whom their American captors knew nothing inflamed public opinion in every corner of the earth.

Then, faced with a widening insurgency in Iraq, the Bush team suspended military operations against the main insurgent groups, effectively granting them sovereignty over the ground they held. Thus the insurgents were able to mount more efficient attacks on Americans throughout the summer of 2004. Unsurprisingly, these insurgent groups' victories over the Americans proved to be an irresistible incentive for the interim Iraqi government installed on June 28, 2004, to somehow buy them off. By midsummer 2004, it had become difficult to imagine a fruitful role for America in Iraq.

The character of any foreign government matters principally insofar as that government sponsors or allows activities that impact us—directly or indirectly. The urgent question in Iraqi politics was whether the Sunni minority would continue to exercise disproportionate power. How this would be resolved was of some importance to America because the Sunni minority that had prospered under Saddam had absorbed anti-Americanism, and reinforced it in the process of fighting the Americans to reestablish their privileges. Hence American interest was limited to preventing the return of the Baath Party to power. But the Bush team did not see things this way. Rather, it looked on Iraqi politics as the proving ground for its theory that democracy would end terrorism.

Throughout the summer the U.S. government prepared to reverse its grant of effective sovereignty to the main insurgent groups, principally the Sunni ones in and around the city of Fallujah. Doing so was a necessary condition for restoring some of the U.S. armed forces' prestige and hence safety, as well as for holding the national Iraqi elections that President Bush had designated as the symbol of political success. But taking Fallujah in November, necessary as it had become, was not sufficient for the safety of American forces, nor did it achieve Bush's definition of political success. The insurgency continued to increase the number of Americans and Iraqis killed. More significantly, it succeeded in making itself the political representative of Iraq's Sunni minority. Whereas in late 2003 only about 25 percent of the Sunni population identified with the insurgency, by late 2004 some 40 percent did.

The future of Iraq indeed would be decided by Iraqis—but not at the ballot box. The political process ran much deeper, and in a sense had long been predetermined. Slowly, the Bush team faced reality. Iraq's Shiite majority wanted to maintain a unified Iraq—but only on condition that it rule the country well-nigh absolutely. Its second, nonnegotiable, preference was simply not to be ruled by the Sunnis. The largest minority, the Kurds, though it preferred independence, was willing to be part of Iraq—if the country were a federation looser than either the Shiites or the Sunnis would tolerate. But the Kurds' nonnegotiable preference was autonomy. The Sunnis were eager to be not just part of Iraq, but demanded many of the privileges they had enjoyed for centuries. Its nonnegotiable preference was to safeguard itself against the Shiites who are bent on doing to them what they had done to the Shiites—and which the Shiites were sure to do. Hence as the balloting scheduled for January 2005 approached, it became clearer that the several communities had already made their choices. The largest Sunni party declared that it would lead the Sunni population in civil war unless the voting was postponed and some system adopted that would not force Sunni Arabs to be governed by Shiites and Kurds. It made its point by stepping-up violence against the provisional government. The other groups reacted predictably. Hence while the outcome of the voting was not in doubt, the history of Iraq would be ultimately written by what each group actually managed to do to the others.

Navigating the intricacies of Iraqi domestic politics was not self-evidently in America's national interest. The more the American government supported some and opposed others—equally ineffectively—the more it fed hatred and contempt, and the more it led Iraqis as well as the rest of the world to forget the most important thing of all: that America had overthrown its enemy Saddam, and stood ready to do the same to any other enemy. Saddam had not been able to put up any opposition, and neither would any other regime. Foreign populations can be controlled only by their own regimes. But America has the power, as well as the absolute right to demand that each regime neither do nor allow anything that harms America. The War on Terror would have to drive this fact into millions of heads—and to cut off those that would not act accordingly. Unfortunately, the high cost and scant returns of America's venture into the details of Iraq's domestic life will make George W. Bush and future presidents less likely to attack other regimes, and hence less fearsome.

Fortunately, the regimes whose death would give us peace have enemies who are eager to kill them. Their methods are unlikely to be kind, gentle, or democratic. It is enough for our peace that there be people who have their own reasons for destroying the people and culture—the regimes—that are the effective causes of violence against us. And it is enough for us to tip the balance against our enemies—provided of course that we judge correctly who they may be.

Americans, no less than foreigners, are the only ones who can determine the character of their regime, the way they live. Only we can determine what kind of peace will be ours—what we will put up with and what not. The test of victory or defeat is what happens in America.

On the most obvious level, the disappearance of security measures is the surest indication of peace, while their permanence is final proof of the opposite. To maintain otherwise is the opposite of sophistication. Simplicity is the truest sophistication.

II: Winning a Battle and Losing the Peace

MAGNIFICENT, BUT WAS IT WAR?*

"C'est magnifique, mais ce n'est pas la guerre." Thus in 1854 did a French observer dismiss the Light Brigade's charge into the Russian guns at Balaklava during the Crimean War. War consists less of shooting than it does of figuring out objectives worthy of killing and dying for, and then of applying means proportionate to the ends. Because the British commanders in the Crimea had not thought through the relationship between ends and means, the Light Brigade's heroism produced only dead bodies.

One year after the Gulf War, are we, too, compelled to say that it was magnificent but that it was not war? Yes and no. Yes, in the sense that the U.S. achieved disproportionately less than its massive and techni- cally flawless military effort warranted—and precisely because George Bush failed at the essential test of thinking through what the enemy was about, what our objectives should be, and what we had to do to achieve them. But no, in the sense that there can be little doubt that the world is better off—at least for a little while—than it would have been had the war not been fought.

By 1990 Saddam Hussein had become a clear and present danger to his Arab neighbors, to Israel, and to the world. His well-equipped, million-man army was developing medium-range ballistic missiles, and was within a year or two of producing atomic bombs. Saddam had already begun to overawe the region. At his insistence, Saudi Arabia and the Gulf Emirates had canceled billions of dollars' worth of debts

*This chapter originally appeared in Commentary, April 1992.

he had incurred during his war against Iran (1981-88). They were increasingly receptive to his calls for raising the world price of oil. And he was successfully portraying himself to the impoverished Arab masses as their champion against plutocratic rulers and, of course, against Israel.

In 1990, one could see over the horizon a time when Saddam's nuclear weapons could shield whatever horrors he might choose to sponsor in the Middle East, and whatever convulsions his manipulations of the price of oil might force upon the world's economy. Today, by contrast, Saddam is under siege. The flower of his air force is interned in Iran, the wrecks of about half his tanks litter the vicinity of Kuwait, and his ability to replenish his power by selling his country's oil is restricted. A goodly portion of his nuclear weapons program has been wrecked. His political power in the Arab world is diminished.

Saddam's regime, however, may be compared to a bacterial infection that has been treated with enough antibiotics to make the patient feel better, but not enough to kill it. The patient has every reason to fear that in time the infection will become more virulent, and meet less resistance, than before.

The core of Saddam's regime, its police, emerged unscathed from the Gulf War. He has reestablished his army, especially his six Republican Guard divisions, and has begun to play hide-and-seek with the international inspectors who are supposed to supervise his disarmament. As the CIA recently reported, the essence of the Iraqi nuclear program—its personnel—is intact and can be expected to produce weapons a few years after import restrictions are eased. Saddam knows, as do his neighbors, that absent America's will to go to war again, there is every historical reason to believe that restrictions will fade away and that domestic hiders will prevail over foreign seekers.

Saddam's Kuwaiti, Saudi, and other neighbors are politically weaker than ever, having shown that they can survive only through the support of infidels. Hence Saddam is well-positioned to resume both his military and his political threats. That is why his neighbors are beginning to make plans for living in his shadow—plans not so different from those they were making in 1990. Israel too has every reason to be worried. The principal long-term effect of the Gulf War seems to be a growing animosity toward Israel in the U.S., and the development of a Washington-Damascus axis.

Many who praise President George H. W. Bush for making war on Saddam cannot understand why he did not finish it. Yet Bush's handling of the beginning and middle of the war was no less capricious, no more rational; no more respecting of the historical norms of war than was the end. Throughout, Bush showed a phobia against elaborating policy through the clash of ideas and thereby failed to clarify what he was really after, and whether this or that measure would achieve the desired result.

To make matters worse, he was not surrounded by self-respecting advisers like Dean Acheson, James Forrestal, or even Harold Brown—men who, right or wrong, would argue their point, and help the president they served reach informed decisions. Instead, books such as Jean Edward Smith's *George Bush's War* and Bob Woodward's *The Commanders* confirm one's impression that Bush's advisers were yes-men. They also agreed with Bush's preference for keeping Congress from exercising its responsibility to declare (or not to declare) war. But Congress too has taken a dislike to open discussion and accountable decisions. As a result, the U.S. government collectively made a series of decisions that would have seemed as absurd in the light of open discussion as they now seem in retrospect.

When the Iraqi threat loomed, the U.S. government appeased. When Saddam invaded Kuwait, the U.S. government treated the invasion as the problem to be solved rather than as a symptom of the problem, which was Saddam Hussein's hostile priorities. By focusing on the Kuwaiti symptom rather than on the Iraqi disease, Bush put himself in the worst of positions: Iraq could meet his maximum demand, and yet win the confrontation. During the war, Bush and his team finally came to see that they had to eliminate Saddam or lose. Yet no sooner did Bush have Saddam in his power than the same advice he had received during the years of appeasement, plus fear of the responsibilities of victory, convinced him to let the Iraqi dictator go.

The first and most difficult prerequisite for fixing the mistakes of the past is admitting them. But before that, one must understand them.

The roots of the Gulf War go back to the U.S. government's decision in 1956 to sabotage Britain and France's defense of their contractual rights in the Suez Canal. Britain soon responded by renouncing all its commitments "east of Suez," and ever since then the U.S. government, while refusing to take on the role of colonial power, has tried any number of schemes to bring to the oil-rich Persian Gulf the friendly stability that the British had enforced in the past. As befits self-contradictory attempts, these schemes have all failed. First, in the aftermath of Suez, the U.S. counted on the Baghdad Pact, which tied Turkey, Iraq, Iran, and Pakistan into an alliance that geographically connected NATO Europe with America's Asian allies. This paper alliance fell apart in 1958 when Abdul Karim Kassem, an admirer of Egypt's Gamal Abdel Nasser (whom the U.S. had made a hero in 1956), took power in Baghdad and gave Iraq the first of a series of regimes that have been as nasty at home as they have been abroad.

For the next twenty years, the U.S. depended on the Shah of Iran to act as its "pillar" in the region. So axiomatic was the Shah's importance that the U.S. government considered discussions of flaws in his regime to be in bad taste and lacking in "realism." That, and not any lack of information, is why the Shah's total collapse in 1979 came as such a great surprise to Washington.

Soon thereafter, when President Jimmy Carter faced the "nightmare scenario" that the Persian Gulf—Europe's and Japan's principal source of oil—might be conquered by a now-hostile Iran, and possibly by the Soviet Union, he reluctantly proclaimed as a "doctrine" that the U.S. would fight to prevent it. But it was only under George Bush in 1991 that the Carter Doctrine was actually brought into play, albeit against a new devil, Saddam Hussein.

Yet this same Saddam Hussein had for the previous ten years been regarded as growing into the role of pillar previously played by the Shah and as (in the words of Brent Scowcroft, Bush's National Security Adviser) "a reasonably responsible member of the international community." During Iraq's war against Iran, Saddam had been seen as the bulwark against Washington's *bete noire du jour*, the Ayatollah Khomeini's "Shiite fundamentalism." And so, in 1981, when Israeli bombers destroyed Iraq's Osirak nuclear reactor, the U.S. government's best and brightest trooped to Capitol Hill to express heartfelt rage. Bobby Ray Inman, the deputy director of the CIA, accused Israel of having set back a delicate plan to make Saddam play a useful role in the region. (Indeed, the CIA would soon supply Iraq with satellite photos of Iranian units.) In March 1982, the State Department removed Iraq from the list of states sponsoring terrorism—and kept it off despite the fact that the PLO's Abu Abbas and others continued to operate out of Baghdad. In 1982 also, the U.S. began to give Iraq credits for the purchase of American grain. In 1987, the U.S. uncritically accepted Iraq's explanation that its attack on the USS Stark (which cost thirty-seven American lives) was an accident. In 1988, while the world (and much of the U.S. Congress) gasped at Saddam's gas attack on a Kurdish village, the U.S. government concluded that it too might have been an accident of the Iran-Iraq war. In 1990, the U.S. Ambassador to Iraq, April Glaspie, apologized for a Voice of America (VOA) editorial that had criticized Saddam as a "brutal dictator." Secretary of State James A. Baker III, angry at the VOA, insisted that all of its broadcasts dealing with Iraq be cleared by his (supposedly wiser) staff. On the eve of the invasion of Kuwait, the State Department killed a VOA editorial restating the U.S. commitment to its friends in the Gulf.

During 1990, as Saddam stepped up his anti-Israel, anti-Saudi, and anti-American rhetoric, plus pressure on Kuwait for territorial concessions and money, the question arose of what he wanted. The consensus in the administration was that he wanted nothing that was incompatible with U.S. interests. On July 24, 1990, Baker cabled instructions to Glaspie for her dealings with the Iraqi government. The next day she met with Saddam and followed her script: the U.S. sought good relations with Saddam; the president would not be unhappy to see the price of oil rise to $25 a barrel; the U.S. had no opinion on the substance of conflicts between Arab states, and specifically on Saddam's quarrel with Kuwait.

The day before Iraq's invasion, with Saddam's divisions poised on the Kuwaiti border, Assistant Secretary of State John Kelly told the House Foreign Affairs Committee that the U.S. had no obligation to intervene on behalf of any country in the Persian Gulf. On August 2, 1990, the day of the invasion, Glaspie was quoted as being surprised that Saddam had taken all of Kuwait. She and the administration had expected him to take only a part, and had not been particularly concerned.

On the morning of August 2, President Bush met with the National Security Council to consider the Iraqi invasion. The desultory conversation came to a unanimous conclusion by default: the Persian Gulf was too far away and Iraq too powerful for the U.S. to affect events except through a gigantic effort. Besides, although Saddam had done more than all but one (low-ranking) intelligence analyst had expected, he was not threatening any vital American interests. Nor were Iraqi troops mistreating civilians. Later that day Bush spoke with Egypt's President Mubarak and Jordan's King Hussein, who shared these views and thought that the Arab countries might well reach some sort of settlement. Saddam might keep a few pieces of Kuwait, and the Kuwaiti royal family might have to move to Switzerland, but nothing much would change. When, then, did the U.S. government go on to make Iraq's invasion of Kuwait *a casus belli*?

Because that same afternoon Bush spoke with British Prime Minister Margaret Thatcher, who convinced him that Saddam was Hitler, Kuwait was the Rhineland, and this was 1936. Thatcher having, in the words of the Manchester Guardian, performed a "backbone transplant" on him, Bush now declared: "This will not stand." Thereafter, he consistently denounced Saddam as evil and affirmed that he would stand up for good. But in turning against Saddam, Bush seems never to have asked himself a number of necessary questions: What is it about Saddam that I object to? Is it the invasion of Kuwait? Is it the possibility that he might invade other countries? Is it that he might exercise the wrong kind of leadership in the Arab world! Was I dreadfully wrong in trying to get along with Saddam while I knew that he was building nuclear weapons and awesome conventional forces but thought that he was going to take only part of Kuwait? If I was not dreadfully wrong, then what difference does the invasion of Kuwait make? Why am I even thinking of sending Americans to kill and die in the Arabian desert? And if my policy of relying on the strongest regional power in the Gulf—regardless of its internal character—was mistaken, or if it quite simply failed, am I willing to adopt the alternative? Am I willing to interfere in the internal affairs of the Gulf countries to make sure that they respect one another as well as the interests of the West?

Since the decision to send American troops was made without answering such questions, different sets of people within the government were left to develop their own diagnoses and prescriptions. The National Security Council staff and the Defense Department civilians—the hawks who focused on the president's dictum that the invasion of Kuwait must not stand—saw U.S. forces as a shield behind which the U.S. and the UN would squeeze Iraq until Saddam realized that the costs of occupying Kuwait exceeded the benefits. Then he would pull out. But these people did not consider that perhaps the real problem—the military and political primacy of a hostile Iraqi regime—was broader than Saddam's occupation of Kuwait and could not be fixed by a pull-out. For after Iraqi troops had retreated a few miles and the Americans had gone back to the other side of the globe, the problem might well be worse.

The "doves"—James Baker's State Department, backed by the editorial page of the New York Times—thought that the situation was comparable not to Hitler's occupation of the Rhineland in 1936 but to the Soviet Union's occupation of Eastern Europe. Hence their prescription was to "contain" Iraq with a political-military commitment analogous to NATO. But this group did not realize that what had worked in Europe was—physically, socially, and politically—a non-starter in the Persian Gulf. Whereas two generations of American personnel had enjoyed Germany's beer, frauleins, and conferences on the Rhine or in the Alps, American endurance of a Saudi populace at least as forbidding as the burning sand could be measured only in months. Moreover, whereas the Soviet Communists' anti-American appeals had found resonance only in a small and decreasing percentage of Europe's population, Saddam's call to rally against an army of Christians, women, and Jews on Muslim soil appealed to a large and growing population of Arabs. NATO in the Gulf or, as the columnist William Safire of the *Times* dubbed it, Gulfo, should never have received a second thought.

The point is that Bush and his people should have seen that the problem lay in the very existence of Saddam's regime. As such, it presented the U.S. with only two real alternatives: either to overthrow and replace that regime with an acceptable one (or at least to overthrow it and retain the capacity to crush any unacceptable successor), or to do whatever necessary to appease it. One is reminded of Machiavelli's rule of thumb: enemies are either to be caressed or extinguished. Yet since the two real alternatives were so demanding, the Bush administration preferred not to look at either, but to imagine that there existed easier diagnoses and prescriptions somewhere in the middle. One reason the Bush administration was so unclear about what it wanted in the Gulf was that it avoided domestic debate and concentrated on securing authorization for its plans from the United Nations, and above all from Mikhail Gorbachev.

Perhaps the most pernicious, and the least warranted, of the hangovers from the Vietnam era is the Beltway conservatives' veneration of presidential prerogative and their mistrust of the American people. Never mind that, at every point of the Vietnam decade, public-opinion polls were more hawkish than administration policy. Never mind that, whenever presidents have undertaken vigorous action abroad—from Nixon's Cambodian invasion to Bush's invasion of Panama—public opinion has rallied behind them and dragged Congress along. It was still an article of faith in the Bush White House that the American people could not be trusted to hear the real number of troops being sent to the Gulf without gagging, that they would not stand for any talk of offensive warfare, and that they would not tolerate the killing of

Saddam Hussein—even after the polls showed that some 80 percent of Americans wanted him dead.

It was also White House dogma that Congress was a treacherous enemy. Again, never mind that Congress has asserted itself in foreign affairs only when presidents have been hesitant, and that presidents who press their foreign agenda on Congress invariably win. Never mind, too, that the Constitution confers upon Congress alone the power to declare war. The Bush administration still did everything in its power to prevent Congress from exercising its responsibility, including, in the end, proposing that a congressional debate be held the week after it had planned to start hostilities.

This attachment to executive prerogative is most unconservative. Indeed, it stems most immediately from the belief of the liberal so-phisticates in the Kennedy and Johnson administrations that they could manage the Vietnam conflict to a mutually acceptable solution if only they could resist the American people's simplistic demand, echoed by Senator Barry Goldwater, to "win or get out." But as Colonel Harry Summers points out in *On Strategy*, not declaring war turned out to be the biggest mistake the U.S. made in Vietnam. Summers shows that when entering major commitments—war quite as much as marriage— the most important thing people can do is declare their intentions. This is not so much out of "a decent respect for the opinions of man-kind" as because declaring commitments forces people to face the implications of what they are doing, and presses them to "do it right" or not at all.

During the Gulf War the Bush administration's self-styled conser-vatives, far from negating the Vietnam heritage, personified it in the sense that they too thought themselves more sophisticated than the people, and they too feared that a declaration of war would limit their flexibility. Instead of Congress, therefore, it was foreign leaders with whom George Bush worked out what U.S. forces would and would not do in the Gulf. But these leaders had their own priorities.

Gorbachev played both sides. He supported Bush's demand that Saddam leave Kuwait, but he clearly opposed interference in the in-ternal affairs of Iraq. The great importance that Bush placed on acting in concert with Gorbachev is one of the principal reasons the U.S. never made changing the Iraqi regime part of its policy. Egypt's Presi-dent Mubarak, Syria's dictator Hafez al-Assad, and other Arab lead-ers also helped to entangle U.S. policy. These Arabs were willing enough for the U.S. to save them from Saddam. But they asked Bush to pay for the privilege of doing so by distancing the U.S. from Israel. And, as we shall soon see, they were instrumental in Bush's decision to preserve Saddam's regime.

As in Vietnam, then, America's war in the Gulf was essentially military, conducted largely without regard to creating specific postwar conditions. "First we're going to cut it off, then we're going to kill it," said the chairman of the Joint Chiefs of Staff, General Colin Powell, referring to America's primary focus, the Iraqi army in Kuwait. But the bombing of central Iraq that accomplished the cutoff also gave the U.S. its main opportunity to affect the postwar world. To the limits of the intelligence information available (which was not very good), the U.S. Air Force set back Iraq's nuclear and chemical weapons establishment. It also dropped bombs on military headquarters. But—true to repeated declarations by Bush and Powell—the U.S. never targeted any individual. Indeed, when, during the last week of the war, the U.S. Air Force located Saddam Hussein and asked for permission to bomb him, the president said no. He would kill the draftees, not the drafter.

Ironically, killing the Iraqi army was not a prerequisite for a real victory. Because the bulk of it was dug into the Kuwaiti sands, pinned down by U.S. air power, the Iraqi army could not have stopped any U.S. move either to Baghdad or to support the self-determination of Kurds and Shiites. Any such move would have doomed Saddam. But U.S. military leaders nowadays do not think in such terms. For them, high strategy means flanking maneuvers. Hence, war meant killing the Iraqi army.

To kill the Iraqi army the U.S. planned first to secure control of the air by destroying radars, communications, aircraft, and other equipment associated with air defense; second, to destroy the military's command, control, communications, and logistical systems; third, to destroy up to one-half of the tanks, planes, and people in the bunkers. Having done this, U.S. ground forces would flush the remaining Iraqis out of their bunkers, exposing them to the full fury of U.S. combined arms.

The Americans would be able to approach Iraqi positions in relative safety because accurate fire from airplanes and helicopters would keep the Iraqis' heads down. Meanwhile, an encircling maneuver from the west would trap the survivors and make them prisoners. The U.S. armed forces were confident that they could execute what they had planned. And they did, brilliantly.

Once defeated, the Iraqi army began to dissolve, much as the slave armies of the region have done after every defeat they have suffered since the time of Alexander the Great.[1] Had the historic pattern been allowed to play itself out, the long-oppressed subjects of the tyrant's empire, who had already taken arms, would have been joined by a rabble of defeated troops, and would have found that the tyrant's defenders had melted away or had killed him themselves. But George Bush arrested that pattern. Forced to choose between, on the one hand, superintending Iraq's revolution and reconstruction, and, on the other, saving Saddam and thus permitting him to seek hegemony another day, he chose the latter.

Thus, Bush's unilateral cease-fire of February 27, 1991, saved two heavily armed Republican Guard divisions from being disarmed or destroyed. Immediately after the cease-fire, the U.S. had to deal with thousands of prisoners of war who were eager to take refuge indefinitely in American-held territory, or to fight Saddam, or simply to wander home. On orders from Washington, U.S. forces turned them over to the Iraqi army, sending an unmistakable signal that since the army had nothing more to fear from the Americans, civilians should start fearing the army again. Later, civilian refugees flocked to U.S.-held territory. On orders from Washington, U.S. forces sent them back. Same signal.

On March 3, 1991, General H. Norman Schwarzkopf forbade Iraqi commanders to fly their helicopters or fixed-wing planes, and made a partial exception for supply flights. Ten days later, the world learned that, immediately, the Iraqis had begun using helicopters to bomb and strafe rebellious Kurds and Shiites.

The rebellions had been incited a bit by the CIA, more by Bush's February 15 call for the Iraqi people to overthrow Saddam, but most of all by the near-dissolution of Saddam's army. Yet even though U.S. policy had quickly stopped this dissolution, the Kurdish and Shiite rebels had been able to take control of the major cities in their respective regions.

The rebels, however, had no aircraft and no means of defending against aircraft. Hence the Iraqi army's use of helicopters would doom them. Between March 13 and March 24, Bush issued warnings to Iraq against so using helicopters. But he did nothing to enforce the warnings, and his lieutenants told the press that they were "rhetorical." Finally, on March 27, the *New York Times* reported that Bush, at a

---

1. *The pattern has been noted by, among others, Xenophon, Livy, and Machiavelli— not the bedside companions of the Bush administration.*

meeting with his seven top military and national-security advisers, "reaffirmed" a policy "to let President Saddam Hussein put down rebellions in his country without American intervention."

Bush, it turns out, had made this choice at the urging of "Washington's Arab allies," who did not want to see the "splintering of the country"—i.e., who wanted Iraq's Sunni Arab minority to continue ruling Kurds and Shiites. Over the following days high administration officials told reporters that these wise Arab (and Soviet) allies, backed by the wise CIA, were confident that after the army had reestablished the empire, "someone from Hussein's own group" would do him in. Bush and his advisers seem never to have asked why Saddam would let this happen, or if it did happen, why a successor similar to Saddam would be preferable to a splintered Iraq—or to a democratic Iraq—or why it would be an acceptable result after the expenditure of blood and treasure.[2]

During March and April, by the rule "I slaughter, therefore I am," Saddam restored his authority at home, and some of the regional prestige that he had lost in the military rout. The Republican Guard, having escaped the Americans through no merit of its own, took out its rage on Shiite and Kurdish civilians. They shelled and rolled over them, raped and murdered so genocidally as to send millions fleeing for the nearest border. The borders nearest the Kurds were snowy mountains, where they died at the rate of up to 1,000 per day.

Bush claimed that the Gulf War had been a great moral victory. But Saddam's conspicuous carnage challenged Bush either to acknowledge that his victory had made things worse, or that it had been incomplete and that further military involvement was needed. Bush equivocated: he extended humanitarian aid to the refugees under U.S. military protection, while doing his best to withdraw that protection as soon as he could do so without embarrassing himself before American voters.

As UN "peacekeeping troops" replaced Americans in town after town, the Iraqi secret police would tighten its grip. Within hours,

---

2. *A year later, with Saddam still in power, the Saudis would be giving Bush the opposite advice—to stir the Kurds and the Shiites into revolt yet again, but this time supporting them with air strikes. But neither the Saudis nor their supporters in Washington would be able to explain why the administration should do something under the relatively difficult conditions of 1992 that it had chosen not to do in 1991, when it would have been easy.*

pro-Saddam posters would appear on the walls, and ordinary people would refuse to be seen with reporters. The people of Iraq behaved as if Saddam had won the war.

The Saudi and Kuwaiti governments also did not behave as if America had won. When the U.S. government asked the Saudis to take the lead in eliminating the Arab world's state of war with Israel, they responded by adding another hundred American companies to the list of those whom they boycott for doing business with Israel. The Saudis did cut out their subsidies to the PLO, but they increased their aid to Syria, which used it to buy Scud-C missiles to be aimed at Israel. Then the Saudis cut production of crude oil enough to cause the price to rise roughly to where it had been in August 1990, before Saddam's occupation of Kuwait was challenged. They had to be aggressive on oil and Israel, explained the Saudis, because Saddam had renewed his propaganda to the Arab masses, charging Saudi Arabia with being a tool of the Zionists and the Americans.

Once again, the U.S. government, unwilling to involve itself decisively in the Middle East yet desirous of influence, felt obliged to approve as its surrogates in the region (this time, Syria and Saudi Arabia) adopted policies harmful to the American people. And once again, the government considered criticism of its surrogates to be in bad taste and lacking in realism.

"No one," wrote Clausewitz, ought to start a war "without first being clear in his mind what he intends to achieve by that war and how he intends to conduct it." It was good that the U.S. went to war against Iraq, but because George Bush and his team violated Clausewitz's basic rule, they cannot now fully enjoy the fruits of peace. And neither can the rest of us.

THE GULF WAR*

TO THE EDITOR OF COMMENTARY:

Evidently displeased with President Bush's management of the war in the Gulf,...Angelo M. Codevilla ["Magnificent, But Was It War?," April] endeavors, albeit unconvincingly, to catalogue the purported errors of Bush's ways. Though he concedes implicitly that the state of

*The following edited exchange of letters and comments appeared in the July 1992 issue of Commentary.

affairs in the Gulf region is "better," Mr. Codevilla nevertheless remains frustrated, because Bush's objectives were not as extended as he might have preferred.... Saddam Hussein is still in power....He was neither appeased nor replaced, and Mr. Codevilla views this as a disaster. Is it?...Mr. Codevilla touches on an important matter without completing his analysis. He acknowledges, correctly, that American citizens would have liked to see Saddam Hussein "dead," but he does not address the concomitant question: how many of their sons and daughters were (are?) they predisposed to sacrifice in pursuit of that end? He offers no answer. Moreover, since intelligence-gathering has not yet reached the pinnacle of an exact science, it was perfectly reasonable for Mr. Bush—and his advisers—to project the possibility that Saddam Hussein might be replaced by a successor regime. It did not happen. Yet President Bush is not politically indictable for that failure.

Finally, Mr. Codevilla cites Clausewitz, who counseled that no war should be undertaken by a nation without its leaders first postulating means and ends. In my opinion, Bush was faithful to this prescription. His means passed the test of proportionality. Now let us consider whether his ends were accomplished.

Were Kuwait's borders restored? Was its territorial integrity sustained?...Was Saddam Hussein's attempt at extortion frustrated? Were nations the world over assured of continuing access to oil at reasonable world prices? Was Iraq's capacity to wage nuclear, chemical, and biological warfare crushed, if not as yet...totally eliminated? Was relative stability in the Middle East secured?

I submit that despite Mr. Codevilla's pessimism and disappointment, the foregoing questions are answerable in the affirmative.

ELLIOTT A. COHEN
NEW YORK CITY

TO THE EDITOR OF COMMENTARY:
Angelo M. Codevilla, commenting on the aftermath of Desert Storm,...draws attention to the March 27, 1991 story in the *New York Times* reporting our betrayal of the rebellions against Saddam Hussein at the behest of our "Arab allies." But he omits the report in the *Times* (and the *Washington Post*) of April 2, 1991 that National Security Adviser Brent Scowcroft went to the Middle East on March 26 (according to the *Post* account) for consultations that included "Saudi interest in the situation in Iraq and future relations between Saudi Arabia and

Iraq under Saddam Hussein" (according to the *Times* account). The question is: did Scowcroft go for "consultations" or instructions? The lead story in the *Washington Post* of April 2 opened as follows:

> Iraqi Kurdish rebels, pressed hard by relentless attacks from government forces, retreated into the mountains of northern Iraq yesterday as their leader, Massoud Barzani, urged the United States, Britain, and France to stop "genocide and torture against our people."

The plight of the Kurdish people was not deemed fit to print on the front page of the *Times* that day....Quite clearly, we approved policies harmful to the Kurds. And we certainly approved policies harmful to Israel, demanding that it accept Scud attacks passively, and sitting back while yet another of its fierce enemies, Syria, augmented its own stockpile of missiles aimed at the Jewish state.

DAVID R. ZUKERMAN
BRONX, NEW YORK

TO THE EDITOR OF COMMENTARY:
Angelo M. Codevilla's otherwise brilliant article is fatally flawed by one crucial omission: it does not deal at all with the U.S. contention that Iraq's forces were massing on the southern border of Kuwait for an immediate attack against Saudi Arabia.

There is a range of possibilities. The most straightforward is that there were genuine aerial and satellite photographs which showed a pre-invasion buildup massive enough to convince the Defense Department and the Saudi rulers that an imminent threat to Saudi Arabia existed. If that was so, much of Mr. Codevilla's narrative and argument loses its force. President Bush would have had valid reasons for changing his mind about letting Saddam Hussein get away with the rape of Kuwait.

The only reasons to justify his omission, then, would be either that Mr. Codevilla has cause to believe that the photographs were not genuine but were "edited," or that they did not really convince the Defense Department but were used to convince the Saudis, who were less sophisticated in the interpretation of high-altitude surveillance data.

If Mr. Codevilla had cause to distrust the official story, however, the omission would not be justifiable either. U.S. conduct would then be a case of acquiring war powers by fraud comparable only to the Tonkin Gulf incident.

FELIX KAUFMAN
ANN ARBOR, MICHIGAN

ANGELO M. CODEVILLA WRITES:
   Elliott A. Cohen sees my central point: George Bush fought the Gulf War without regard to its natural end—the removal of the reason why we were moved to fight in the first place, namely, Saddam Hussein and his regime. But Mr. Cohen somehow concludes that Saddam's removal is a personal preference of mine. He concedes that killing Saddam would have been nice, but rhetorically asks how many American lives I would have been willing to sacrifice for what, he implies, would have been icing on the cake. "Were [not] Kuwait's borders restored?" and so forth, he asks. I remind Mr. Cohen and, alas, Mr. Bush that the distinction between ends and means is not a matter of personal preference. How would we judge a malpractice suit against a surgeon who removed all but the root of a tumor and then claimed that the operation had been a success because the patient felt better, who asked why he should have spilled more blood just to remove the last 10 percent of the malignancy, and who protested that removal of the tumor's root was a personal preference? Surely we would point out that the patient did not submit to the operation just to be cut open and sewn up again, but rather that if he agreed to shed any blood at all it was so he could be rid of his life-threatening problem. George Bush sacrificed hundreds of Americans and killed tens of thousands of Iraqis while going out of his way to preserve Saddam Hussein. We should all be asking: should *any* human life have been sacrificed *except* for the purpose of destroying Saddam and his regime? Note also that, had the U.S. government chosen the proper strategic objective— the destruction of Saddam's regime—the U.S. armed forces would not have had to fight the bulk of the Iraqi army. When Saddam sent his army to Kuwait, he left himself uncovered. It took all the combined brains of George Bush, Richard Cheney, and Colin Powell to reverse Douglas MacArthur's commonsense principle, "hit 'em where they ain't," and to concentrate on the target with the highest military resistance and the lowest long-term political consequences.
   David R. Zukerman makes a good point. Although the U.S. news media eventually carried enough sickening pictures of the horrible

consequences that George Bush's decision had for millions of Kurds and Shiites, the media clearly let Bush off the hook. They attributed to Bush a mistake at the margin rather than, as they should have, a fundamentally flawed policy. The reason for this is that while U.S. media executives will occasionally see evil in Third World dictators, principle and habit prevent them from concluding that the U.S. is ever justified in doing away with them. The media's points of reference— Mikhail Gorbachev, the European Left, and the European Community Commission—had strongly warned the U.S. against deposing Saddam. So while the media decried the bloody result of a botched war, they were hardly eager to explore the reasons why it had been botched. As for Israel, fashionable opinion now has stuck it into the same near-outlaw category as America itself.

Felix Kaufman [suggests that the administration went to war with a fraudulent rationale]: Did the Bush administration acquire war powers by a kind of fraud? Its pretenses were not so much false as they were empty. The administration sought power, not to serve a hidden agenda but while refusing to articulate one. Neither the Saudis, nor the U.S. Congress, nor, I suspect, George Bush himself would have agreed to wage a $70 billion war that would leave the Saudi and Gulf regimes less domestically legitimate than ever, an Iraq solidly in Saddam's hands, and a U.S. government that had shot its bolt in the region for a least a generation. My point is that a lack of intellectual clarity can have terrible consequences.

III: Victory and Defeat

Victory: What It Will Take to Win*

As Americans mourned on the night of September 11, many in the Middle East celebrated. Their enemies, 280 million people disposing of one-third the wealth of the earth, had been bloodied. Better yet, Americans were sadly telling each other that life would never be the same as before—and certainly not better.

The revelers' joy was troubled only by the fear that an angry America might crush them. For a few hours, Palestinian warlords referred to the events as *Al Nachba*—"the disaster"—and from Gaza to Baghdad the order spread that victory parties must be out of sight of cameras and that any inflammatory footage must be seized. But soon, to their relief, the revelers heard the American government announce that it would not hold them responsible. President George W. Bush gratuitously held out the cachet of "allies" in the war on terrorism to nations that the U.S. government had officially designated as the world's chief sponsors of terrorism. Thus Yasser Arafat's, Saddam Hussein's, and Bashar al Assad's regimes could enjoy, *undisturbed*, the success of the anti-Western cause that alone legitimizes their rule. That peace is their victory, and our lack of peace is our defeat.

Common sense does not mistake the difference between victory and defeat: the losers weep and cower, while the winners strut and rejoice. The losers have to change their ways, the winners feel more secure than ever in theirs. On September 12, retiring Texas Senator Phil Gramm encapsulated this common sense: "I don't want to change the way I

This essay originally appeared in the Claremont Review of Books, *Fall 2001.*

live. I want to change the way they live." Common sense says that victory means living without worry that some foreigners might kill us on behalf of their causes, but also without having to bow to domestic bureaucrats and cops, especially useless ones. It means not changing the tradition by which the government of the United States treats citizens as its masters rather than as potential enemies. Victory requires killing our enemies, or making them live in debilitating fear.

The flood of authoritative commentary flowing from the U.S. government and the media soon washed common sense out of America's discourse. The conventional wisdom is foursquare in favor of the "War on Terrorism." But it defines that war in terms of an endless series of ever more sophisticated security measures at home; better intelligence for identifying terrorists; and military as well as economic measures to "bring to justice" the shadowy al-Qaeda network. Notably, this flood averts attention from the fact that sowing terror in order to get America to tie itself in rancorous knots is the principal element of several governments' foreign policy. It also discourages questioning the competence of the U.S. officials under whose guidance, in a single decade, America became the object in much of the world of a fateful combination of hatred and contempt. In short, the conventional wisdom envisages no effort to make mourners out of revelers and vice versa.

There will surely be more attacks, and of increasing seriousness. That is because the success of the September 11 attacks and of their aftermath has mightily encouraged America's enemies, and as we shall see, no security or intelligence measures imaginable stand any chance of diminishing the opportunities for successful terrorist attacks. Why should America's enemies stop doing what has proved safe, successful, and fun?

Let us first examine the attitudes and policies of the U.S. government that guarantee defeat—in fact, are defeat itself. Then we will be able to see more clearly what victory would look like, and how it could be achieved.

Part I: Anatomy of Defeat

The U.S. government's "War on Terrorism" has three parts: "Homeland Security," more intelligence, and bringing al-Qaeda "to justice." The first is impotent, counterproductive, and silly. The second is impossible. The third is misconceived and is a diversion from reality.

SECURITY IS ILLUSORY

The nationally televised statement on October 31 by Tom Ridge, President Bush's head of Homeland Security, that the national "alert" and the new security measures would last "indefinitely," is a conclusive self-indictment. The Homeland Security office's vision of the future for ourselves and our children and our children's children involves identification cards for all, with biometric data and up-to-the-minute records of travel, employment, finances, etc., to be used to authorize access to places that are vulnerable to terrorist attack. This means that never again will the government simply trust citizens to go into a government office, a large building, a stadium, an airplane, or for that matter merely to walk around without what the Germans call *Ausweis*—papers. Checking everyone, however, makes sense only if officials will never be able to tell the difference between the average citizen and the enemy—and if the enemy will never be defeated.

But to assume such things is deadly. Unable to stop terrorists, Homeland Security will spend its time cracking down on those who run afoul of its regulations. In Chicago's O'Hare Airport, for example, a man was taken off an aircraft in handcuffs for having boarded before his row number had been called. Tom Ridge, with the demeanor of every state trooper who has ever pulled you over for exceeding 55 miles per hour, reassured Americans that he has the authority to order the shoot-down of civilian airliners. As Machiavelli points out in his *Discourses*, security measures that hurt, threaten, or humiliate citizens engender hatred on top of contempt. No civil libertarian, Machiavelli teaches that true security comes from armed citizens to whom the government is bound by mutual trust. America fought Nazi Germany, Imperial Japan, and the Soviet Union without treating the public as potential enemies, and without making officials into a protected class. By governing from behind security screens, America's leaders today make our land less free and prove themselves less than brave.

Impotence worsens contempt. In *The Prince*, Machiavelli points out that no defense is possible against someone who is willing to give up his life to kill another. In our time we have seen suicide gunners and bombers shred Israel's security system, surely the world's most extensive. Studies carried out by the CIA's Counterintelligence Center generalize the lesson: Whereas terrorist attacks against undefended targets have a rate of success limited only by the terrorists' incompetence, the rate of success against the most heavily defended targets hovers around 85 percent. In short, the cleverest, most oppressive defensive measures buy very little safety. In America, the possibilities for terrorist attack are endless, and effective security measures are inconceivable. How many school buses roll every morning? What would it take to toss a Molotov cocktail into ten of them at precisely the same time? How easy would it be to sneak into a Safeway warehouse and contaminate a case of breakfast cereal? What would it take to set afire a gasoline tanker in a U.S. port?

Security measures actually magnify the effects of terrorism. The hijackings of September 11 have set in motion security measures that shut down airports on receipt of threats or merely on the basis of technical glitches in the security system itself. Similarly, attacks on the food distribution system, the schools, ports, etc., would cripple them by setting in motion attempts to make them secure. Indeed, manipulating the security system in order to cause disruption must rank high on the agenda of any competent terrorist. What's more, any successful attack through, or around, the security systems (remember, such attacks are very likely to succeed) proves that the government cannot protect us.

On top of this, most security measures are ridiculous on their face. Airport security is prototypical. Everyone who flies knows that September 11 ended forever the era of hijacking, and not because of the ensuing security. In fact, hijacking had become possible only because of U.S. policy. Bowing to pressure from the Left in the 1960s, the U.S. government failed to exercise its right to force Castro's Cuba to return hijackers, and instead defined security as disarming passengers. This succeeded in disarming everyone but hijackers. By 1969, Cuba's immunity had encouraged Arab governments to get into the hijacking business. The U.S. government's response to failed policy, however, was not to reverse it, i.e., to attack foreign governments involved with hijacking and to empower passengers to defend themselves. Rather, the government reemphasized its approach. The official instructions to passengers (in force on September 11) read like an invitation to hijackers: "Comply with your captors' directions"; "Relax, breathe deeply"; "If told to maintain a particular body position, talk yourself into relaxing into that position, you may have to stay that way for a long time." Indeed. U.S. security policy *guaranteed* the success of the September 11 hijackings.

But the first plane that hit the World Trade Center forever ended the free ride for hijackers by showing that the federal regulations exposed passengers to death. The passengers on United Airlines flight 93 violated the regulations (for which they technically could have been prosecuted—remember "you must comply with all federal regulations, posted signs and placards, and crew member instructions") and they attacked the hijackers, who unfortunately were already at the controls of the plane. Had they disobeyed minutes before, they would have saved themselves. Since then, a few incidents aboard aircraft have shown that the only function that henceforth a sky marshal might be able to perform would be to save a would-be hijacker from being torn apart by the passengers.

Despite the fact that anti-hijacking measures are now superfluous, the U.S. government now requires three checks of the same identity documents before boarding an airplane, and has banned more items that might be used as weapons. These now superfluous measures would have been futile on September 11. The hijackers would have satisfied any number of document checks, and could have carried out their operation using as weapons things that cannot be excluded from aircraft, such as nylon stockings; or even barehanded, using martial arts. Nor could the gun-toting, camouflage-clad soldiers who nowadays stand out like sore thumbs in America's airports have done anything to prevent September 11.

For passive security to offer any protection against enemies while reducing aggravation of innocents, it must focus very tightly on the smallest possible groups who fit terrorist profiles. In America's current war, terrorists are overwhelmingly likely to be a tiny, mostly visible minority—Arabs. But note that even Israeli security, which carries this sort of profiling to the point of outright racial discrimination, reduces the success of terrorist attempts only marginally.

INTELLIGENCE IS IMPOSSIBLE

Are America's intelligence agencies culpable for failing to stop September 11? No. But for the same reasons that they could not have prevented that atrocity, it is futile to suggest that they might help punish those responsible for it and be able to prevent future terrorism. It is impossible to imagine an intelligence system that would deal successfully with any of the three problems of passive anti-terrorism: security clearances for most of the population; the multiplicity of targets that must be defended as well as the multiple ways in which they can be attacked; and an unlimited stream of possible attackers.

Imagine a security investigation in which neither the investigators nor the evaluators can ask or even listen to anything about the subject's ethnic identity or political or philosophical beliefs, never mind sexual proclivities. This is the system in force today for clearing a few people for "Top Secret—Codeword" information, which concerns nuclear weapons, among other things. How could the U.S. government deny access to a job in Homeland Security, or as an airline pilot, to an Arab Muslim opposed to U.S. policy in the Middle East, for example. Consequently, although The Card (the American equivalent of the Soviet Internal Passport) would contain all sorts of data on your personal life, it would do nothing to impede terrorism. The first act of terrorism committed by a properly credentialed person would dispel any illusion. Alas, the routine occurrence of such events in Israel has not shaken official faith in documentation.

To protect against future terror, U.S. intelligence would have to gain foreknowledge of who, precisely, intended to do what, where, when, and how. It cannot do this both because of fundamental shortcomings and because the task is beyond even the best imaginable system.

Roughly, U.S. intelligence brings to bear against terrorism its network of communications intelligence (COMINT) and its network of human collectors. The value of COMINT with regard to terrorism has never been high and has been diminished by the technical trends of recent decades. The exponential growth in *the number of sources* of electronic communication—cell phones, computers, etc. —as well as *the volume* of such communications has made nonsense of the standard U.S. practice of electronic sorting of grains of wheat in mountains of chaff. Moreover, the advent of near-perfect, cheap encryption has ensured that when the nuggets are found, they will be unreadable. It would have been a fluke had U.S. intelligence had any COMINT data on September 11 prior to the event. It has had none since. If any of the thousands of CIA human intelligence collectors had acquired prior knowledge, the surprise would have been even greater. These collectors simply are not in contact with any of the people who are involved with such things. CIA people work in embassies, pretend to be diplomats, and have contact only with people who normally see diplomats. Human intelligence means human contact. To make contact with terrorists, the CIA would have to operate the way the Drug Enforcement Agency does—becoming part of the drug business. But nobody at CIA knows how to do that, is capable of doing that, or wants to learn. As for the FBI, alas, they are cops who get pay raises not so much for accurate intelligence as for the number of people they put behind bars.

Imagine, however, that U.S. intelligence were excellent in every respect. What could it contribute to passive anti-terrorism? The (new, much improved) official doctrine of the new CIA-FBI Joint Counterintelligence Office states that the intellectual point of departure for counterintelligence and counterterrorism must be identification of the U.S. assets and secrets that enemies are most likely to attack. Then analysts should identify the ways in which enemies might best wage the attacks. Once this is done, they can investigate whether in fact these attacks are being planned, how, and by whom. When analysis of "what" leads to knowledge of "who," the attacks can be frustrated. This approach makes sense as regards counterintelligence, because the targets of the attacks are few and the attacks themselves have to be in the form of slow-developing human contacts or technical deceptions. But it makes no sense with regard to terrorism because the assets that are vulnerable to attack are practically infinite in number and variety, and the modes in which they are liable to be attacked are legion. There cannot be nearly enough investigative resources to explore every possibility.

Hence counterterrorist intelligence has no choice but to begin with the question "who?" Answering this question as regards those who are preparing attacks is difficult in the retail sense, and irrelevant on the wholesale level. Both the difficulty and the irrelevance stem from the fact that those who perpetrate terrorist acts are the equivalent of soldiers in war—there are lots of them, none is remarkable before he shoots, and there are lots where they came from. How would the Drug Enforcement Agency's intelligence operate if it tried to target mere drug couriers or petty salesmen? Its agents would haunt the drug dens, cultivating petty contacts a few of which might be recruited into trafficking. By the same token, today's CIA and FBI (in the unlikely event they could manage the cover) would haunt mosques, Islamic schools, and so forth, in the hope that some of their contacts might be among those recruited for terrorism. Very occasionally all this hard work would be rewarded by a success. But all this would amount to picking off a few drops from a fire hose.

That is why intelligence is useful only in the service of intelligent policy, that is, policy that aims at eliminating the people whose elimination would turn off the hose. But as we shall see, the identity of such people is discoverable not by espionage but by intelligence in the ordinary meaning of the word. It is in this regard that U.S. intelligence is most defective. For example, since September 11, for want of sources of its own, the CIA has been accepting information on terrorism from the intelligence services of Syria and of Yasser Arafat's PLO— outfits whose agendas could not be more opposed to America's.

The gullibility of U.S. intelligence is not merely an intellectual fault. The CIA's judgment is corrupted by its long-standing commitment to certain policies. It is only a small exaggeration to say that radical Arab nationalism was invented at the CIA. Secretary of State John Foster Dulles, when speaking to his brother, CIA director Allen Dulles, about the granddaddy of Arab radicalism Gamal Abdel Nasser, used to call him "your colonel" because his takeover of Egypt had been financed by the CIA. Franz Fanon, the father of the anti-American Left in the Third World, was so close to the CIA that he chose to die under the Agency's medical care. Within the government, the CIA long has championed Arafat's PLO, even as the PLO was killing U.S. ambassadors. Under the Clinton and George W. Bush administrations, CIA Director George Tenet has openly supported the fiction that Arafat's "Security Forces" are something other than an army for the destruction of Israel. Before Iraq's invasion of Kuwait, the CIA's National Intelligence Estimate described Saddam Hussein as no threat to the region and as ready to cooperate with the United States. These are not mere errors.

Intelligence officers are most corrupted by the temptation to tell their superiors what they want to hear. Thus in September, CIA prevailed upon the intelligence service of the Czech Republic to cast doubts on reports that Mohammed Atta, the leader of the September 11 attacks, had twice met in Prague with Iraqi intelligence as he was preparing for the attacks. The Czech government later formally disavowed its service's denial and affirmed the contacts between Atta and Iraq. But the CIA insists that there is no evidence that these two professional terrorists met to discuss terrorism. Gardening, perhaps?

When weapons-grade anthrax began to appear on Capitol Hill and in U.S. post offices in October, attention naturally turned to Iraq, whose regime had run the world's largest or second-largest program for producing it. But the FBI in November, after failing to discover anything whatever concerning the provenance of the anthrax, officially gave the press a gratuitous profile of the mailer as a domestic lunatic. The domestic focus of the investigation was doubly foolish. Even if Saddam Hussein had not thought of anthrax attacks on America before October

2001, the success of the attacks that did occur, as well as the U.S. government's exoneration of foreigners, well-nigh ensured that Saddam would quickly get into the business of spreading the disease among us. Why shouldn't he? Moreover, the further "identification" of the source of the anthrax by an unidentified "intelligence source" as "some right-wing fanatic" aggravated the naturally worst effect of foreign wars: to compound domestic rivalries.

The use of intelligence not to fight the enemy but to erect a bodyguard of misimpressions around incompetent policy is not a sign of brilliance.

The third pillar of the Bush strategy, the hunt for Osama bin Laden and military action first and foremost against the Taliban, is equally problematic.

AL-QAEDA IS NOT THE PROBLEM

In life as in math, we judge the importance of any part of any problem or structure by factoring it out. Does the equation still work? Does the building or the argument still stand? Imagine if a magic wand were to eliminate from the earth al-Qaeda, Osama bin Laden, and Afghanistan's Taliban regime. With them gone, would Americans be safe from Arab terrorists? No way. Then what good does it do for the U.S. government to make war on them and no one else? Why not make war on those whose elimination would eliminate terrorism?

Talk of bringing bin Laden "to justice" would sound less confident were ordinary rules of evidence to apply. The trial of bin Laden would be a nightmare of embarrassment for U.S. intelligence. Any number of uncorroborated reports from sources both unreliable and with an interest in deflecting U.S. anger away from Arab governments have painted bin Laden and his friends as devils responsible for all evils. This picture is attractive because it tends to validate decades of judgments by U.S. policymakers. The only independent test of these reports' validity came in 1998, when President Clinton launched a cruise missile strike against what "sources" had reported to be al-Qaeda's germ warfare plant in Khartoum. It turned out to be an innocent medicine factory. None of this is to deny that bin Laden and his friends are America's enemies and that their deaths would be good for us. But people like bin Laden are far from the sole practitioners of violence against Americans and the people and conditions that brought forth all these violent anti-Americans would soon spawn others like them.

Moreover, even if bin Laden had ordered September 11, as he boasts in a recruitment video, the fire that it started in America's house has been so attractive to potential arsonists that America will not be able to rest until they are discouraged. Getting bin Laden won't help much.

The Taliban are mostly irrelevant to America. Typically Afghan and unlike the regimes of Syria, Iraq, and the PLO, the Taliban have little role in or concern with affairs beyond their land. They provide shelter to various Arabs who have brought them money and armed help against their internal rivals. But Afghans have not bloodied the world. Arabs have.

The loyalty of the Taliban to their Arab guests is of the tribal kind. The moment that the Taliban are under serious threat, they probably will give the foreigners up. But absent the complicity of someone who knows where bin Laden is hiding, it is inconceivable that U.S. intelligence would find bin Laden's location and dispatch Special Forces that could swoop in, defeat his entourage, and take him out. It is surprising that no one has yet lured the U.S. into such an operation—and into an ambush. Destroying the Taliban regime in Afghanistan was always the only way of getting bin Laden, for what little that is worth.

From the beginning of U.S. military operations in Afghanistan on October 7, the lack of strategy for ousting the Taliban was evidence of incompetence. Since then, obvious changes in the character of operations belied U.S. spokesmen's claims that the war is "on schedule," and confirmed that those who planned the operation made no intellectual connection between the military moves they were making and the political results they expected. During the first weeks, U.S. actions were limited to bombing "fixed targets," mostly primitive air defenses and mud huts, unrelated to the ongoing civil war in Afghanistan. Only after it became undeniable that the only force that could make a dent in the regime was the Northern Alliance did U.S. bombers begin to support the Alliance's troops—but tentatively and incompetently. All war colleges teach that bombs from aircraft or artillery are useful in ground combat only insofar as they fall on enemy troops so close in time to the arrival of one's own infantry and armor that they render the enemy physically unable to resist. Whether in the two World Wars, in Vietnam, or in Kosovo, whenever significant amounts of time have passed between bombs falling on defenders and the arrival of attackers, the defenders have held. The Afghan civil war is very much a conventional war. Nevertheless, U.S. officials began to take seriously the task of coordinating bombing and preparing the Northern Alliance for serious military operations only after more than a month of embarrassment. In the initial days and weeks, the operation was a show of weakness, not strength.

The U.S. government's misuse of force was due to its desire to see the Taliban regime lose and the Northern Alliance not win—impossible. When the Alliance did win, the tribal nature of Afghanistan guaranteed that the tribes that stood with the losers would switch sides, and that they would sell to the winners whatever strangers were in their midst. This, however, underlined the operation's fundamental flaw: just as in the Persian Gulf War, the objective was so ill-chosen that it could be attained without fixing the problem for which we had gone to war. We could win the battle and lose the war.

Hence the worst thing about the campaign against Afghanistan was its opportunity cost. Paraphrasing Livy, Machiavelli tells us "the Romans made their wars short and big." This is the wisdom of the ages: where war is concerned, the shorter and more decisive, the better, provided of course that the military objective chosen is such that its accomplishment will fix the problem. By contrast, the central message of the Bush administration concerning the "War on Terrorism" is hardly distinguishable from that of the Johnson administration during the Vietnam War: This war will last indefinitely, and the public must not expect decisive actions. In sum, the Bush administration concedes that the objectives of its military operations will not solve the problem, will not bring victory. Whatever its incidental benefits, the operation is diverting U.S. efforts from inconveniencing any of America's major enemies, and it is wasting the American people's anger and commitment.

You Can't "Spin" Defeat

Sensing mounting criticism at home and abroad for ineffectiveness, President Bush addressed the world and the nation on November 8. But he did not address the question that troubled his audiences: Do you have a reasonable plan for victory, for returning the country to the tranquility of September 10? Conscious that economic activity and confidence in America were sinking, he tried to rally the public by invoking the battle cry of Todd Beamer, the passenger on Flight 93 who attacked the hijackers: "Let's roll!" But the substance of what he said undercut the spirit. Rather than asking Americans to take security into their own hands, he asked Americans for indefinite tolerance of restrictions on their freedom. Typical of the result was a *New York Times* interview with a young laid-off professional. When he watches the news, he said, "it feels like the world is going to hell, like nothing is going to get better." That is defeat.

What would victory look like?

PART II: VICTORY

For Americans, victory would mean living a quiet and peaceable life, if possible even less troubled by the troubles of other parts of the world, even freer from searches and sirens and friction and fear, than on September 10. Hence all of the U.S. government's actions subsequent to September 11 must be judged by how they relate to that end. So what should be the U.S. government's practical objectives? Who is the enemy that stands in the way? How is this obstacle to be removed? In sum, as Thucydides' Archidamus asked the Spartans, "What is to be our war?"

THE TRANQUILITY OF ORDER

Our peace, our victory, requires bloody vengeance for the murder of some 5,000 innocent family members and friends—we seek at least as many deaths, at least as gory, not to appease our Furies, nor even because justice requires it. Vengeance is necessary to eliminate actual enemies, and to leave no hope for any person or cause inimical to America. Killing those people, those hopes, and those causes is the *sine qua non* of our peace—and very much within our power.

Fortunately, our peace, our victory, does not require that the peoples of Afghanistan, the Arabian Peninsula, Palestine, or indeed any other part of the world become democratic, free, or decent. They do not require any change in anybody's religion. We have neither the power nor the right to make such changes. Nor, fortunately, does our peace depend on making sure that others will like us. We have no power to make that happen. Neither our nor anyone else's peace has ever depended on creating "New World Orders," "collective security," or "communities of power." International relations are not magic. Our own peace does not depend on any two foreign governments being at peace with each other. It is not in our power or in the power of any third party to force such a peace except by making war on both governments.

Much less does our peace depend on a "comprehensive peace" in the Middle East or anywhere else. It is not in our power to make such a peace except by conquering whole regions of the world. Our peace and prosperity do not depend on the existence of friendly regimes in any country whatever, including Saudi Arabia. That is fortunate, because we have no power to determine "who rules" in any other country.

Virtually all America's statesmen until Woodrow Wilson warned that the rest of mankind would not develop ideas and habits like ours or live by our standards. Hence we should not expect any relief from the permanent burdens of international affairs, and of war. Indeed, statesmen from Washington to Lincoln made clear that any attempt to dictate another people's regime or religion would likelier result in resentment abroad and faction at home than in any relief from foreign troubles. We can and must live permanently in a world of alien regimes and religions. The mere difference in religion or mode of government does not mean that others will trouble our peace. Whether or not any foreign rulers make or allow war on America is a matter of their choice alone. We can talk, negotiate, and exercise economic pressure on rulers who trouble our peace. But if they make war on us we have no choice but to make war on them and kill them. Though we cannot determine who will rule, we surely can determine who will neither rule nor live.

What do we want from the Middle East to secure our peace? Neither democracy nor a moderate form of Islam—only that the region's leaders neither make nor allow war on us, lest they die. We have both the right and the capacity to make sure of that. But is it not necessary for our peace that the countries of the region be ruled by regimes friendly to us? No. By all accounts, the Saudi royal family's personal friendship with Americans has not affected their aiding and abetting terror against us. It is necessary only that any rulers, whatever their inclinations might be, know that they and their entourages will be killed, surely and brutally, if any harm to Americans originates from within their borders. Respect beats friendship. Do we not have to make sure that the oil of the Middle East continues to fuel the world economy? Is this not necessary to our peace? Indeed. But this does not burden us with the impossible task of ensuring that Saudi Arabia and the Oil States are ruled by friendly regimes. We need only ensure that whoever rules those hot sands does not interfere with the production of the oil that lies beneath them. That we can do, if we will.

In sum, ending the war that broke out on September 11 with our peace will require a lot of killing—to eliminate those in any way responsible for attacking us, and those who might cause further violence to us or choke the world's economy by troubling the supply of oil. It turns out that these mostly are the same persons. Who then are the enemies whose deaths will bring us peace?

It's the Regime, Stupid

When the suicide pilots of September 11 died, they made nonsense of the notion that terrorism was perpetrated by and on behalf of "senseless" individuals, and that the solution to terrorism lay in "bringing to justice" the bombers and trigger pullers. If this notion were adhered to, the fact that the terrorists had already gone to justice should have ended the matter, except for some ritual exhortation to states to be a bit more careful about madmen in their populations.

But these terrorists were neither madmen nor on the edges of society. They came from well-established families. They had more than casual contacts with the political movements and intelligence services of their own regimes and of neighboring countries. They acted on behalf of international causes that are the main sources of legitimacy for some regimes of the Middle East, and are tolerated by all. These causes include a version of Islam; a version of Arab nationalism; driving Westerners and Western influence from Islamic lands; and ridding the Arab world of more or less pro-Western regimes like that of Egypt, Saudi Arabia, and the Emirates. Moreover, peoples and regimes alike cheered their acts. In short, these acts were not private. Rather, they were much like the old Western practice of "privateering" (enshrined in Article I of our own Constitution, vide "letters of Marque and Reprisal"), in which individuals not under formal discipline of governments nevertheless were chartered by governments to make war on their behalf.

Since the terrorists of September 11 are dead and we sense that their deeds were not merely on their own behalf but rather that they acted as soldiers, the question imposes itself: Whose soldiers? Who is responsible? Whose death will bring us peace?

Islam is not responsible. It has been around longer than the United States, and coexisted with it peacefully for two hundred years. No doubt a version of Islam—Islamism—a cross between the Wahhabi sect and secular anti-Westernism, is central to those who want to kill

Americans. But it is neither necessary nor sufficient nor possible for Americans to enter into intra-Muslim theological debates. Besides, these debates are not terribly relevant. The relevant fact is that the re-definition of Islam into something harmful to us is the work of certain regimes and could not survive without them.

Regimes are forms of government, systems of incentives and disin-centives, of honors and taboos and habits. Each kind of regime gives prominence to some kinds of people and practices, while pushing others to the margins of society. Different regimes bring out different possi-bilities inherent in the same people. Thus the Japanese regime prior to World War II changed the meaning of the national religion of Shinto from quaint rituals to militant emperor-worship. Germany meant vastly different things to the German people and to the world when it was under the regime established by Konrad Adenauer, rather than the one established by Adolf Hitler. In short, regimes get to define them-selves and the people who live under them.

Note that Palestine's Yasser Arafat, Iraq's Saddam Hussein, and Syria's Assad family have made themselves the icons of Islamism de-spite the fact that they are well known atheists who live un-Muslim lives and have persecuted unto death the Muslim movements in their countries. Nevertheless, they represent the hopes of millions for stand-ing up to Westerners, driving Israel (hated more for its Westernness than its Jewishness) out of the Holy Land, and undoing the regimes that stand with the West. These tyrants represent those hopes be-cause they in fact have managed to do impressive anti-Western deeds and have gotten away with it. The Middle East's memory of the Gulf War is that Saddam tried to drive a Western lackey out of Kuwait and then withstood the full might of America, later to spit in its face. The Middle East's view of Palestine is that Arafat and the Assads cham-pion the rights of Islam against the Infidels.

Nor are the Arab peoples or Arab nationalism necessarily our en-emies. America coexisted peacefully with Arabs for two centuries. In-deed, the United States is largely responsible for pushing Britain and France to abandon colonial and neo-colonial rule over Arab peoples in the 1950s. U.S. policy has been unfailingly—perhaps blindly—in favor of Arab nationalism. It is true that Egypt's Gamal Abdel Nasser founded Arab nationalism on an anti-American basis in the 1950s. It is true that in 1958 the Arab Socialist Party's (Baath) coup in Iraq and Syria gave Arab nationalism a mighty push in the anti-American direction. It is true that the Soviet Union and radical Arabs created the

Palestine Liberation Organization as an anti-Western movement. But it is also true that Jordan, Saudi Arabia, the Emirates, and, since 1973, Egypt have been just as Arab and just as nationalistic, though generally more pro-Western.

How did the PLO and the Baath regimes of Syria and Iraq gather to themselves the mantle of Arab nationalism? First, the Saudis and the Emirates gave them money, while Americans and Europeans gave them respect and money. Saudis, Americans and Europeans gave these things in no small part because the radical Arabs employed terrorism from the very first, and Saudi, American, and European politicians, and Israelis as well, hoped to domesticate the radicals, buy them off, or divert them to other targets—including each other. Second and above all, we have given them victories, which they have used as warrants for strengthening their hold on their peoples and for recruiting more terrorists against us.

Today, Iraq, Syria, and the PLO are the effective cause of global terrorism. More than half of the world's terrorism since 1969, and nearly all of it since the fall of the Soviet Union, has been conducted on behalf of the policies and against the enemies of those three regimes. By comparison, Libya, Iran, and Sudan have been minor players. Afghanistan is just a place on the map. Factor these three malefactors out of the world's political equation, and what reason would any Arab inclined to Islamism or radical nationalism have to believe that such causes would stand a chance of success? Which intelligence service would provide would-be terrorists with the contacts, the money, the training to enter and fight the West or Israel? For whom, in short, would they soldier?

The Iraqi, Syrian, and the PLO regimes are no more true nationalists than they are true Muslims. They are regimes of a party, in the mold of the old Soviet Union. Each is based on a narrow segment of society and rules by physically eliminating its enemies. Iraq is actually not a nation-state but an empire. The ruling Baath party comes from the Mesopotamian Sunni Arabs, the smallest of the empire's three ethnic groups. The ruling faction of the party, Saddam's *Tikriti*, are a tiny fraction of the ruling party. The Assad family that rules Syria is even more isolated. The faction of the local Baath party that is their instrument of power is made up almost exclusively of Alewites, a neo-Islamic sect widely despised in the region. It must rely exclusively on corrupt, hated security forces. Yasser Arafat rules the PLO through the *Fatah* faction, which lives by a combination of buying off competitors with money acquired from the West and Israel, and killing them. Each of the regimes consists of some 2,000 people. These include officials of the ruling party, officers in the security forces down to the level of colonel, plus all the general officers of the armed forces. These also include top government officials, officials of the major economic units, the media, and of course the leaders of the party's "social organizations" (labor, youth, women's professional, etc.).

All these regimes are weak. They have radically impoverished and brutalized their peoples. A few members of the ruling party may be prepared to give their lives for the anti-Western causes they represent, but many serve out of fear or greed.

The Gulf War and the Arab-Israeli wars proved that their armies and security forces are brittle: tough so long as the inner apparatus of coercion is unchallenged, likely to disintegrate once it is challenged. Killing these regimes would be relatively easy, would be a favor to the peoples living under them, and is the only way to stop terrorism among us.

On Killing Regimes

It follows that killing regimes means killing their members in ways that discredit the kinds of persons they were, the ways they lived, the things and ideas to which they gave prominence, the causes they espoused, and the results of their rule. Thus the Western Allies de-Nazified Germany not by carpet-bombing German cities, which in fact was the only thing that persuaded ordinary Germans that they and the Nazis were in the same boat. The Allies killed the Nazi regime by killing countless Nazis in battle, hanging dozens of survivors, imprisoning hundreds, and disqualifying thousands from social and economic prominence. The Allies promised to do worse to anyone who tried Nazism again, left no doubt in the minds of Germans that their many sorrows had been visited on them by the Nazis, and made Nazism into a dirty word.

Clearly, it is impossible to kill any regime by killing its people indiscriminately. In the Gulf War, U.S. forces killed uncounted tens of thousands of Iraqis whose deaths made no difference to the outcome of the war and the future of the region, while consciously sparing the much smaller number who made up the regime. Hence those who want to "bomb the hell out of the Arabs" or "nuke Baghdad" in response to September 11 are making the same mistake. Killing must be tailored to political effect. This certainly means invading Iraq, and perhaps Syria, with ground troops. It means openly sponsoring Israel's invasion of the PLO territories. But it does not mean close supervision or the kind of political reconstruction we performed in Germany and Japan after World War II.

It is important that U.S. forces invade Iraq with the stated objective of hanging Saddam and whoever we judge to have been too close to him. Once those close to him realize that this is going to happen and cannot be stopped, they will kill one another, each trying to demonstrate that he was further from the tyrant than anyone else. But America's reputation for bluff and for half measures is so entrenched that the invasion will have to make progress greater than in the Gulf War in order for this to happen. At this point, whether or not Saddam himself falls into U.S. hands alive along with his subordinates, it is essential that all be denounced, tried, and hanged on one charge only: having made war on America, on their own people, and on their neighbors. The list of people executed should follow the party-government's organization chart as clearly as possible. It is equally essential that everyone who hears of the event be certain that something even more drastic would follow the recrudescence of such a regime. All this should happen as quickly as possible.

After settling America's quarrel, America should leave Iraq to the peoples who live there. These would certainly break the empire into its three ethnic constituents: Kurds in the north, Mesopotamian Sunnis in the center, and Marsh Shiites in the south. How they may govern themselves, deal with one another and with their neighbors, is no business of ours. What happens in Iraq is simply not as important to us as the internal developments of Germany and Japan were. It is enough that the Iraqis know that we would be ready to defend whatever interest of ours they might threaten. Prestige is a reputation for effective action in one's own interest. We would have re-earned our prestige, and hence our right to our peace.

In the meantime, we should apologize to Israel for having pressured her to continue absorbing terrorist attacks. We should urge Israel to act decisively to earn her own peace, which would involve destroying the regime of the PLO in the West Bank and Gaza. Israel could do this more easily than we could destroy Saddam's regime in Iraq. The reason is that the regime of the PLO, the so-called Palestine Liberation Authority, is wholly dependent on Israel itself for most basic services, from money and electricity to telecommunications, water, food, and fuel. Moreover, the PLA's key people are a few minutes' driving distance from Israeli forces. A cutoff of essentials, followed by a military cordon and an invasion, would net all but a few of these terrorists. The U.S. could not dictate how they should be disposed of. But it would make sense for Israel to follow the formula that they deserve death for the harm these criminal gangs have done to everyone with whom they have come in contact, even one another. With the death of the PLO's gangsters, Palestinian politics would be liberated from the culture of assassination that has stunted its healthy growth since the days of Mufti Hussein in the 1920s.

After Iraq and Palestine, it would be Syria's turn. By this time, the seriousness of America and its allies would speak for itself. A declaration of war against the Assad regime by the U.S., Israel, and Turkey would most likely produce a palace coup in Damascus—by one part of the regime eager to save itself by selling out the others—followed by a revolution in the country. At that point, the Allies might produce a list of persons who would have to be handed over to avert an invasion. And of course Syrian troops would have to leave Lebanon. Americans have no interest in Syria strong enough to require close supervision of successors to Assad. But Turkey's interest might require such supervision. The U.S. should make no objection to Turkey's reestablishment of a sphere of influence over parts of its former empire.

Destroying the major anti-Western regimes in the Middle East might come too late to save the moribund government of Saudi Arabia from the anti-Western sentiments that it has shortsightedly fostered within itself. Or the regime might succumb anyway to long-festering quarrels within the royal family. In any case, it is possible that as a consequence of the Saudi regime's natural death, the foreigners who actually extract and ship the oil might be endangered. In that case, we would have to choose among three options: 1) letting the oil become the tool of whoever might win the struggle (and taking the chance that the fields might be sabotaged in the war); 2) trying to build a new Saudi regime to our liking; or 3) taking over protection of the fields. The first amounts to entrusting the world's economy to the vagaries of irresponsible persons. The second option should be rejected because Americans cannot govern Arabs, or indeed any foreigners. Taking over the oil fields alone would amount to colonial conquest—alien to the American tradition. It would not be alien, however, to place them under joint international supervision—something that Russia might well be eager to join.

Our Own Worst Enemies?

What stands in the way of our achieving the peace we so desire? Primarily, the ideas of Western elites. Here are a few.

Violence and killing do not settle anything. In fact they are the *ultima ratio*, the decisive argument, on earth. Mankind's great questions are decided by war. The battle of Salamis decided whether or not there would be Greek civilization. Whether Western Europe would be Christian or Muslim was decided by the battle of Tours. Even as the U.S. Civil War decided the future of slavery and World War II ended Nazism, so this war will decide not just who rules in the Middle East, but the character of life in America as well.

Our primary objective in war as in peace must be to act in accordance with the wishes and standards of the broadest slice of mankind. In fact, the standards of most of mankind are far less worthy than those prevalent in America. America's Founders taught this, and forgetting it has caused harm. Alliances must always be means, never ends in themselves, and as such must be made or unmade according to whether or not they help secure our interest. Our interest in war is our kind of peace. That is why it is mistaken to consider an ally anyone who impedes the killing of those who stand in the way of our peace. With allies like Saudi Arabia, America does not need enemies.

When involved in any conflict, we should moderate the pursuit of our objectives so as to propitiate those moderates who stand on the sidelines. Individuals and governments stand on the sidelines of conflict, or lend support to one side, according to their judgment of who will win and with whom they will have to deal. "Extremist" is one of many pejorative synonyms for "loser." The surest way to lose the support of "moderates" is to be ineffective. Might is mistaken for right everywhere, but especially in the Middle East. Hence the easiest way to encourage terrorism is to attempt to deal with "the root causes of resentment against us" by granting some of the demands of our enemies.

Learning to put up with security measures will make us safer, and is a contribution we can all make to victory. On the contrary, security measures will not make us safe, and accustoming ourselves to them is our contribution to defeat. The sign of victory over terrorism will be the removal of security measures.

The Arab regimes that are the matrices of terrorism have nothing going for them except such Western shibboleths. Their peoples hate them. Their armies would melt before ours as they have melted before

Western armies since the days of Xenophon's Upcountry March. They produce nothing. Terror is their domestic policy and their foreign policy.

The regimes that are killing us and defeating us are the product of Western judgments in the mid-twentieth century that colonialism is wrong and that these peoples could govern themselves as good stewards of the world's oil markets. They continue to exist only because Western elites have judged that war is passé.

It is these ideas and judgments, above all, that stand in the way of our peace, our victory.

IV: 2002—What Now?

VICTORY WATCH: ARE WE WINNING YET*

" In the end, there was no one so small or weak that they could not do them harm." Montesquieu, The Greatness of the Romans and Their Decline

By New Year's Day, Afghanistan's Taliban regime was history and the Bush administration was basking in the aura of success. But auras are not realities—especially in war.

Were the victims of September 11 avenged? There is no evidence that anyone killed in Afghanistan had a role in the September 11 attacks. Was America now safe from terrorism, or at least safer than it was? No one suggests that any significant proportion of the leaders or followers of anti-American terrorism were killed, or that hopes for their cause were defeated. So what exactly did sweeping away the Taliban do to bring America the peaceful security necessary to our way of life?

The proof that it did nothing is that success in Afghanistan coincided with intensification of the security measures that have darkened American life since September 11. Only the relaxation of the security measures' grip, a return to the habits of trust that had made America unique, would constitute victory. Would forthcoming operations in the "war on terrorism" trigger such a return? Alas, attempts to engage officials in the Bush administration in such questions inevitably resemble a hospital dialogue:

> Doctor: Good news. The operation was a complete success. We removed the targeted tissue using the latest and most advanced

*This essay appeared in the Claremont Review of Books, *No. 2, Winter 2002.*

61

techniques medical science has to offer. We are planning several more operations, each designed for assurance of similar success.

Family: Great! Thanks! That means you are now taking the life-support tubes out of our patient, right? When will he be back to normal?

Doctor: The medical staff will discuss only the professional qualities of our procedures. New life-support tubes are going into him every day, and as we said, each successive operation is sure to be more successful than the previous one. You must have patience.

Family: Sure, but patience for what, and for how long? What do you mean by success? If the procedures are so successful, why more life support? Are you doing anything that would let him go home?

Doctor: We are making no plans at this time for the removal of life support. It is enough for us that our operations are related to his condition, and that they have high technical merits.

Family: What sense does that make? We've heard that you rejected or postponed indefinitely some operations that some experts say would actually cure him. Why?

Doctor: They might or might not cure him. And they would be expensive.

Family: But money's no problem for us. Besides, your operations will keep him as a medical guinea pig indefinitely. Why not try the only ones that anyone argues will effect a cure?

Doctor: Well, you see, those measures would be disruptive to the medical profession. Doctors here and elsewhere would think badly of us for abandoning protocols most of us have followed for years. To do so would be to concede that we have not been very good doctors.

Family: Maybe you aren't.

WHAT HAPPENED IN AFGHANISTAN AND WHAT DID NOT

After abandoning an embarrassing three-week effort to defeat the Taliban regime without handing a victory to their Northern Alliance foes, the U.S. government used modern communications and close air support to facilitate that victory. The Taliban ceased to exist. As predicted here, Afghans of all stripes eagerly killed or turned over to Americans the Arabs who had bolstered the losing faction.

Many of the perhaps 2,000 Arabs who died in Afghanistan, and perhaps a few of the more numerous Afghans who died, were unfriendly to America. But because there is no evidence that anyone who died had anything to do with September 11, the Afghan campaign did not avenge America. Perhaps some of those who died might have harmed America had they lived. Hence America is much better off for their deaths. But these deaths did not shut off the pipeline of violent young men who believe that America is more contemptible than it is evil.

Whose deaths might have shut off this pipeline? Conceivably, killing Osama bin Laden in a way that would have discredited him might have helped. But the U.S. government did not find him, and would not have known how to discredit him if it had. Simply killing him would not have blunted his message: America may kill some servants of Allah's cause, but it cannot protect itself or defeat that cause. Bin Laden's claim that countless others would fill his place was no idle boast, while the U.S. claim that al-Qaeda was the proximate cause of anti-American terrorism was belied by the U.S. "homeland security" measures, which waxed even as al-Qaeda waned.

WHAT HAPPENED TO OSAMA BIN LADEN?

When it became clear last November that the Taliban would be defeated, it also became clear that if bin Laden remained in Afghanistan, he would end up in American hands. Since America would destroy any other regime that harbored him, he became a deadly liability to any host. In American hands alive, he might have implicated anyone who had ever associated with him—especially governments whose purposes he had served. In American hands as a dead trophy, he would be a liability to his cause. But if he was never found, he would serve his cause as a living legend. More important, those governments who had succored him knew that obliging the Americans to continue searching for him would deflect America's ire from themselves. And in fact those Americans who successfully argued against attacking Iraq also cited the continuing need to search for bin Laden. Because bin Laden is worth more to his associates dead than alive, it is a safe bet that he died at their hands and will never be found. Take a lesson from *The Godfather Part II*: Don't bother looking for the assassins. Those who sent them have long since killed them.

Chasing Mice

After a groaning December debate over whether to follow up victory over the Taliban with the destruction of the Iraq regime, the Bush administration decided to send American forces to hunt down some anti-American small fry in the boondocks of the Philippines and Somalia, to leave Saddam Hussein alone, and to continue supporting a Palestinian state. The reasons that U.S. officials give for this are remarkably truthful: Although the vast majority of Americans would welcome a decisive war against Iraq, the administration does not wish to displease those elements of elite opinion who would regard it (correctly) as a departure from the post-World War II habit of not doing away with America's enemies. Moreover, while centrist leaders of Italy, Spain, and Turkey would cheer at the undoing of Saddam Hussein's regime and the end of Yasser Arafat's Palestinian Authority, the leftist European leaders so dear to much of U.S. elite opinion would be displeased, and the Saudi royal family would be frightened.

The administration did not try to make a case that chasing mice in the Philippine and Somali operations would make America safer than operations against Iraq or the Palestine Authority—just that more people in Washington would be comfortable doing one thing rather than another.

Dancing Around Wolves

In war, however, true comfort comes only from defeating the enemy. Taking comfort from the deaths of recruits to the enemy's cause is a short-term illusion. The terrorists' chief weapon is the will to attack, and they will attack so long as their causes have hope and credit. That hope and that credit is embodied by regimes, and success or failure is defined by the fate of regimes. On the anniversary of the Persian Gulf War in January, Saddam Hussein gave yet another speech to the Arab world, credibly claiming that America's power had dwindled in eleven years and would surely drop further. He has allowed acolytes to praise him on Arab TV for the success of September 11. As it became clear that the post-September 11 U.S. government was no more capable of mustering the will to topple him than had its predecessors, Hussein sat firmly in the saddle. He warned the Arab world that its chief preoccupation would have to be satisfying the demands of the warriors being mobilized in the great anti-American struggle.

The Saudi regime got the message. Those who follow the region's affairs have always known that the impotent, faction-ridden, terminally corrupt Saudi regime has stayed a step ahead of internal implosion and external attack by paying ransom to the threat *du jour*. Thus the Saudis have fed the Iraqi regime and the Palestinian movement that bit them, as well as the Islamist movement within its own borders. Saudis recruited by Iraq or other anti-American and anti-Saudi regimes but financed by the royal family have been in the forefront of anti-American terrorism. Yet the Saudi regime has enjoyed U.S. support resulting from its many friendships in America, many bought and paid for. Now, however, the threats from Iraq and other anti-American forces are so strong, and support from America against those threats so irrelevant, that the House of Saud is being forced to cut its ties with America—with as little disruption as it can manage. This, of course, is likelier to speed its overthrow than to retard it.

What matters is that keeping Saudi Arabia "on our side" — in practice, allowing the Saudi regime to be on both sides at once — has been terribly important to U.S. policy. For the sake of not upsetting the Saudis, the first Bush administration did not finish off the Iraqi regime in 1991, and for that sake the current Bush administration decided that the "war on terrorism" would not be waged against any Arab country. Considering that America's attackers are almost 100 percent Arab, this amounts to beating around the bush, if not the bushes dancing around the wolves—in any case, nothing serious, like war.

DECLARING VICTORY ON LIFE SUPPORT

America is at war to establish the kind of peace in which we can live American lives. While the U.S. government's actions abroad thus far have not had serious consequences on America's enemies, the U.S. government's actions at home have had consequences at once serious and laughable. There are checkpoints, and not just at airports, where the people doing the checking are more likely to be terrorists than those being checked. Moreover, because of political correctness, old ladies are being searched while young Arab men are not. Washington D.C. is a fortress. *New York Times* columnist Thomas Friedman half-joked that the next step in security will be for passengers to fly naked. Nakedness will not suffice, however, to prevent the smuggling of biological warfare powders. For that, body cavity checks would be required. And then there is the fact that with all the armed security

---

personnel around, the easiest way to penetrate the security is to forge credentials or just buy uniforms. In the few instances in which persons have tried to penetrate these security systems, they have succeeded.

Nevertheless, Homeland Security Czar Tom Ridge and Attorney General John Ashcroft staked much on the gratuitous prediction that the 2002 Winter Olympics in Salt Lake City will be terror-free because the U.S. government is spending $400 million on the *dernier cri* in security programs. Just one terrorist success, and the aura vanishes.

By forgoing attempts to defeat the causes of anti-American terrorism as well as the regimes that support those causes, and by placing its bets on security measures, the government has endangered not only America's security but her liberty.

VICTORY WATCH: WHAT WAR?*

"For them, war would consist of fighting as little as possible." Charles de Gaulle, War Memoirs, Vol. I, *on Franco-British policy between September 1939 and June 1940.*

By spring 2002, the Bush administration's pretense that it was making "war" had worn thin. The Bush team had invoked war, but aimed its military operations and diplomacy chiefly at minimizing the discomfort of "friendly" Arab governments. Intent on not displeasing, the Bush team let itself be diverted from fighting the terror states into restraining Israel. And yet these "friendly" governments, in thrall to the terror states of Iraq, Syria, and the Palestinian Authority, were practically accessories in the terrorist attacks on America. All of this calls for something of a postmortem on the war.

Rather than destroy enemies whose leaders' deaths would make the American people safe from terrorist attacks, the Bush team went out of its way not to identify any enemy except the "shadowy" al-Qaeda—as if a private organization could freely organize worldwide mayhem from Arab police states without being one of their tools.

This essay originally apeared in the Claremont Review of Books, Spring 2002.

So far, the Bush team's discussions of strategy amount to wish lists, unrelated to acts of war. Hence, rather than conveying readiness to force others to choose between being killed or accepting America's version of peace, the Bush diplomacy conveyed readiness to accept others' ever-pricier promises of peace. This is what "peace processes" are all about: one side vainly seeks to avoid the reality of war.

Yet reality does not long permit the self-indulgences of phony war. That is because once the killing starts, one side's reluctance is the greatest encouragement for the other to fight. And the longer wars go on, the more possibilities they offer to the bold. That is why any government that stints its pursuit of victory in order to preserve its favorite current arrangements inevitably finds that others impose their own agendas on the conflict.

In sum, the "war on terrorism" did not veer off course in the spring: it wasn't on track from the beginning.

NEVER ON TRACK

The Bush team decided, from the start, to make war on "terrorism" (an abstract noun) rather than on real people. Nearly a century's experience should have taught Americans that to rid the world of certain abstract nouns—e.g., "militarism" (1917), "war" (1928), "aggression" (1941, 1950, 1990, etc.), or "poverty, hunger, disease, and ignorance" (Vietnam)—while making it safe for "democracy," would take ruling the globe with an iron hand. But latter-day American statesmen have eschewed matching military means to political ends. This has made U.S. foreign policy insolvent, unserious.

By nature, armed force only can kill certain people and regimes. Who to kill is the decision that defines any war. In September 2001, in response to an attack on America by Arabs traveling on passports from "friendly" Arab countries on behalf of causes supported by those countries' governments and embodied by the terror states of Iraq, Syria and the Palestinian Authority, the Bush team decided to kill people in Afghanistan and to overthrow the Taliban regime. No one argued that this would make America safe from the rising enmity of the Arab world, or definitely avenge the attacks of September 11. Indeed, the Bush team acknowledged that Arab governments were abetting this enmity and warned that it would have to root out Arab enemies. But it deferred the whole matter to an undefined "next phase," because it did not want to displease "friendly" Arab governments. Saudi Arabia conditioned its support of the war on Americans' not killing any Arabs at all. Thus the Bush administration allowed the war to go off the serious track—at least temporarily.

But the temporary threatens to become permanent. Deference to the Saudi and Egyptian governments—the reason that the first Bush administration had stopped short of Baghdad in 1991—dictated once again the deferral of action. The completion of the U.S. war in Afghanistan did not usher in the "next phase" in which America would fight its enemies in the Arab world. Instead, American troops would scour the ends of the earth for al-Qaeda. Pursuant to intelligence reports of sophisticated terrorist nerve centers in northeast Afghan caves, U.S. troops stormed the caves—and found nothing of the sort. But real information could not trigger action against Arab states. In the March 25 issue of *The New Yorker*, Jeffrey Goldberg reported that Saddam Hussein was making use of elements of al-Qaeda to fight the Kurds in northern Iraq. Yet this report coincided with the Bush team's admission that planning for any invasion of Iraq was deferred to 2003, if then.

Why? Because nothing that happened on September 11 had changed the Bush team's primary objective in the Middle East—maintaining the status quo—or its evaluation of what the status quo required, namely, the good graces of Saudi Arabia and Egypt. Alas, to ask dubious allies to support a course of action that one has already shown the willingness to defer and redefine, amounts to asking for further pressure to defer, redefine, and derail.

ON THE ENEMY TRACK

Following the Saudis' lead, America's Arab "friends" persuaded the Bush administration to abstain from rooting out America's enemies in the Arab world and devote itself to restraining Israel from striking at its enemies in the Middle East. The Arab powers persuaded the Bush team to turn from America's war to a role in *their* war, and on *their* side.

In the 1990s, Saddam Hussein's Iraqi regime had become the leading force in the Arab world. Despite losing half his military forces in the 1991 Persian Gulf War, Saddam won over the region's most virulent elements by surviving to thumb his nose at America and denouncing all manifestations of Arab collaboration with the United States. By adroit, vehement propaganda, money, and murder, he and the leaders of the other terror states personified the identification of Islam with anti-Westernism. Their movement, which included political and philanthropic as well as terrorist activities, grew fat and strong on the protection money extorted from the Saudi royal family. By the turn of the century its message that America, its Jews, and their "Zionist entity" were polluting Arab lands had forced America's Arab "friends," notably including the Saudi royal family, to follow their fears more than their friendships.

To shift the Bush team from America's war to their own, the Arab terror regimes had first to manufacture one. The spring of 2002 saw a dramatic increase in the level of attacks by various Palestinian forces against Israel. These assaults, which included suicide bombing, inflicted half as many casualties on Israel as had the 1967 war. This new war served no interest of the ordinary Palestinians. It made their lives immeasurably worse materially, and subjected them to constant danger of execution as "collaborators" for failure to back the war. Note also that suicide bombing was anything but the action of autonomous individuals. The bombers' families received sums of money that amounted to compelling endowments, supplied publicly by the Saudi royal family and Saddam's Iraqi government.

The Saudi royal family's demands were straightforward: The Bush team must intervene by interposing American bodies between Israel and the Palestinians in exchange for Saudi promises to intercede with the Palestinians. But note that our Arab "friends" also promised that in any quarrel between America and the terror states they would stand, publicly at least, with...the terror states. To do otherwise would undermine their stability, which the Bush team would not desire, right? By the end of April, President Bush had bought this line and had committed American officers to "oversee" (with no power to compel) the Palestinian Authority's promise to keep certain malefactors in prison. He promised to send more Americans, and had in fact already put the brakes on Israel's own war on terrorists.

Did the Bush administration not know that Americans, thus interposed, would become the occasion of endless diversions? Did the administration not care about avenging September 11, about fighting all terrorists, about erasing distinctions between terrorists and those who harbor them? They probably did know and care—just not enough to change longstanding foreign policy priorities and intellectual habits, not to mention the people who run U.S. intelligence and diplomacy.

THREE MONKEYS

"See no evil, hear no evil, speak no evil" describes U.S. intelligence in
the war on terrorism. Nine months after September 11, U.S. intelligence still has no idea who most of the hijackers were, where the
operation was organized, by whom, or who paid for it. Our professionals concluded that, except for Osama bin Laden, the identity of
America's enemies is a mystery. Still, they are certain that our enemies are amateurs, unconnected with professional intelligence
services.

Start with the Saudi hijackers. The photos and names released by
the U.S. government match flight manifests with visa files from U.S.
consulates. But the only pictures of the hijackers from security cameras are of persons other than the ones in the visa files and flight
manifests. Indisputably, the hijackers used stolen identities. That is a
mark of a major-league intelligence service. (The Saudi government
prevented independent investigation of who the hijackers really were.)

The hijacking itself bore marks of professionalism: the hijackers
used sophisticated chemical sprays and methods of rapid entry into
the cockpits, they had mastered navigation beyond what had been
taught them in their U.S. flight schools, and they had turned off the
planes' transponders—which also had not been taught them in the
flight schools.

Then there is the $100,000 that financed the U.S. part of the mis-
sion. Mohammed Atta, an Egyptian, reportedly got it after a meeting
in June 2000 in Prague with Ahmed al Ani, an Iraqi intelligence officer
who specialized in handling terrorists. The account from which the
money came had been professionally scrubbed of the owner's identity. On April 9, 2001, Atta made a 72-hour trip to see al Ani again.
Two weeks later, the trained "soldiers" in the hijacking left Saudi Arabia
for America. Did the two terrorists talk about the lingerie business?

From all this, a reasonable person—also knowing that Iraq has a
facility where terrorists train to take over Boeing aircraft—might conclude that September 11 had been organized by Iraq, with connections
in Saudi Arabia and Egypt.

But the CIA paid attention to trails that the hijack operation had
chosen not to cover. On September 9, Atta wired $15,000 back to a
different account. This one had an unhidden owner—an associate of
Osama bin Laden. Osama had done it! And Atta had left his flight
manual in a car he had rented in his own name. He only knew what

he learned in flight school! See? An amateur operation planned in one of those fabulous Afghan caves.

If Wishes Were Strategy

With the help of the CIA, the Bush team imagines the world somewhat as follows: nearly all the world's governments see terrorism as a threat to themselves as well as to civilized life, and are more-or-less willing to cooperate in rooting it out. The problem is that the Gulf War and the Israeli-Palestinian conflict have inhibited modernization and secularization in the Muslim world. The key to defeating terrorism is the cooperation of friendly, progressive governments in the Muslim world. To get that cooperation, we must ensure the survival of those governments. To do that, we must cool any conflicts that raise popular ire against them and America. This means any American attack on Iraq would be counterproductive. It would call forth more terrorism than it would prevent, and would directly endanger friendly governments. This also means cooling the Arab-Israeli conflict, whatever the cost. Once Egypt, Saudi Arabia, Jordan, and maybe Syria and the Palestinian Authority too, can afford to be as friendly to America as is Pakistan, then liaison between their intelligence services and ours will leave the terrorists nowhere to hide. The war on terrorism will be won by police measures.

Reality

Success fuels hope of victory, which fuels effort. By this spring, only American policymakers could fail to understand that the Saudi government's diplomatic overtures to Teheran and above all to Baghdad, as well as its assumption of the role as their advocate in the West, implied its recognition that it was living at its enemies' sufferance. Any number of troublemakers in the region surely saw in the Saudi government's weakness the chance of their lives. There is little doubt that someone will seize that chance and that the House of Saud will first split and then fall, which in turn will convince more people in the region to try for power and glory. That is what real wars are made of. As stability, the Bush team's premise and objective, disappears, the Bush team finally will have to confront the choice that it worked so hard to avoid: between paying the price of victory and that of defeat. And it will have to do this from a well-earned position of disadvantage.

Governments bend to those they fear, and bite those they hold in contempt. The Bush team's conduct of the "war" made the Arab world less afraid of America. How could that be, given all the bombs America dropped on Afghanistan? Simple. The Arab world knew all along that America could drop those bombs. It wondered, however, would America dare to drop them in order to alter the balance of power among the Arabs themselves? By dropping them on Afghanistan, America answered, no. "Friendly" Arabs' estimate of America's capacity to protect them from threats foreign and domestic also dropped. America seemed weak again when the Bush team recoiled from the Arab world's brandishing of the ultimate terror weapon, suicide bombing. Count on it: the next stage of the war will feature suicide bombings on American streets.

V: Hamlet's Pieces

THE PATH TO VICTORY:
A SYMPOSIUM ON THE WAR

The following exchange of views involves five distinguished commentators who reviewed the published accounts of my analysis of American policy. When the discussants have referred to specific articles, I have indicated in brackets the corresponding chapters in this book.*

WILLIAM F. BUCKLEY JR.
EDITOR-AT-LARGE, NATIONAL REVIEW

One of the deposits of Angelo Codevilla, with almost every one of his essays, is deep, heavy *gloom*. His analysis is so shrewd, his sense of human nature and its drives so highly developed, he confidently tells us what is going to happen, and it is quite awful. In the first of his essays [Chapter III] for the *Claremont Review of Books* he explained, at some length, that there is no way in which the United States can protect itself from continued acts of terrorism. The reason is as simple as that the American people do not live surrounded by a moat, which means that there are 10,000 concentrations of people every day—in movie theaters, stadiums, parades, tourist centers, college graduation quadrangles—who are targets for terrorists; to be sure, terrorists one degree less ambitious than those who brought off the attacks of September 11.

He was right, there is no way we can protect ourselves. He was wrong in predicting that these assaults would ensue. In the most recent

This chapter originally appeared in the Claremont Review of Books, Fall 2002.

issue [Chapter IV] Mr. Gloom tells us that there will be suicide bombings on American streets. "Count on it."

Well, I'm not going to count on it any more than on Codevilla's
forecast for the weeks following September II, but with that demur-
ral, I am with him on his overall analysis of deficient U.S. strategy. In
that first essay, I thought him arresting and persuasive when he wrote
that the personalization of the September massacre was precisely what
we needed to do. We did it, to be sure, to Osama bin Laden, but he
was never a large enough target. I myself wrote, soon after September
II, that we had a great deal to fear from actually finding and shooting
bin Laden, which would have left us theatrically triumphant, queen
bee inert in our hand, while the swarm continued its depredations.
Something much larger than bin Laden needed decapitation, and I
liked also that Codevilla declared that a great deal was to be gained by
precisely condemning a real enemy—Saddam Hussein, a head of
state—to death. Executing Saddam Hussein in Baghdad would not
absolutely eliminate the hive, but the mailed fist would have been felt,
and the consequences of it would still the hands of most of the terror-
ist-minded who think themselves agents of a political ideal.

Codevilla is right that from the beginning we have feared the consequences of living up to our own rhetorical demands. If we truly set out
to "declare war" on those who shelter terrorists, let alone dispatch
them, we'd be at war all over the place. Call it a world war. We needed
a manageable target, and Iraq was it. It is, I think, too late to generate
what would have served us so well, strategic marksmanship. Codevilla
was right. He usually is. Count on it.

FRANK GAFFNEY
PRESIDENT, CENTER FOR SECURITY POLICY

Angelo Codevilla's essay "What War?" [Chapter IV] dissected with
characteristic brilliance the problems with the Bush administration's
response to the attacks of September IIth. The good news is that,
since that critique was published several months ago, President Bush
and his national security team have corrected some of the policy and
strategic defects identified by Codevilla. The bad news is that they
have not done so across the board.

First, consider the positive steps: In the months since "What War?"
was written, the president's determination to remove Saddam Hussein
from power has been formally and repeatedly declared. This decision

reflects an appreciation not only that it was a grievous mistake to have allowed the Iraqi despot to remain in power eleven years ago but a belief that he will become a vastly more dangerous foe for the United States and its allies if not toppled forthwith.

Preparations to effect such a change of regime appear to be proceeding, involving military movements, diplomatic consultations, and other measures. This presidential direction reflects a decided departure from the notion that Codevilla has correctly ascribed to successive American governments—namely, that regional stability can only be achieved by preserving the status quo. If President Bush has his way, at least one Arab foe will be taken out before this war is over. Equally important are the administration's recent pronouncements to the effect that the United States is no longer going to legitimate, work with, and otherwise prop up the so-called "reformers" in the Iranian government. If the president is also serious about helping the people of Iran achieve their liberation, the status quo in the Persian Gulf could be changed beyond recognition—and very much to the advantage of U.S. interests and those of others who cherish freedom.

In the past few months, President Bush has also taken important steps to counter the Arab bait-and-switch aimed at implicating this country in what Codevilla correctly calls "their war"—the long-running and relentless campaign to destroy Israel. By declaring that numerous, systemic political and leadership changes must precede the establishment of a Palestinian state and American recognition of same, Mr. Bush has created a new opportunity to return the focus of America's war back where it belongs.

Finally, there are, in addition to the foregoing, signs that the Saudi Arabians are losing the privileged status they have enjoyed and exploited in Washington over the past few decades. To be sure, this is partly a product of American popular revulsion at: the Saudis' involvement in the September 11 attacks; their lack of cooperation in investigating this and other acts of anti-U.S. terror; their support for suicide bombers in Israel and Wahhabist-sponsored recruitment, indoctrination, and terrorism elsewhere around the globe; the excessive influence exercised by the Saudi Ambassador Prince Bandar, the array of former U.S. officials and ambassadors on his payroll and the various subversive political, media, and ostensibly theological organizations they have created in this country over the past four decades; and the House of Saud's repressive, indeed Talibanesque, application of Sharia law against women, non-believers, and U.S. service personnel.

Still, the sea-change is palpable and if not reversed will prove to be of enormous strategic import.

While these and similar steps are promising correctives to several of the serious policy defects Professor Codevilla identified a few months back, they will only contribute to a genuine victory in the present war if further actions are taken without delay. These include:

- Equipping, training, funding, and otherwise empowering the Iraqi National Congress to serve as an effective opposition umbrella group in Iraq—an essential ingredient to the liberation of that country and to giving it a chance for peace and stability post-Saddam.

- Providing whatever financial, informational, and material support is needed to help the Iranian people end the theocrats' misrule in Teheran.

- Working closely with non-Wahhabist Muslims in this country and abroad to counter the effects of that sect's virulent anti-American and anti-Western pedagogy and recruitment while cutting off Saudi support for same.

- Taking the war in appropriate ways to all of our enemies, not just al-Qaeda.

- Complementing other defensive measures at home by building and deploying at once effective protection against ballistic missile attack.

To accomplish any, let alone all, of these prerequisites for victory in the war begun on September 11, the Bush administration must adopt one of Angelo Codevilla's most trenchant recommendations: It must change not only "longstanding foreign policy priorities and intellectual habits, [but] the people who run U.S. intelligence and diplomacy." Only by staffing the State Department and CIA with individuals who want the president to succeed in the present war—and who are willing to help him do so—is there a chance of avoiding an outcome in which, when it is over, the question will be "What victory?"

Mackubin T. Owens
Professor of Strategy and Force Planning, U.S. Naval War College

There is little of substance in Angelo Codevilla's series on the terror war with which I would quibble. He is especially on target when he criticizes the whole concept of homeland security. He is also dead right when he formulates in his first installment [Chapter III] the four attitudes that traditionally have informed the U.S. approach to the use of force.

The problem with the series is Codevilla's failure to give any consideration to prudence in the development and implementation of policy and strategy. This failure creates an unrelenting negativism that can only end in defeatism. Codevilla's apparent inability to distinguish between the Clinton and Bush administrations when it comes to international relations and the use of force is akin to suggesting in 1861 that there was no difference between the Buchanan and Lincoln administrations.

Indeed, Codevilla puts me in mind of nothing so much as the Radical Republicans who harried Lincoln throughout the Civil War. Eschewing prudence and ignoring the political conditions that Lincoln faced, they constantly criticized him for his timidity. But had they prevailed in forcing their policies on Lincoln, the Union cause most likely would have been lost in 1862.

We praise Lincoln for his prudence in navigating the minefields of American politics during the Civil War. President Bush deserves the same consideration. In accordance with the dictates of prudence, he, like Lincoln, has skillfully modified his policy in order to adapt to changing circumstances. This is not insignificant.

In fact, only a blind man could fail to note the substantial differences between the Bush and Clinton administrations. Bush's State of the Union speech laid out a new foreign policy. The Bush administration now has a declared policy of regime change and preemption. And perhaps most significantly, President Bush, having "given peace a chance" in the Middle East, now essentially has thrown the weight of the United States behind Israel. In other words, President Bush has begun to implement all the policies that Codevilla advocated in his first article, albeit not as quickly as the good professor would like.

But that's the point. For political reasons, President Bush was not able to effect these changes immediately any more than Lincoln was able to proclaim emancipation in 1861. Such a step surely would have led to the Union's loss of Kentucky and Missouri—and possibly even Maryland. The political cost of precipitous action to President Bush likewise would have been high.

I don't think I need to remind Codevilla that the essence of prudence is the ability to adapt the universal principle to particular circumstances. The right policy, as Codevilla argues, is to effect regime changes in states such as Iraq and to abandon the "evenhanded" approach to the Arab-Israeli dispute. But prudence dictates when and how the policy is to be implemented, which in turn depends a great deal on the circumstances. For instance, Codevilla decries the fact that we have not yet attacked Iraq. But he must know that current conditions, mostly having to do with weather, climate, and the "tyranny of distance," do not favor military action for a few more months. Precipitous action in the Gulf would be as risky as an Allied attempt to invade Europe would have been in 1942 or 1943.

An insistence upon rapid action also ignores the greatest military advantage the United States possesses—dominance of the world's "commons," *viz.*, the sea, space, and air. This advantage means that the United States does not have to strike rapidly. We can bide our time until conditions are optimal. We don't need to risk precipitous action.

Codevilla also ignores some other points. To begin with, he seems adamant that there is a single response to terrorism. But as the Prussian "philosopher of war" Carl von Clausewitz wrote over a century and a half ago: "The first, the supreme, the most far-reaching act of judgment that the statesman and commander have to make is to establish...the kind of war on which they are embarking; neither mistaking it for, nor trying to turn it into, something that is alien to its nature. This is the first of all strategic questions and the most comprehensive." But it is also the most difficult because the answer ultimately depends on the interaction of the belligerents. Since both sides can adapt and change, the kind of war we will be fighting will not necessarily remain constant but will be mutable and may change as conditions change.

Finally, Codevilla seems to believe that his proposals will assure a final victory. But surely he is familiar with what Clausewitz had to say about the finality of war: "[E]ven the ultimate outcome of a war is not always to be regarded as final. The defeated state often considers the outcome merely as a transitory evil, for which a remedy may still be found in political conditions at some later date."

Codevilla is fond of citing Machiavelli. Perhaps, in the political context of a democratic republic, he should think more in terms of Aristotle. The issue is not the right policy, but when it is prudent to implement it.

NORMAN PODHORETZ
SENIOR FELLOW, THE HUDSON INSTITUTE, AND EDITOR-AT-LARGE, COMMENTARY

Angelo Codevilla's critique of the American government's response to the attacks of September 11 is the most intellectually formidable of any I have seen. There is no disagreeing with much of what he says about the weaknesses of the CIA and the FBI; about some of the methods by which the administration has thus far been trying to make us more secure; and about the confusion that has resulted from its original misconceptions regarding the nature of the Arab regimes and the war they have been waging against Israel.

Yet in Codevilla's own opinion, even if the CIA and the FBI were perfect, we would still remain vulnerable to terrorist assault. "There will surely be more attacks, and of increasing seriousness," Codevilla assures us, including "suicide bombings on American streets."

Yes; and yet, as of late July, none of this has (thank God) materialized. It is a great puzzle, and despite much strenuous lucubration I have been unable to come up with a persuasive explanation. Perhaps, then, for all the missteps our government has taken in this area, it has been doing something right. Perhaps enough terrorist "sleepers" in the United States have been arrested to frustrate their immediate designs. And perhaps the grilling of all those prisoners in Guantanamo has yielded information that has further hampered such designs.

But Codevilla not only ridicules the Bush administration's "homeland security" measures as ineffective; he also casts a cold eye on its conduct of the war abroad. In his judgment, the campaign in Afghanistan has taken on the wrong enemy in the wrong place for the wrong reasons and by the wrong means.

Here again, however, even granting some of his criticisms, perhaps this campaign actually has disrupted the terrorist network, and perhaps those daisy cutters have sufficiently frightened the state sponsors of terrorism to induce second thoughts about the desirability of other operations that were in the offing. The terrorist dog that has not (yet!) barked would strongly suggest that this indeed is what has been accomplished by the pursuit of al-Qaeda and the toppling of the Taliban.

I am wholeheartedly with Codevilla when he asserts that we ought to "kill" the regimes in Iraq, Syria, and the PLO, which together "are the effective cause of global terrorism" (though I cannot fathom why he omits Iran and its satellite Lebanon from this list or, for that matter, our putative "friends" Saudi Arabia and Egypt, both of whom have incited and financed Palestinian suicide bombing). I am with him, too, when he adds that we should destroy these regimes "as quickly as possible" by capturing their leaders and then subjecting them to punishments ranging from execution to imprisonment to banishment from public life—just as we did with the Nazis.

But I part company with Codevilla entirely when he tells us that in the highly unlikely event that we were to do all this, our best course would then be to pack up and go home. So long as the successor regimes do not make war on us, he declares, it is none of our business how they govern themselves. The "kind of political reconstruction we performed in Germany and Japan" is out because "what happens in Iraq is simply not as important to us as the internal developments of Germany and Japan were."

Yet Codevilla never explains why the character of the successor regimes in Iraq, Syria, and the Palestinian Authority would be of no great concern to the United States. In any case, I strongly disagree with his view. I would remind Codevilla of his own observation that the Middle East as it exists today was created not by Allah but by the West after the First World War. From this much else follows along with our right to get rid of a bunch of murderers and thugs who have now turned on us.

Indeed, as against Codevilla, I would argue that, having helped these criminals assume and keep power, we now also have a right and a responsibility to leave behind a better system. And by "better" I, unlike Codevilla, mean more than merely a group of regimes that will be afraid to threaten us again. I mean a system that will at least contain the potentiality for an evolution toward democracy and economic health. If necessary, we should ensure that this happens precisely the way we did in Germany and Japan: through temporary imperial control that would clear enough political space for the sprouting of indigenous alternatives.

Codevilla is convinced that even if so grand an ambition were attainable, the American people are unsuited to pursuing it. Well, my sense of things is that most of us now yearn for the nation to perform the great and glorious deeds of which, time and again, it has proved itself capable.

As for George W. Bush, Codevilla thinks that all he wants is to maintain the status quo. But to believe this requires brushing off the Bush Doctrine as first enunciated in the president's great speech of September 20, 2001 and then fleshed out in three subsequent addresses. In these statements, Bush repudiated moral relativism; officially adopted an understanding of terrorism as dependent upon states that must be held accountable for sponsoring it; asserted a lawful determination to launch a preemptive attack on Iraq (and any other countries that seek to equip terrorists with weapons of mass destruction);

and at long last placed Israel's war against terrorism into the context of our own.

Taken seriously, those four speeches undermine much of Codevilla's account. But what is more important, for all the mistakes the president may have committed, and even if his actions are bound to fall short of his promises, Bush's formal statements are infused with so much force of their own that not all the Colin Powells in all the chancelleries of the world can in the long run fully succeed in denying them their due.

DAVID TUCKER
ASSOCIATE PROFESSOR OF DEFENSE ANALYSIS, NAVAL POSTGRADUATE SCHOOL

Angelo Codevilla says that the current war on terrorism consists of homeland security, more intelligence, and bringing al-Qaeda to justice. This war is a failure in his view because homeland security is silly, impotent, and counterproductive; more intelligence, an impossibility; and bringing al-Qaeda to justice, misconceived and a diversion. The war on terrorism should be, according to Codevilla, the destruction of Iraq, Syria, and the Palestinian Authority and the hanging of every member of the ruling parties of those states, which "are the effective cause of global terrorism." This mayhem is necessary in order to achieve what Codevilla believes should be the objective of the war: "Americans…living a quiet and peaceable life, if possible less troubled by the troubles…of the world, even freer from searches and sirens…than on September 10."

Codevilla is a tough guy. But he is wrong about the current war and wrong in his own prescriptions. First, the current war. Codevilla's criticism of homeland security and intelligence (the human component of which he has misunderstood for years) can be dismissed out of hand. His argument amounts to saying that they are no good because they are not perfect. No one claims they are. No one believes that "passive anti-terrorism" suffices. That something is not sufficient does not mean that it is not necessary. At great length, Codevilla smashes a straw man.

His claim that going after al-Qaeda is a diversion rests on the assumption that terrorist organizations are just fronts for state intelligence services. They are not. They gain from the assistance of such services as states benefit from the actions of terrorists, but terrorist organizations arise and exist independently of state support. Consider

one example: contrary to what Codevilla implies, terrorists made suicide bombing an effective weapon against the United States long before Iraq and others started giving martyr bonuses to the bombers'
families. Another example: Codevilla says that the use by terrorists of
stolen identities is a mark of support by major league intelligence
services. Are the Iraqis responsible for the current problem of identity
theft in the United States? Are they responsible for the acquisition
around the world on a daily basis of passports and visas through
bribery? The terrorists opened bank accounts with phony social security numbers that no one bothered to check. As it would be self-de-
feating to ignore the aid provided to terrorists by states, so it is self-
defeating to ignore the autonomous capabilities of violent clandestine
organizations. Codevilla misunderstands and underestimates our enemies.

What of his prescriptions? Without the bombast, Codevilla's objectives are banal: peace and the domestic security status quo ante. The
latter is unattainable. If there were no terrorists, others would still
seek to exploit our vulnerabilities at home. Chinese military officers
have described how to do this in their writings. Instead of longing for
some imagined past, it would be better, in light of our fundamental
principles, to think seriously about the changes we might make.

Codevilla believes this unnecessary because he proposes to destroy
those abroad who would threaten us at home. But we will not be able
to stop with Iraq, Syria, and the Palestinian Authority. What about
Iran? Codevilla is oddly silent about the Islamic republic, although it
has provided more support to terrorists than either Iraq or Syria. What
about China? Enemies are endless and so, on Codevilla's argument,
will be our regime destroying wars. Is endless war-making compatible with his objective of "Americans...living a quiet and peaceable
life"? Why will those we attack not attack us at home with terrorism?
Worse, will not our endless warfare and slaughtering and hanging
abroad inevitably and adversely affect our republican way of life at
home?

Codevilla apparently thinks his plan will work either because we
will slaughter enemies faster than our slaughtering makes new ones
or because our strutting will cow our enemies. He is proposing attri-
tion warfare without regard for either the character of the enemy we
face or the domestic and international politics in which we must operate. Codevilla epitomizes the worst of narrow conventional military
thinking made, if possible, even worse in his case because shorn of
the restraint that comes from responsibility.

Conservatives and conservative publications should beware of tough-guy posturing. In this case, extremism in the defense of liberty is a vice and moderation in the pursuit of justice would be a virtue.

ANGELO M. CODEVILLA RESPONDS:

In three articles [Chapters III and IV] over the past year amounting to some 15,000 words, I applied the classical notion of victory—is there any other that fits the word?—to the "War on Terrorism." The gist of the articles is that victory means having your own kind of peace, that in our case it means not having to worry about terrorist attacks or suffering "security measures"; that we can achieve this only by undo-ing the regimes that embody terrorist causes; and that the Bush team, rhetoric aside, is longer on domestic police measures than on counter-ing hostile regimes.

The *Claremont Review of Books* asked five prominent persons to cor-rect and amplify both the concept and my application of it. None of the brief comments claims that we have victory, or that it is in sight, or says anything about what it would look like. Three try to square their "support of the president" with lack of victory by expressing confidence, to one degree or another, that Mr. Bush will somehow produce victory in the future. One is wroth that I think ill of official policy, indeed that I dare to think of victory at all. Another regrets the lack of intellectual focus that is a precondition of victory. Neverthe-less, each points to some substantive issues concerning the "war," on which I will remark.

Norman Podhoretz admits in principle the validity of my criticisms of the post-September 11 U.S. policy, and then asks whether *maybe* the fact that certain events have not yet happened means that my criticisms *may be* invalid. If Podhoretz, a master of argument, thought it possible to make a stronger attack on criticisms he would prefer were invalid, he would have made it. And in fact Podhoretz disagrees with me forthrightly on the important issue of whether the U.S. gov-ernment ought to take responsibility for the internal affairs of defeated enemies.

Frank Gaffney admits the validity of my criticisms and then argues that since my articles were written, President Bush *has begun to do* the things that I consider necessary for victory. He concludes with a list of other things that the president *must* do, lest my criticisms be restored to full validity. This is good Washington hortatory form. Gaffney does not mistake words, or even beginnings, for real policy—much less results. He is less sure that the president will carry through with what he has begun, much less with what he has not begun, than that he *had better* do as Codevilla and Gaffney prescribe. But does victory amount to following a set of policy prescriptions?

Mackubin Owens, however, seems to mistake rhetoric for policy. Whereas Frank Gaffney says that the president *must* mean what he says, Owens seems to believe that what the president says amounts to actions *already successfully carried* to term. For him, the fact that the Bush team has not yet done the things that bring victory is a sign of moderation and prudence. Hence, Owens raises a question worth pondering: In war, what is prudence?

David Tucker is outraged that anyone should think that such a victory, a life as safe as that before September 11, were possible. There are too many enemies, we are too vulnerable, and too many people at home and abroad ("the domestic and international politics in which we must operate") don't want it. Yes, we must oppose our foreign enemies, but moderately—meaning that we should not think of eliminating them. And we must "think seriously about the changes we must make," presumably to our own way of life. Recall that I began my first essay [Chapter III] by invoking Phil Gramm's practical definition of victory and defeat: "I don't want to change the way I live. I want to change the way they live." Tucker disagrees diametrically. He directs animus against those who would challenge the wisdom of "responsible officials" who share his views. He specifically associates his judgment with those of the U.S. intelligence services. Instructive choice.

William F. Buckley Jr. has been more correct about more things than any person alive. His minor point, that I predict gloomy doom, is half correct. I have written that the Bush administration's current "war" policies naturally lead to bad results. Mismanaged wars usually do. In the 1960s, not even the gloomiest analyses of U.S. policy in Vietnam forecast the changes in American society that it would engender. And at the time, no one was proposing the kinds of across-the-board degradations of American life that today are the alternative to victory. Buckley's major point—entirely correct—is that this war, like all wars, requires choosing a military target such that killing it yields the war's aims. That is my point as well. But Buckley adds that the time for such "strategic marksmanship" is past. He's gloomier. But who's right?

NATION-BUILDING?

Norman Podhoretz's comments continue a conversation begun a decade ago on the first anniversary of the Gulf War when, as editor of *Commentary*, he published a controversial article of mine [Chapter II], "Magnificent, But Was It War?" Podhoretz—barely—let me argue that although U.S. troops had won the battle of Kuwait, the U.S. government had lost the Gulf War. Expelling Saddam from Kuwait, I argued, had been the wrong objective. Because Saddam's presence in Kuwait was but a symptom of the problem—a successful anti-American regime—getting him out of Kuwait would give us brief symptomatic relief only. Podhoretz disagreed. Substitute "terrorist" for "Iraqi regime," and his comment now is his argument a decade ago: "perhaps this campaign actually *has* disrupted the [Iraqi regime,] and perhaps those daisy cutters *have* sufficiently frightened [the Iraqi regime] to induce second thoughts about the desirability of other operations that were in the offing." By weakening Saddam's regime, Bush the Elder had effectively fixed the problem itself. I argued that weakened though Saddam was, he would parlay his natural geographic advantage and the fact of his very survival into a strategy for the deliberate, long-term propagation of anti-American causes in the region. Those causes now dominate the region.

So, protestations of faith in official policy aside, Podhoretz now agrees with me that we ought to kill the regimes that embody those causes—more regimes than I proposed. He notes Bush the Younger's "great speech of September 20, 2001," and that, "taken seriously," this and other speeches undermine my criticism of the war. Podhoretz would *prefer* to take the speeches seriously. But he does not take them much more seriously than I do.

Podhoretz wants to go further than Bush, and further than I proposed or propose to go. Forthrightly, he argues for establishing in Iraq (and, logically, elsewhere as well) "temporary imperial control that would clear enough political space for sprouting of indigenous alternatives." And he hopes that those alternatives would involve "democracy and economic health." In this he joins a respectable group ranging from historian Paul Johnson to the *Washington Post* who recognize now that the U.S. decision in the 1950s to chase Franco-British imperialism from the Middle East opened Pandora's box. They agree with me that "the West, not Allah," thus created today's Middle East and put it in the hands of "a bunch of murderers." They recognize that, left to themselves, the locals are not likely to be decent, prosperous, peaceful, or friendly. In this they are admirably ahead of the State Department and CIA, who continue to be blinded by the mirages that they themselves conjured up three generations ago.

But we cannot undo that wrong. Thanks in part to America, Europe so changed character that it is now part of the problem rather than the solution. Imperialism is a difficult, un-American art. Neither Podhoretz nor I know of any Americans fit for or inclined to imperial service. We are also without any compelling set of teachings to impart that would cancel out the massive damage to local cultures that the "best and the brightest" from our universities wrought when they sold the Germans and Japanese secular socialism. The rebirth of Germany and Japan occurred because the remnants of Christian Democratic and Taisho democratic culture, respectively, were strong enough. Nevertheless, the Americans almost managed to make Adenauer and Yoshida into discredited puppets which is what the next generation of Americans succeeded in doing to Thieu and Ky in Saigon. Today, the fact that Afghanistan's Hamid Karzai lives surrounded by a praetorian guard of American troops augurs badly for "nation-building" there.

So if we cannot take responsibility for making the peoples of the Middle East into other than what they are, if we cannot make them like us, what can we do? We can earn their respect by killing our enemies. Though we cannot make good regimes, we *can* kill harmful ones. Distinguishing between the relatively harmful and harmless, between the more and less friendly, is the simple beginning of wisdom. Plato grounds the argument of his *Republic* on the observation that dogs do this well. So far however, the U.S. government has killed lots of people whose deaths have not made us safe, and spared the regimes that hate us.

I suggest, and prefer to believe that Norman Podhoretz agrees, that our own intellectual and moral insufficiencies are our main problem in this war. Is it not interesting that the kind of Americans who used to urge deference to the Soviet Union now urge deference to the Islamic world?

WHAT WILL IT TAKE?

Frank Gaffney proposes an impressive list of prescriptions for victory, with which I agree entirely. Some, the Bush team has promised to buy.

Others it has not—yet *inshallah*, as they say. But before considering whether victory is the sum of these or any prescriptions, we should note how difficult they are to implement in the teeth of the elite culture shared by the Bush team.

Regime change. Recall that during the Cold War only discredited right-wingers such as Ronald Reagan and a minority of his advisers braved the scorn of "the best and the brightest" (including most of the two Bush teams) by suggesting that the Soviet regime could not be housebroken, much less reformed, and that U.S. policy should aim at its death. Indeed, few in Washington or academe even know what the word "regime" means. After September 11, I called attention to the fact that terrorism is not the aberration of individuals but the product of regimes when I wrote, "It's the regime, stupid!" But when Deputy Defense Secretary Paul Wolfowitz said that our war should aim at undoing several regimes, the Bush team publicly disowned him.

Think of the policies and practices, and of the people who embody them, that would have to be changed to focus on regimes. "Dual Containment" of Iraq and Iran has been in place for a decade. "Peace Processes" vis-à-vis the Arab-Israeli conflict—paying the nastiest Arabs not to be so nasty—have been the staple of U.S. policy since before 1967. When we speak of states that finance terrorism, we must include the United States, which funnels millions (while the European Union funnels billions) to the PLO.

Think of the disastrous ideas and of the people who have made careers pushing them. Sure, some officials will deny that they ever espoused them, and climb higher yet on the new wave. Hence it is amusing to see Richard Haver, who in the 1980s, as Bobby Ray Inman's protégé, championed Saddam Hussein's moderation and malleability, now touted as the Defense Intelligence Czar in the "war on terrorism." Had the Inman-Haver line prevailed in U.S. foreign policy, it would have been impossible for Israel to destroy Saddam's reactor, and Iraq would have become a nuclear power. Such flip-flops can work. But the Bush team's addiction to people with bad records is a mortgage on good policy.

The Arab bait and switch. Back in 1953, Gamal Abdel Nasser told his officers that he had discovered the secret of success against the West: Don't attack in uniform with flags flying. Rather, send irregulars. Hail the cause for which they fight—your cause—but disavow any involvement with them. Nasser did not imagine that Western statesmen lacked the raw mental capacity to understand his ploy. Rather, he figured that they were so morally undermined by their commitment to the ideal of the equality of peoples, so morally incapable of fighting for their own interests, that they would go along with the game.

And for half a century, they have. Thus, after Arabs bloodied America on September 11 in behalf of causes supported by all Arab governments, the U.S. has taken no action against any Arab government. Gaffney rightly notes it as news that President Bush, after supporting the creation of a Palestinian state, after crediting the patently fraudulent "Saudi peace initiative," after massively restraining Israel, has *verbally* conditioned the continuation of this attitude on "numerous systemic, political, and leadership changes" in the Palestinian Authority, if not in Saudi Arabia itself. President Bush may have seen through the "bait and switch" intellectually. But the "bait and switch" was never an intellectual problem.

The privileged status of Saudi Arabia. There are signs, writes Gaffney, that the Saudi royal family may be losing its privileged status in Washington, and that it should no longer be confident of exercising vetoes over U.S. policy. Good. Whence came that status and that veto power? From two of the American elite's moral shortcomings.

The first is straightforward: Lots of Americans are eager to be bought. By guaranteeing seven-figure incomes to former U.S. ambassadors to Saudi Arabia, the royal family assures itself that current U.S. ambassadors will do what it takes to earn a pension that dwarfs what the U.S. taxpayer will provide. By favorable treatment of oil executives who put pressure on politicians on their behalf, the royal family buys itself a potent lobby. Awareness that the average American might begin paying attention to such routine corruption accounts for the signs that Gaffney mentions.

The second is less evident, more significant, and more difficult to eradicate. How did the Saudi royal family get the money with which it propitiates so many Americans? Lots of oil comes from Saudi Arabia. But is it written in the stars that the oil money should go to the royal family? If the money were to go exclusively to those who found the oil, who provide the expertise, the labor, and the equipment to get it out of the ground and into the world's gas tanks, or who defend the fields, very few Arabs—and no Saudi royals at all—would get anything. They get what they get because Western elites think they have a right to it, because the elites believe that all peoples are naturally sovereign over the ground they occupy, and because Westerners know no grounds for distinguishing legitimate regimes from robber bands. This peculiar ideology is neither self-evident nor compelled by intellectual rigor. Until 1973, Westerners, not Arabs, decided what "royalties" the royals should get. Having less lucre, these Arabs were unable to finance the terrorism and corruption that have fouled our lives since the 1970s. Paying such sums is symptomatic of the same moral confusion and corruption that made it okay to be bought.

Finally, Gaffney's premise is that President Bush must live up to his words. Richard Perle recently mused for the record that President Bush, having spoken as he did on September 20 and in his 2002 State of the Union Address, cannot mount the podium of the House of Representatives in 2003 without having begun at least to dismantle the "Axis of Evil." But taking such actions will not be easy. It will be tempting, certainly to many in his administration, for Bush to announce instead: "No war against Iraq. Long live Saudi stability. Homeland Security forever!"

We can see, then, that victory is more than the sum of the parts that Frank Gaffney has assembled so well. These policies are indeed the body of victory. But to live, that body must have a mind and soul capable of sustaining its parts. Good policies are necessary, but not sufficient. At countless points in any struggle, there must arise temptations to misinterpret or to deviate. One must know why the policies are correct, and have cultivated shame of doing the wrong thing.

PRUDENCE AND THE PILL

Aristotle defines prudence as the application of means most apt to achieve the good end. I'm sure Mackubin Owens agrees with that. All human actions, indeed, all processes of nature—so teaches Aristotle—are ordered each to its peculiar end. The natural end of war is victory, just as the natural end of farming is produce. Prudence is essential to farming, not for its own sake but so that we may eat the fruits of the field. Prudence is essential in war so that we may live in the safety that is the fruit of victory. Just as we cannot eat prudence instead of corn, prudence cannot shield us from our enemies. The proof of prudence or lack thereof is neither in rushing forward nor in holding back, but in good results.

Owens praises Bush for not having done certain things—*yet*. But according to the dictionary, and even more according to Aristotle, it makes no sense to pin the label prudence on speaking rather than acting, or for that matter on acting instead of speaking. Prudence involves good deliberation that leads to good actions. The two must go together, which is why it makes little sense to use the term prudence prospectively.

Much of Owens' comments consist of truisms, e.g., "prudence dictates when and how the policy is implemented, which in turn depends on the circumstances." He applies them to concrete circumstances only once: an invasion of Iraq after September 11, he claims, would have been impractical (and is now impractical) because of "weather, climate, and the 'tyranny of distance.'" Prudently, we must ask: Compared to what? Afghanistan?

Last time I looked, Afghanistan was almost as inaccessible as Mongolia or Tibet, whereas Iraq had a sea coast. I am confident that the Naval War College's maps, like mine, show that no point in Afghanistan is closer to any part of the United States or Europe, never mind to our fleet bases, than the farthest point of Iraq is. Iraq is largely flat, whereas Afghanistan is one mountain range after another. As for "weather and climate," the U.S. invaded Afghanistan rather than Iraq precisely at the time when the weather was nicest in Iraq and getting worse in Afghanistan.

Above all, from the standpoint of prudence—remember, it points to results, not action or inaction—invading Afghanistan *proved to be* imprudent because Afghanistan *proved not to be* the enemy's "center of gravity" (see Clausewitz). The proof? Even though the military operation was successful, the Bush team (rightly) acted as if the threat of terrorism to Americans was undiminished.

The Best and the Brightest

Whereas Owens defends the Bush administration's hesitancy as part of what he believes is the optimal pursuit of victory, David Tucker praises it because he believes that the pursuit of victory itself is a terrible thing.

Tucker calls my proposals for victory "bombast" and "tough-guy posturing." Does he claim that I would not intend to do the things I propose? Only in that case would the terms apply. Or does Tucker fault me for truly intending to do them? Note that President Bush has endorsed much the same things in his speech of September 20, 2001, and in his State of the Union Address of 2002, but repeatedly makes it clear that he has no plans to do them. Why does Tucker not apply the dictionary definition of "bombast" and "posturing" to that? Answer:

Tucker does not object to speaking loudly and carrying a small stick. He really does believe that destroying one's enemies is a bad thing. This of course was the position of the best and the brightest. Tucker's arguments against trying for victory recall those of 40 years ago: Robert Osgood and Thomas Schelling and McGeorge Bundy and Robert McNamara, not to mention those of the Henry Kissinger of the late 1960s and 1970s, and later, Strobe Talbott. "Enemies are endless," and the attempt to secure ourselves through victory means endless war. If we succeed in defeating one set, "others will still seek to exploit our vulnerabilities at home." Besides, peace and security are "unattainable." The real danger to America is "extremist" Americans who are "shorn of the restraint that comes from responsibility" and "epitomize the worst in narrow military thinking." Straight out of McNamara's *In Retrospect*. All this talk of victory is an excuse for avoiding "thinking seriously about changes we might make" in our own way of life. Straight out of the fountainhead of 1960s anti-Americanism, William Appleman Williams' *The Tragedy of American Diplomacy*.

Tucker also has the U.S. intelligence community on his side. Full disclosure on my part: Between 1977 and 1985, my job was to oversee the budget and quality of operations of the U.S. intelligence community on behalf of the Senate Select Committee on Intelligence. During painfully detailed reviews of operations, analyses, post-mortems, proposals, and even more painful involvement in internal controversies at the highest levels, after having written volumes of classified documents, including (largely) the 1980 transition report for William Casey and Ronald Reagan, I came to highly critical conclusions about the agencies' understanding of their craft. In the open literature, I published *Informing Statecraft* (1992). I am the principal author of the eight-volume series *Intelligence Requirements of the 1980s* (Roy Godson, editor, 1979-1985) as well as of many articles. Two directors of Central Intelligence have asked me to help senior officials think through their problems, and I have taught courses in intelligence classified at the Codeword level.

Tucker accuses me of "saying they are no good because they are not perfect." In fact, I think U.S. human intelligence is almost perfectly incompetent. What other term should we apply to the following record? Whenever we have gotten windfalls of information about our agent networks in key countries, it has turned out that all or nearly all were actually working for hostile intelligence services and feeding us information cooked to their masters' tastes. In the case of Cuba, it was 100 percent. In the case of East Germany, it was all but three. In the case of the Soviet Union, Aldrich Ames and Robert Hansson turned over the names of all Russians who were working for us and, since they were in charge of vetting all new recruits, made sure that we accepted as real agents every single courier of disinformation that the KGB sent our way.

The causes of this gullibility are less the occasional traitor than faults of the system. First, neither in the CIA nor in the FBI is the quality control function of counterintelligence independent. It's as if Arthur Andersen were actually a subsidiary of Enron. Second, CIA and FBI officials have too often been rewarded for telling higher-ups what they want to hear.

The agencies' performance in the war on terrorism has been all too predictable. Lacking sources of their own, they depend on Arab liaison services. CIA sources boasted to *Time* magazine that America now gets much of its strategic information about "al-Qaeda" and the September 11 conspiracy from one Muhammed Haymar Zammar, who, the Syrian General Security directorate tells us, it has in prison. We do not know the relationship between Syria and Mr. Zammar, because Americans are not allowed to see him. CIA submits written questions to the Syrian government, which then gives us what it claims are Mr. Zammar's answers. CIA expresses satisfaction because the Syrians may be torturing those answers out of Zammar. What reason does the CIA have to believe that those answers are coming from Zammar at all, rather than from meetings of Syrian and other Arab officials who bat around the question: What do we want the Americans to think today?

It so happens that what the Arab governments want the U.S. government to think—namely that terrorism is the spontaneous reaction of good people throughout the Middle East to scandalously pro-Jewish U.S. policy, that the U.S. government has at least as much to fear from its own "extremists" as it does from Arabs, and that as Tucker put it, "terrorist organizations arise and exist independent of state support"—is precisely what much of the U.S. government wants to hear. Consider the events of July 4, 2002, when, after an Egyptian carried out a suicide mass shooting of Israelis and Americans at Los Angeles International airport, the FBI spokesman declared: "There is nothing to indicate terrorism."

Our intelligence agencies love "Homeland Defense." Under its umbrella, they get budgets, promotions, and, so far, a free pass not to worry about how they treat ordinary Americans. There is no reason, however, for the rest of us to agree.

STRATEGIC MARKSMANSHIP

William F. Buckley Jr. elsewhere has written wisely and passionately on the stupidity of the U.S. government reacting to terrorism by Arabs for Arab causes by acting as if each and every human being was as likely to be a terrorist as any other human being. Buckley knows that this kind of "Homeland Security" is the alternative to victory, and that it is a ruinous alternative. Also, more clearly than professional students of war, Buckley absorbed the common sense of Clausewitz's insight that seriousness in war—or more correctly, war as opposed to mere violence—means striking at the enemy's "center of gravity," that set of persons or things that, if knocked over, will rid you of your problem. Thus do ordinary soldiers shoot at the other side's officers.

Herein, Buckley writes that, for the reasons I have explained, Iraq's Baathist regime is the center of gravity of terrorism. But why is it too late to generate strategic marksmanship? Granted, such things are better done sooner than later, but why not later rather than not at all? The choice is perpetual.

The opposite of strategic marksmanship, the opposite of targeting the leaders of foreign governments, is for the U.S. government to make life harder, less full of confidence, for Americans at home and ultimately to discredit itself as well as those who support it.

Only the dullest believe that the "security measures" that now inconvenience and humiliate grandmothers, Medal of Honor winners, and Al Gore (he was searched at an airport recently) reflect the capacity of the U.S. government to protect us. People know in their bones that they reflect incompetence. Buckley, along with Podhoretz, thinks it significant that no major terrorist blow has struck us since the anthrax attacks that shut down the Capitol in October—only the suicide shooting at LAX on July 4. But clearly the only reason why not worse has happened is that no one has tried. If they had, none of the security measures would have stopped them. As I pointed out in my original article, Israel's pervasive security measures had only the tiniest effect on the suicide bombing campaign. But the cost of failed security measures—in Israel, America, or anywhere else—goes far beyond lives lost and property damaged.

Insecurity, lack of confidence in those in charge—these are poison for economic life. Economies run on confidence. The economic boom that ended the Great Depression began only after it became clear that the Axis was going to be defeated. Ronald Reagan built the U.S. economy quite as much by giving the impression that America could not be messed with as he did with his tax cuts. The boom of the 1990s followed the impression—bolstered by the Gulf War—that the demise of the Soviet Union meant free rein for the global economy. Such golden dreams are out of the question so long as executives are subjected to identity checks on their way to meetings, investors fear the next news shock, and consumers, whenever they fly, have to walk past troops armed with automatic weapons.

Confidence is even more essential to polities than to economies. Nothing destroys a people's confidence in its way of life more surely than the impression that the people-in-charge are incompetent, and nothing earns that impression more surely than a government's failure to provide safety. That is why the U.S. government's failure to win (in the true sense of the word) the war on terrorism, failure to restore "a quiet and peaceable life," would have consequences for America far worse than the ones that befell when "the best and the brightest" botched the Vietnam War.

Bad as that war's consequences were for America as a whole, however, they were worse for American conservatives. The war was not their doing. This was a Liberals' war, run by Liberals, who regarded Barry Goldwater and William F. Buckley, Jr., as more reprehensible than Ho Chi Minh. Moreover, those who ran the war engendered changes in American society that were anathema to conservatives. Nevertheless, a misguided patriotism moved conservatives to "support the president" when others abandoned him. Thus conservatives were left holding the bag for the defeat. Successive generations learn that the whole mess was due, as Jimmy Carter put it, to an "inordinate fear of Communism," and that "through defeat we found our way back to our own values." The "war on terrorism" is not the doing of conservatives. Its causes—indulgence of Third Worldism in general and of Arab tyrannies in particular, and most particularly the failure to finish the Gulf War—are things that conservatives from Buckley to Robert Bartley unanimously inveighed against. Nor is the "war on terrorism" being waged as conservatives would like. It would be a raw deal if conservatives, following their natural inclination to "support the president," were left holding the bag for yet another botched war.

VI: Hamlet's Choice

VICTORY WATCH: WAR AT LAST?*

"All ye shall be offended because of me this night: for it is written, I will smite the shepherd and the sheep shall be scattered abroad." Matthew 26:31

"The best way to protect you is to find those killers one at a time and bring them to justice." George W. Bush, October 31, 2002

Beginning on September 11, 2001, the Bush administration coupled words appropriate to foreign war with actions that amounted to police work. This reflected intramural ambivalence, perhaps unresolved because of George Bush's own confusion or indecision. But by November 2002, events were forcing the Bush team to choose between making war on Arab regimes and turning American society inside out in a futile effort to protect it—between destroying the regimes that embody the causes for which terrorists fight, and bringing the terrorists "to justice" one by one.

TO BE OR NOT TO BE

Consistently, President Bush sought to avoid this choice, perhaps failing to understand the difference between war and police action, or imagining that he could reconcile two contradictory lines of policy by pursuing both. To be sure, he gave the impression that he would wage foreign war: he called for no distinction between the terrorists and those who help or harbor them, only between those who would fight

This essay appeared in the Claremont Review of Books, Winter 2002.

95

alongside us and those who wouldn't. At the same time, however, Bush belied such words by an invasion of Afghanistan calculated less to cut off terrorism at the roots than not to disturb those roots—the Saudi, Syrian, and Palestinian regimes. Indeed, the Afghan invasion seemed to belie the thesis that America's objective in the current war was "regime change." In a similar twist, Bush verbally "delegitimized" Yasser Arafat's Palestinian regime, but continued to protect it and to demand that Israel make it a state.

But by mid-2002 Palestinian suicide bombers (paid by Iraq and Saudi Arabia), and the American public's increasing impatience for results in the "war on terrorism" had forced to the top of Bush's agenda whether or not to make war on the Iraqi regime. This led to a belated, half-hearted assertion of Iraq's links to terrorism, and to the new official reason for "regime change," namely that Iraq threatens the world with "weapons of mass destruction."

Had Bush finally chosen to make war? No. In fact he authorized Secretary of State Colin Powell to state that disarming Iraq would be the equivalent of "regime change," and agreed to one more round of "weapons inspections" in Iraq—guaranteed to find no weapons and put off the day of reckoning. He repeated so often and so sincerely that he had not decided on any means to achieve his ends that even the courtly George Shultz accused him of playing Hamlet.

What was he doing for real? On November 5, 2002, a U.S. remote-controlled Predator drone flying above Yemen fired a Hellfire missile into a car carrying six Arabs whom U.S. intelligence had identified as members of al-Qaeda. This was the first admitted instance in which U.S. forces had fired on anyone outside Afghanistan. This action rose to the level of Israel's strikes against persons believed to belong to terrorist organizations. Like Israel's strikes however, it underlined that the targets were individuals. Because such strikes are not aimed at regimes or causes, they are not measures of war but police actions, adjuncts to "security measures" that no one expects to have protective effect—or ever to end.

The Bush team urged Americans to be patient and vigilant...against one another in general and against no one in particular, lest Muslims in general (and Black Muslims and Arabs in particular) be offended. U.S. intelligence operations were essentially unchanged from before September 11. The Bush team forestalled independent investigation of the intelligence agencies' incompetence, and assured Americans that their government would protect them. In October 2002, however, an American who had adopted the name Muhammed crippled the Washington metropolitan area for three weeks with thirteen random shootings. Charles Colson and Daniel Pipes, among others, have written about the fact that the overwhelming majority of Islamic chaplains in America's prisons are Wahhabis, trained and paid by Saudi Arabia, and that the religion they preach to imprisoned criminals (mostly blacks) amounts to blaming America for their troubles. One could hardly imagine anything more incendiary: young men, already inured to violence, already looking for reasons to feel good about themselves and for hating the people who frustrated them and now punish them, being told that, yes, they really are strangers in the enemy's midst, that out there are millions and millions of people, colored like them, who are better than Americans and are with them in thinking ill of America. It does not take many such recruits to terrorism to make big changes in American life.

In October, we saw the havoc that John Muhammed and his acolyte, John Lee Malvo, caused with the barest of resources. Had they possessed a little training in terrorist technique they would not have been caught. What could a dozen or two such teams do to America? Preparing quicker ways to seal off highways is a path not to victory but to modern Israel's agony.

By fall, the Bush administration's (and the Republican Party's) standing with the American public depended on one factor: President Bush had convinced the American people that he was preparing to make war against America's enemies, and needed support. He could not afford to be seen as reneging on his promises of action, especially out of regard for "allies" whom the American people had learned to disdain. He could stay on his perch only if he got off the edge of indecision and actually made war—successfully. Yet at the beginning of November, the Bush team was as likely to try to "find those killers one at a time" (lots of luck!) as it was to wage war. The two enterprises, in this context, are as different as defeat and victory.

VICTORY MEANS KILLING CAUSES

Where did all the Nazis go? Where are all those Communists who so recently made up a movement with roots and branches in every corner of the world? Recall for a moment the Communist movement's breadth and depth. The Communist Party was just the tip of the iceberg. Every political party, every labor union, every newspaper, every school, every profession, every social organization had sympathizers with Communism who played a significant role in its life. What made Communism so strong? What made democratic politicians (Reagan excepted) afraid to say that it was evil? No one argued that the Soviet Union recruited every Communist, pulled every string on Communism's behalf throughout the world. It did not have to, any more than the sun has to reach down and turn every sunflower to make it follow its path. Where now are all those people, young and old, who would argue and demonstrate, and scheme and spy and kill and betray for the grand cause of Communism?

They were no more when the Soviet Union was no more, just as sunflowers would cease to exist were there no sun. As for those ferocious Nazis whom the *New York Times* (all by itself, without orders from Berlin) once thought were the wave of the future, only the name remains, as a hackneyed insult. Human causes are embodied by human institutions. With them they flourish, with them they die. Communists and Nazis everywhere ceased to be a problem when the regimes that inspired them died.

Terrorist acts against America are a subset of Arab anti-Americanism, which itself is a subset of the hatred and contempt for America that exists in various forms around the world, prominently within U.S. borders as well. To be rid of those who would commit terrorist acts against America, we must deal with the fact that anti-Americanism—both its hatred and contempt for us—has become institutionalized in regimes whose very existence inspires such acts.

Why do people hate? Sometimes, because they have suffered what they consider to be wrongs. America's Founders counseled us to have as little political intercourse as possible with foreign peoples, not to interfere in their affairs, precisely because we have little control over what others will consider offenses. Mostly however, people hate not because of anything others do, or even because of who others are, but because they tend to blame others for their own unhappiness. Hence, it is not in the power of America or of any other country to reduce others' hate for it. Even as American troops were liberating France from the Nazis, French intellectuals were telling each other that America was a dastardly enemy. The point is that such attitudes are the problems of the people who have them. We can't change them. The essence of the volumes being written (the best by Bernard Lewis) on "the roots of Muslim rage" is that this rage comes from resentment of their own failures, and is very much their problem.

Our problem is that many of today's Arabs, like yesterday's Germans, like the (unlamented) Soviets, and unlike today's Frenchmen or Germans, have set up regimes that are living, breathing, spawning expressions of hate against us. True, we had something to do with establishing those very regimes. To that extent, Arabs have a legitimate beef against us. But we cannot do anything that would force them to hate us less. Even if, God forbid, we were to fulfill their most strident demand—turn ourselves into raging Jew-haters, and destroy Israel for them—we would earn not less hate but even more contempt.

Contempt is the active ingredient of anti-Americanism. And others' contempt for us is entirely our fault. People have contempt for those they consider impotent. The deadliest contempt is reserved for those who have, or seem to have, great power but somehow cannot use it. Contempt is the bite that the jackal inflicts on the stricken or befuddled lion. It is a cheap substitute for courage. Contempt for America makes vile European intellectuals feel like men. Flouting America with impunity, declaring moral superiority over it, bribing its businessmen and politicians, allows Arab dictators—whether they call themselves kings or presidents—to pretend that they are world statesmen instead of bandits of the desert. And it is our fault, because we let them get away with it.

Terrorism is not a militarily serious matter. All the world's terrorists combined cannot do as much damage as one modern infantry battalion, one Navy ship or fighter squadron. Nor is terrorism such a bedeviling challenge to intelligence. It is potent only insofar as terrorism's targets decide to deny the obvious and pretend that the terrorists are acting on their own and not on behalf of causes embodied by regimes. Terrorism is potent only against governments that deserve contempt. The U.S. government earned the Arabs' contempt the hard way, by decades of responses to terrorism that combined impotent threats, solicitude for the terrorists' causes, outright payments to Egypt and the PLO, courting Syria, a "special relationship" with Saudi Arabia, and a pretense that Islam was as compatible with American life as Episcopalianism. Killing individuals who do not count engenders hatred, while sparing those who do count guarantees contempt.

Victory against terrorists requires precisely the opposite approach: expend little or no energy chasing the trigger pullers and bombers. Rather, make sure that any life devoted to terror will be a wasted life. This means leaving no hope whatever for any of the causes from which the Arab tyrannies draw such legitimacy as they have: people who give their lives for lost causes exist more in novels than in reality. It means discrediting and insofar as possible impoverishing (rather than paying for) Arab regimes that foster opposition to America. It means using military force to kill the regimes—the ruling classes—of countries that are in any way associated with terrorism.

Such regimes cannot be other than matrices of terrorism; they are riding tigers. Should the people who run them try to change, they would perish at the hands of internal enemies. America cannot possibly reform them. The choice is to suffer them, their causes, and their terrorist methods—or to kill them.

⟨⟩⟨⟩

VICTORY WATCH: CONFUSION AND POWER*

"Above all, let us avoid the policy of peace with insult.... The worst policy for the United States is to combine the unbridled tongue with the unready hand."
Theodore Roosevelt

"Just win, baby." Al Davis, owner, Oakland Raiders

By mid-winter 2003, President Bush and his team had spoken so long and so vehemently, and had moved so many troops, as to well-nigh guarantee that spring would bring either military success against Iraq, or the administration's discredit. Moreover, the Bush team's internal confusion and delay had so eroded the American people's precious post-September 11 resolve, as well as foreigners' support for America, that the president and his secretary of state had to scramble to build support for war. Even after the president's State of the Union address, and Secretary Powell's dramatic February 5 appeal to the United Nations, the Bush team remained of two minds about whether to change Iraq's regime or merely "disarm" it. The president had not resolved disagreements over whether anti-American terrorism is the work of renegade individuals, or of regimes that use them as cut-outs. Nor

*This essay appeared in the Claremont Review of Books, Spring 2003.

had he explained what part military action against Iraq would play in the "war on terrorism." Was it a diversion from the "war," as some in the administration charged, or was it, as others maintained, the war's proper centerpiece?

At the outset of the "war on terror," the Pentagon argued that the path to victory lay in changing hostile Arab regimes. President Bush, however, sided with Colin Powell's State Department, the CIA, as well as the earlier Bush administration's "best and brightest," and rejected the connection between regimes and terrorism (except for friendless, hapless Afghanistan). He chose to work with Saudis and other "friendly" Arab regimes against "shadowy networks," and to track down killers "one at a time."

By summer 2002, Bush somehow decided that Saddam's regime had to be toppled. Whatever his reasoning, he did not break with his earlier decision's premises and with the advisers who personified them. He spoke not of "regime change" but of "disarming" Saddam. He claimed that he had not decided whether to attack, and that he thought it necessary, or at any rate useful, to obtain the endorsement of the UN. This proved too clever by half. Whereas in the summer of 2002 polls had been running heavily in favor of overthrowing Saddam, by January 27, 2003, opposition to attacking Iraq, and to President Bush, had risen sharply.

Common sense would not have expected otherwise. To ask support of anyone, never mind of powers who are declared opponents, for a course of action on which one has not decided oneself, and at the same time to give the impression that one's decision is contingent on such support, is to beg for opposition. More important, once President Bush had given the American people the impression that America needed the UN's blessing to go to war, many Americans took him at his word and disapproved of war without those blessings.

As a preface to discussing America's political-military choices on the eve of the battle with Iraq, it is essential to look at how President Bush and his closest aides framed these choices since September 11.

INSIDE THE WAR CABINET

The *Washington Post's* Bob Woodward has produced a portrait of George Bush and his war cabinet at work, between 9/11 and the downfall of Afghanistan's Taliban regime, that is as detailed as it is accurate. *Bush at War* (2002) is not history, because Woodward focuses so sharply on his portraits, and says little by which the reader might evaluate people, ideas, or actions. But it is excellent raw material for history. To anyone personally acquainted with these persons, Woodward's account has the ring of truth.

In the few passages in which he states facts rather than his subjects' views, Woodward sums up what the reader has already grasped: The war cabinet had a loose grip on the basic facts, did not identify strategic goals, did not separate detail from key questions, made no attempt to relate means to ends, and acknowledged obvious, massive realities and choices only after having proceeded for weeks as if they didn't exist.

Consequently, Woodward writes: "Eighteen days after September 11 they were developing a response, a plan of action, not a strategy." And "the emphasis on such side issues revealed how far they were from solving the main ones." And, five weeks after September 11, "it was critical" to "incorporate military and CIA functions," but it was not being done. As for bombing Afghanistan, after weeks of planning in which the president had insisted that he did not want operations to be like those under President Clinton—bombs falling onto tents and mud huts, "pounding sand" he called it—initial operations in fact amounted to hitting thirty-one meaningless targets. A month after September 11, one participant at a meeting of the National Security Council said: "we need a political vision now." Another commented: "This is FUBAR" (an old military acronym, meaning f—d up beyond all recognition.) Why? Like all human entities, the war cabinet reflected its leader.

When Woodward asked Bush to explain how he led the war, Bush responded with perhaps the book's most revealing passage:

I'm the commander—see, I don't need to explain—I do not need to explain why I say things. That's the interesting thing about being the president. Maybe somebody needs to explain to me why they say something, but I don't feel like I owe anybody an explanation.

And, in fact, Bush neither presented plans of his own, nor synthesized plans from others' contributions. He wanted plans to accomplish vague, often contradictory things. "We need an early blueprint for response." "Have to coordinate public affairs." He demanded "boots on the ground," meaning American soldiers involved against terrorism somewhere. He said next to nothing about what they were to do or what effect they were to have. He wanted to show success, but ventured no view as to what that might mean. He wanted "a demonstration of seriousness" but said little about seriousness itself. He wanted "options" among which he could choose, boxes he could check.

In other words, according to Woodward, Bush led by pulling rank. A stickler for hierarchy, Bush is one of those bosses who calls subordinates by their first names, and even nicknames, while insisting on being called by his honorific. Impatient with intellectual arguments, he was drawn to the bloody-shirt bombast of CIA covert action chief Cofer Black. Only Condolezza Rice dared tell him things that he was likely to regard as unpleasant, and she had to guard her words. The Churchills and Lincolns of this world lead by asking questions that bare the problem's essence. Then, like good coaches, they teach subordinates a game plan and their parts. Not Bush. At one point, he told Rice: "I am the quarterback." She replied: "You are the coach." But Bush saw himself not as teaching, but as demanding "the consensus of six or seven smart people, which makes my job easier." Woodward comments: "He was about to find out that, indeed, the advice might not only be different, but that it could come dressed in language that was not always straightforward."

The confusion began immediately. At 8 a.m. on September 12, CIA Director George Tenet walked into the Oval Office and gave the president some intercepts of associates of Osama bin Laden rejoicing at the previous day's attacks. For Tenet, this was "game, set, and match." For the CIA, anti-American terror amounted to little more than bin Laden's al-Qaeda. Bush believed that Saddam "probably was behind this in the end," but he did not demand to see the evidence for and against contrary hypotheses. He even asked Tenet for a list of which targets in America terrorists were likely to hit. Rather than avow ignorance, Tenet produced a list of guesses. Bush agreed to give the CIA "whatever it takes." Tenet said that much of the money would go to "heavily subsidize" the intelligence services of Arab countries. This would "triple or quadruple" the intelligence available to the CIA. Bush did not question the wisdom of "buying" intelligence from governments whose agendas differ radically from America's. Thus did Bush set the war's goals—implicitly, and on the basis of unexamined assumptions.

At meetings of the National Security Council throughout the rest of that day, "[t]he persistent question was the exact definition of the mission." Defense Secretary Rumsfeld asked: "Are we going after terrorism more broadly than just al-Qaeda?" He suggested that the problem included regimes, primarily Iraq, and that the war should seek to solve the real problem. Secretary of State Powell did not try to define the problem differently, but argued for restricting the mission to al-Qaeda because it would be easier to gain support for that. "Bush made it clear it was not the time to resolve the issue. He emphasized again that his principal goal was to produce a military plan that would inflict real pain and destruction on the terrorists." No one dared ask which ones? And what good would it do to kill one set of people rather than another? Somehow, they would do something in Afghanistan. They would figure out what as they were doing it.

Discussion at the crucial September 15 war council began with the Joint Chiefs of Staff's three options: 1) cruise missile strikes on Afghanistan; 2) add manned bombers; 3) add "boots on the ground." Bush chose option three. But hit what to accomplish what? For Rice, "Afghanistan evoked every negative image: far away, landlocked, hard." Discussion was that vague. Rumsfeld hinted gently that "the worst thing they could do...was to misstate the objective" and that simply moving or killing al-Qaeda or the Taliban would not solve America's problem. Powell steered the discussion away from ends by arguing that: "You're going to hear [objections] from your coalition partners" in case you decide to "do" anything but Afghanistan. And even as regards Afghanistan, he cautioned: "don't go after their leadership." Rumsfeld responded that "any argument that the coalition wouldn't tolerate Iraq argued for a different coalition." The dispute was over whether alliances are ends or means. Bush did not resolve it. He asked, what U.S. forces, what allied ones, when, how, "what's the first wave? What's later?" But he neglected to ask, what do I want to accomplish, and what reason do I have to believe that this action will accomplish what I want?

Since objectives were unclear, "the Pentagon was still coming up dry." And since foreign governments were being asked to provide troops and basing arrangements for operations the ends and means of which the U.S. itself had not decided upon, their commitments were understandably vague. To Bush's impatience, Rumsfeld replied: "Look, we're not able to define a special operation role for our own forces. Until we can do that, how can we talk about others?" But Bush was not in the business of explaining. By the NSC meeting of September 26, he had agreed that "targets...were going to be the air defense systems, military airfields, runways, and other military targets...and boots on the ground may or may not be simultaneous."

When pressed about what the actions he had approved would accomplish, the president said: "Our strategy is to create chaos, to create a vacuum, to get the bad guys moving [so we can hit them]."

"Well, you know," Rumsfeld replied, "our military buildup has already had that effect." The mud huts that America would strike had long since been vacated. "The target list cannot impose much damage on the people we want to impose it on." Thus, two weeks after the September 11 attacks, did the thought wedge itself into the NSC that only the government of Afghanistan could rid Afghanistan of terrorists, and hence that America would have to strengthen rebel forces in Afghanistan. But those forces aimed to change the regime. Did the Bush team want that?

At the NSC meeting of Wednesday, October 3, three weeks after the attacks, the team realized that it had already effectively chosen "regime change." But "the problem was that [they] had not yet figured out how to do it." Nevertheless, on October 7, Bush told the military: "Your mission is defined; your objectives are clear." Meanwhile, Vice President Cheney informed the president that, because of the upcoming winter, "if we're serious about unleashing the Northern Alliance, we need to do it soon." That would mean reorienting the bombing away from the target list on which everyone had agreed over the past month and "on[to] the targets that will make it easier for the Northern Alliance to move." Bush agreed, because he said: "We need the American people to understand we're being successful." It is difficult to avoid the impression that Bush was less concerned with the steak than with the sizzle.

But actual policy did not change, and U.S. pilots continued to pound sand through the middle of October. At the October 15 NSC meeting, after five weeks of non-stop deliberations, the disconnect between the White House word circus and military reality became undeniable. Rice told Rumsfeld privately that it was up to him to craft a strategy. Rumsfeld, Woodward writes, "was stirred up. He went back to the Pentagon and directed his policy shop, headed by Undersecretary [for policy] Douglas Feith, to draft a paper outlining an overall Afghanistan strategy. He wanted it in six hours."

Essentially, Feith came up with the obvious—that only the Northern Alliance could defeat the Taliban, and that close air support was the only way U.S. forces could help. One supposes that over five weeks

Feith (whose "shop" employs about 1,000 people, plus hot and cold running consultants) had thought about matching ends and means in Afghanistan, and in the war as a whole. Such ideas are within the grasp of ordinary mortals. But Woodward shows that planning at the highest level admitted common sense about ends and means only when the alternative of embarrassment was clear and present.

In the end, despite confusion, the power that the United States added to that of the Northern Alliance overwhelmed the Taliban. The president and his administration declared victory, and basked in a year of high approval ratings.

Bush At War deals summarily with "homeland security." Bush was very keen on it. But he dealt with it roughly as he did with military affairs. Bush worried a lot about how America might be hit, and wanted the country "buttoned up." He seemed not to have glimpsed that this is impossible. He said things such as "searching everyone from clergymen to elderly ladies at airports could send a message to terrorists—no matter how you dress or how unlikely a suspect you may appear, no one is immune to scrutiny." He did not ask whether that is worth doing, whether and how it might contribute to victory. Woodward did not write the book to raise such questions. Raising them is our purpose.

THE WAR, AND THE BATTLE OF IRAQ

By making military action appear inevitable, President Bush's State of the Union address and Secretary Powell's UN presentation forced foreign and domestic audiences to consider whether they could afford to be on the losing side of a successful U.S. military operation. Neither address resolved the confusions endemic to the war.

With images from KH-11 satellites, tapes of conversations between Iraqi officers, and evidence of Iraqi purchases of banned materials, Powell argued that Iraq had not complied with UN resolutions regarding weapons of mass destruction. With photos of terrorists in Iraq, he also asserted "a potentially sinister nexus between Iraq and the al-Qaeda terrorist network." The pictures' significance was self evident—but only to those who understand satellite imagery. It was impossible to offer proof of the images' dates. U.S. artists' conceptions of Iraqi mobile biowar labs would have to be accepted on faith. The intercepted conversations certainly were consistent with a cover-up of forbidden programs. But by themselves they proved nothing. Nevertheless, the fact that the Secretary of State bet his country's prestige on a sound and light presentation beamed around the globe was a more certain trumpet for the battle of Iraq than any the Bush team had yet sounded. Still, if the Americans really believed it themselves, why hadn't they made their final decision?

The tentativeness of the connection that Powell made between Iraq and terrorism bespoke the Bush team's long-standing, unresolved internal struggles about "the war."

THE WAR

The only connection President Bush made on January 28 between the battle for Iraq and "the war" was that "outlaw regimes" could "give or sell those weapons to their terrorist allies." But what was the nature of the "alliance" between outlaw regimes and terrorists? Bush had never explained. For a quarter-century, Congress had mandated that the State Department issue yearly reports on states that support terrorism. It was common knowledge in Washington that the reports' depiction of each state's terrorist connections fluctuated with U.S. policy. (In 1982, for example, the report gave Iraq a better grade, as part of the U.S. government's nine-year, misguided attempt to turn Saddam into an ally). In 1993, however, the Clinton administration made the reports irrelevant by embracing the CIA's contention that terrorists were not the foot soldiers and cut-outs of regimes, but were "loose networks" of private individuals imperfectly pursued by regimes. The Defense Department, for its part, had touted evidence of Iraq's provision of stolen identities (and of refuge) to the persons who carried out the 1993 attack on the World Trade Center, the meeting between an Iraqi terrorist handler and Mohammed Atta, the hijack training camp at Iraq's Salman Pak, and so on.

Since George Bush did not question the CIA, he shaped the war on terror according to its view. In the State of the Union, he continued to define "the war" as "against a scattered network of killers," and described its operations as teaching them, "one by one...the meaning of American justice." Bush's fleeting reference to terrorists as "allies" of regimes, like Powell's reference to a "potentially sinister nexus," may have reflected no more than the tactical need to assert at least a tenuous link between the battle for Iraq and "the war." The "nexus" between the battle and the war remained a topic for the president's attention. At any rate, Bush strengthened the CIA's position by placing

a new "Terrorist Threat Integration Center" under its direction. Designed "to make sure the right people are in the right places to protect
our citizens," it stood no chance of doing this.

THE BATTLE

Would America overthrow the Iraqi regime? Bush certainly hinted
broadly at "regime change." He said that "outlaw regimes that seek
and possess weapons of mass destruction" are "the gravest danger in
the war on terror," and that the day Saddam and his regime were
removed would be the day of his people's liberation. He pledged to
bring "freedom" to the people of Iraq. But he stressed even more
strongly that the danger to America consists of Iraq's possession of
certain arms. His only explicit commitment was, "If Saddam does not
fully disarm...we will lead a coalition to disarm him." The confusion
continued.

Supposing U.S. forces were ordered into action, what would they
actually do? Professional military sources are unanimous that they
would use "shock and awe" tactics—the few troops on the ground
would direct accurate fire from the air in order to cut off Iraqi units
from their command structure and from one another, and allow U.S.
units to pass. With Americans moving around them at will, the Iraqis
would surrender even faster than they did during the Gulf War.

But from an operational, as opposed to a purely tactical point of
view, the effectiveness of "shock and awe" is by no means clear. During the Gulf War, Iraqi troops surrendered *en masse* after they had
been cut off in a concentrated deployment far from home, and pounded
for weeks. Many had been killed. They were going to be overrun, and
likely killed. They believed that the U.S. was going to overthrow the
regime. In 2003, it is not self-evident that people will be put in fear of
death by operations designed to produce fear rather than death. Most
important, the fact that Bush does not explicitly aim to change the
regime was sure to compound the deadly memory that the last Bush
had actually turned surrendered prisoners back to Saddam.

What if Iraqi troops did not collapse? U.S. forces would not be prepared for, and Iraqi deployments do not lend themselves to, mass
killing. Pursuing regime change with relatively small forces on the
ground, and in the presence of undefeated Iraqi units, would court
tactical disaster. In the presence of undefeated Iraqi units, search-
and-destroy missions for weapons of mass destruction would *guarantee*

tactical disasters. Too late it would become clear that operations designed for one purpose and pursued for another are less likely to accomplish either than to produce blunders pregnant with catastrophe. Choice is the essence of strategy.

The Bush team's unmade choices could invite ploys to preempt or divert American military power. Saddam might proclaim that troops authorized by the UN could enter Iraq, search for, and take away whatever they pleased. Iraqi forces would not fire unless fired upon. The UN could then unanimously "authorize" a U.S. military incursion, but narrowly tailored to achieve some kind of "disarmament" while respecting Iraqi sovereignty. Part of the Bush team would be tempted to declare that it had achieved its objectives without bloodshed. Bush could agree with Powell that "disarmament" was the functional equivalent of "regime change." The agony of defeat would follow fast.

It is also possible, however, that the U.S. military's advantages over Iraq could overwhelm confused planning. Iraqi troops might well collapse, leading to the shattering end typical of tyrannical regimes. The fate of Saddam could discourage the terror regimes of Palestine and Syria enough so that, under pressure from Israel and Turkey, they would cleanse themselves. Meanwhile, decent Iranians might be heartened to end the terrible regime that, since 1979, had produced misery at home and anti-Americanism abroad. The Saudi royal family could be replaced by persons who actually did useful work and did not feel the need to subsidize the world's terrorists. Following the changes in these regimes, terrorists would no longer hatch faster than we could catch them. After a while, even the Bush administration might consider sending Tom Ridge back to fixing parking tickets.

Magic? Military success is the closest thing to it. If the battle of Iraq turns out so, America will rightly thank the Bush team, confusion and all. If not, we will have to forgive them, for they know not what they do.

VII: Confused Power

Victory Watch: When the Cheering Stops*

"The battle of Iraq is one victory in a war on terror that began on September 11....The war on terror is not over; yet it is not endless." George W. Bush, April 30, 2003

"There has been much talk in Washington about the 'shock and awe' that might result from an air campaign. This is an attempt to induce shock and awe on the ground, as American armor maneuvers near the former power centers of the government and tries to narrow the space where top officials may be hiding." Michael Gordon, New York Times, April 9, 2003

America and the world owe George W. Bush a debt of thanks. Nothing so avenged the victims of September 11 or so shielded Americans from the recurrence of similar disasters as unleashing the U.S. military on the Iraqi Baathist regime, which embodied hate and contempt for America. President Bush's recognition on April 30, 2003, that "Operation Iraqi Freedom" had been the biggest battle yet in the war on terror, *and especially that the war would not be endless,* augurs an intellectual process that may lead to understanding, and then to pursuing, victory in that larger war.

In a nutshell: President Bush ended up making war on Iraq more or less correctly only after having courted political and diplomatic disaster. Immediately after winning the battle, he resumed the policies that had forestalled military success. He reassured the terror regime of Syria, rewarded the terror regime of Palestine, did not scrub the remnants of Baath rule in Iraq, and sought to relieve pressure on the

*This article appeared in the Claremont Review of Books, Summer 2003.

111

Saudi royal family. Most important, any "regime change" abroad remained less certain than the permanence of the post-September 11
changes wrought by security measures in the American regime. Victory or defeat may well depend on George W. Bush's threshold of
embarrassment.

In 1991, as in Vietnam, and as in Korea, America specialized in
winning the battle and losing the war. Whether in 2003 military success in Iraq would break that pattern would depend on the resolution
of intellectual conflicts in Washington.

THE BATTLE OF IRAQ: THE ENEMY

No satisfactory account of the battle of Iraq is possible because—
even after total military success—we lack solid knowledge of what
the enemy was trying to accomplish. We know what the enemy did
and did not do, and we know how he did it. But we have nothing but
conjectures as to why.

Now we know that the Iraqi armed forces fought without operational plans, central command and control, never mind a strategy. We
know that Saddam's inner circle had decided to abandon the regime
well before the battle began. What Saddam had in mind when he so
decided or where he and his key people went, U.S. intelligence hasn't
a clue.

Between October 2002 and March 2003 Saddam Hussein had the
United States in a tightening vise. On one side was Bush's strident
commitment to some kind of victory. On the other side was mounting
opposition to America around the world. In the middle was the key
concession that Secretary of State Colin Powell had squeezed out of
Bush on October 2: if Saddam "disarmed," Bush would finish eating
his words about "regime change." America would claim victory without shooting, and the regime could stay in power. Let the Americans
come into Iraq to search for weapons of mass destruction—but in
peace, with no shooting, accompanied by the UN, and with full respect for sovereignty. Even the U.S. draft resolution had promised the
latter. Bush would look good in the short run, and Saddam would win
in the long. Yet as Bush's March 22 deadline drew closer, Saddam did
not make that diplomatic move, or any other.

Saddam was rightly reputed a master survivor. He knew better
than the Americans how little his weapons of mass destruction were
the basis of his influence in the world, and how much that influence

depended on foiling the Americans again. We now know how little he thought of these WMDs because, weeks or months before the battle, he ordered not just their destruction, but also the chemical decontamination of the instruments involved in their manufacture. He did this even as he was gathering $1 billion in currency in his central bank so he could loot it as he was abandoning his own regime on his own terms. We know not the terms, or why.

Saddam's betrayal of his regime covered his escape. Key to both were some 10,000 *Fedayeen Saddam*, the black-clad criminals that his son Qusay had organized after the 1991 Gulf War in order to terrorize the country back into submission. Saddam deployed them within the Iraqi armed forces and among the population to savage anyone who showed insufficient zeal. He also ordered them to carry out irregular warfare against the Americans. Fear of them froze Iraqis at their posts and prevented their welcoming the Americans. And in fact, the *Fedayeen* accounted for most of the American casualties by fighting disguised as civilians, or by feigning surrender. All of this exposed the *Fedayeen* to execution by the Americans as well as by their enraged fellow citizens once the regime fell. These most loyal and ignorant members of the regime had the greatest need of escape. Yet Saddam betrayed them most cruelly of all.

Also left holding the bag were regime mushrooms (kept in the dark and fed manure) such as Deputy Prime Minister Tariq Aziz, Saddam's token Christian. The *opera buffa* Minister of Information, Baghdad Bob, played Wizard of Oz by delivering briefings canned far in advance in order to fake the existence of a vanished regime.

Partial evidence of Saddam's plan was visible to anyone in Baghdad. As the well-advertised date approached for the beginning of the well-advertised American bombing of "leadership targets" and "military targets," the target palaces and ministries were empty, in the care of forlorn security guards, who watched over meaningless bomb sinks. The military moved to well-advertised safe havens—mosques, schools and hospitals. But it, too, was betrayed, left to take the Americans' blows while the leadership moved who knows where.

The bombs that were scheduled to arrive on March 22, came two days early. Some Iraqis long on the CIA's payroll, told the Agency that Saddam and his sons were spending the night at a particular safe house. CIA told Bush, who on March 20 (Iraq time) directed two F-117s with 2,000-pound "bunker buster" bombs to decapitate the regime. The next day, Saddam spoke on Iraqi TV, probably on tape.

Triggering the strikes through Iraqi double agents, followed by the tapes, Saddam had covered his escape. The strikes gave the Americans plausible cause for declaring him dead, while the tapes fed the Iraqis' fear that he was alive. We still do not know. We do know that Iraqi intelligence had penetrated the CIA's latest plot to encourage senior officers to overthrow Saddam. The intelligence battle was the only one Saddam chose to fight. He seems to have won it.

Ordinary Iraqis, from the Republican Guard to housewives, behaved with one objective in mind: personal survival. Hence some fought perfunctorily before changing into civilian clothes and going home, while others hid their feelings. Was American fire more or less dangerous than *Fedayeen* knives? In short, their behavior swung with the balance of fear.

THE BEGINNING

Since September 2002, the Bush team had vowed that it meant above all to rid Iraq of WMDs. As late as April 10 the White House spokesman said: "That is what this war is about." But beginning in February, President Bush gradually reintroduced into public discourse the link between Iraq and September 11, as well as the expectation that "regime change" in Iraq would usher in much needed changes in the Middle East. But on March 19, Bush announced the goal of Operation Iraqi Freedom: to export the good life. The shell game of justifications reflected the shifting balance of power in the White House. But it neither mollified enemies nor reassured friends. Once the guns began firing, however, any and all objectives depended on collapsing armed resistance.

Pre-programmed strikes in and around Baghdad between March 22 and March 24, by some 3,400 cruise missiles and aircraft sorties, were supposed to "shock and awe" the Iraqi regime into collapse. Simultaneously, the U.S. military plan called for invasion northward from Kuwait by the U.S. Third Infantry Division, the U.S. First Marine Expeditionary Force, and a brigade of British Royal Fusiliers. The Fourth Infantry Division had been scheduled to invade southward from Turkey, but would be redirected to Kuwait and arrive near the end of the fighting. Other U.S. units, including the 101st Airborne Division and various special forces, were dropped or airlifted onto oil fields, airfields, bridges, and into northern Iraq, where they organized Kurdish forces. The movement of troops not preceded by artillery barrages or air strikes, what U.S. planners hailed as an innovative "rolling start," was made possible and prudent by the fact that between Baghdad and Basra and Kuwait, there was little to hit. Rapid advance could secure bridges and oil fields intact. Besides, American forces could count on unchallenged, near instantaneous air cover from fixed-wing aircraft and helicopters every step of the way. Not one Iraqi aircraft would challenge the Americans.

As "shock and awe" was getting under way on March 21, Defense Secretary Donald Rumsfeld said that the Iraqi regime was "starting to lose control" because "their ability to see what is happening on the battlefield, to communicate with their forces, and to control their country is slipping away." But the regime had not tried to see, communicate, or control. Shock and awe did not play to its intended top-level Iraqi audience because that audience was long gone. Gradually, U.S. planners realized that they would have to occupy the whole country in order to convince it that the regime had quit.

Meanwhile, some 80,000 U.S. and British ground troops drove some 15,000 vehicles of all kinds some 100 miles into Iraq in the first thirty-six hours. Regular Iraqi units surrendered on sight, notably the 51st Division. The destruction of two Iraqi armored personnel carriers counted as a major engagement in that drive.

THE MIDDLE

When U.S. Marines and British troops reached the southern city of Basra on March 23, they faced the problem that would typify the middle phase of the operation: Although the city contained no Iraqi forces that could give serious resistance, the city would not surrender. Small amounts of fire came out of it. The *Fedayeen* prevented the city from rising *en masse* to welcome its liberators. Iraqis, especially southern Shiites, had learned bitterly in 1991 not to believe promises of liberation. The Marines moved north, while the British probed inward gingerly lest they take casualties or inflict them on civilians. Basra would not fall until the American successes around Baghdad—the real shock and awe—persuaded the *Fedayeen* that they had been hung out to dry and had better scatter.

In the meantime, however, the Americans moving north past the cities of Nasiriya and Najaf encountered what the press called heavy, unexpected resistance. Heavy compared to what? On March 23, the heaviest day of fighting, 13 Americans were killed—most after a unit of cooks and mechanics had taken a wrong turn. The next largest group of casualties occurred when some *Fedayeen* feigned surrender and then fired. This caused the detail of some more helicopters to escort convoys. Marines took Nasiriya to make sure that nothing from it could threaten transit over the Euphrates bridges. But the notion that Iraqi resistance stalled the drive to Baghdad because of a lack of American troops or heavy equipment, is nonsense.

In fact, beginning on March 25, Mother Nature stalled U.S. forces with a sandstorm. While it lasted, U.S. forces moved up supplies for the destruction of the three Republican Guard divisions that stood in the way to Baghdad.

The End

The Marines advancing from the southeast and the Army from the southwest did not really destroy the Republican Guard around Baghdad. By the time they moved on April 1, four days' work by U.S. aircraft (along with massive defections) had "degraded" three Guard divisions to perhaps a third of their strength. Two American divisions drove through the remnants in four main columns—some forty miles of combat in a little over three days.

The images from CNN and Fox News of American armored vehicles driving along, blasting enemy positions right and left, or watching them being blasted by Apache helicopters or fighter bombers, told a tale confirmed by the casualty figures. Some 20,000 American combat soldiers had driven through a somewhat greater number of Iraqis—perhaps 50,000 men fighting each other with the deadliest of weapons—at the cost of fewer than 50 Americans killed. The final U.S. combat death toll was 124. By April 5, Americans had taken Baghdad airport and mostly surrounded the city. Meanwhile, columns of former Iraqi soldiers who had surrendered to the few U.S. troops operating in northern Iraq were walking happily toward Baghdad in civilian clothes. This was not Stalingrad.

By April 9, the Bush team's decision not simply to crush the enemy and leave, but to export good government, coupled with its failure to decide who would govern, began to haunt the operation. Running the city would require shooting ordinary civilians who defied American rules, and shooting some Iraqi claimants to power who blocked the way for others chosen by Washington. But the State Department and CIA had chosen one set of Iraqis, and the Defense Department another.

The Bush team as a whole disdained shooting, counted on rival Iraqi claimants along with their respective U.S. sponsors agreeing on interim authorities, and on a democratic process for sorting things out. Nonsense.

Machiavelli's prescription for running conquered territory is to arm your clients while disarming the rest—impossible since Bush had not chosen—or failing that, to crush one and all. Instead, the U.S. armed forces were ordered not to govern, and to arrest anyone who tried. Anarchy, anyone? By mid-May, embarrassment led Bush to order U.S. forces to kill (a little) to restore order. But whose order? As Bush waited for serendipity to work out differences between State/CIA, Defense, and their clients, U.S. forces at who knows whose direction, raided the offices of the most pro-American of local factions. "Well, they won't be pro-American anymore, I guess," mused one of the soldiers who carried out the dumb order.

Talk of weapons of mass destruction, judged convenient before the battle, was sure to become an embarrassment afterward. *Of course* Iraq had chemical and biological weapons! Some U.S. Special Forces who had found their hiding places in 2002 had become contaminated and quite sick. But since these substances are almost as easily unmade as they are made, and since the pieces for making them do not have to be kept together, turning their discovery into the test of legitimacy of U.S. policy always amounted to leading with America's political chin. This was the least of the ways in which diplomatic malpractice undermined military success.

DIPLOMATIC MALPRACTICE

Coercive diplomacy is the ingredient that translates the near magic of military success into victory. It shows foreign governments that it is better for them to adjust themselves to the reality created by our military success, however painful that might be for them, than to suffer our forcing on them whatever consequences of that new reality we choose. In the aftermath of America's military success, the magic agenda of cleansing the Syrian, Palestinian, and Saudi sources of terrorism was not about to happen because the U.S. State Department did not practice coercive diplomacy. It had its own agenda. By presenting to these governments proposals that differed only cosmetically, if at all, from those that State had pursued for years prior, State effectively told them that they need not be concerned with any of the things that America could do to them as a result of its military success. Predictably, these governments took this as further reason for contempt towards America.

Here are three instances of the contrast between coercive diplomacy aimed at translating military success into victory, and State Department policy.

SYRIA

As a result of America's success in Iraq, Syria's Baathist regime, surely among the top three purveyors of terrorism, lived exclusively among rocks and hard places. On every side were Americans or America's allies: American forces at sea to the west, and on land to the east, Turkey to the north, and Israel to the south. Each of these alone could defeat the regime easily. Economically, they could strangle it. Moreover, Turkey could cut off Syria's water, or flood it. Whence could help come? Baath had become a dirty word, even in France. Syria was in the legally indefensible position of being the occupying power in Lebanon. Inside Syria, the regime—consisting of the tiny Alewite minority despised by Muslims—stood on shakier ground than even Saddam's had in Iraq. It would not be easy for U.S. diplomacy to make offers that Syria could refuse.

But Colin Powell managed. In mid-April, as Syria cowered, it let on that it was open to an offer of talks. Powell, instead of answering with a list of non-negotiable demands, announced that he would travel to Damascus. Meanwhile, he persuaded President Bush to say publicly that Syria "got the message" and was cooperating. This took the pressure off. Powell arrived in Syria without any demand regarding the freedom of Lebanon or even the arrest and consignment of thousands of known terrorists—only a list of known Iraqi escapees about whom he asked for Syria's help; a request that Syria close some terrorist headquarters; and praise for their having been "helpful...in our global war against terrorism." Predictably, Syria's Assad reacted with contempt. He gave Powell assurances, among other things, that the offices would be closed. The next day, his newspaper, *Al Baath*, conditioned all of the assurances on America fulfilling Syria's agenda regarding Israel. Reporters calling the terrorist offices in Damascus found them open for business. Apparently, this fell below George Bush's threshold of embarrassment.

PALESTINE AND ISRAEL

Not only had Saddam Hussein financed Yasser Arafat's campaign of
suicide bombing against Israel; he had provided the crucial example
that one could succeed against mighty America. Now America had
crushed Saddam's regime. Meanwhile, Arafat had discredited himself
and his movement by acts of terrorism and corruption so egregious
that even Hillary Clinton had been forced to distance herself from the
Palestinian cause. Only George Bush, and he tenuously, was holding
Israel back from utterly destroying it. Again, it was difficult to imagine
America making the Palestine Authority an offer it could refuse. But
again, Powell managed.

The State Department had never abandoned its support of Arafat's
Palestinian Authority. Its stock-in-trade had been the "peace process,"
by which Israel gave Arafat land, autonomy, and money in exchange
for promises of peace. Arafat's stock-in-trade had been to pocket concessions and to use terrorism to demand more. State typically responded by prodding Israel to continue giving in, despite terrorist
outrages. September 11 made this more difficult, although State argued that crafting peace in Israel—meaning satisfying Arab demands
despite Arab terrorism against Israel—was necessary for America's
war on terrorism. When that argument lost traction with Bush, State
fell back to arguing that if the P.A. got itself new leadership, and if it
stopped terrorism, then America should lay on the table a "road map"
by which Arab-Israeli peace might be reached. Further, it argued that
commitment to the road map would help secure Arab and European
consent for the battle of Iraq. Who could object?

It turned out, however, that the Arabs and Europeans were not
mollified. In the fine print, the road map turned out to be worse than
the peace process, and State's sponsorship of it more transparently
fraudulent. Under the road map, State did not require the P.A. to stop
acts of terror. Only to try. State convinced Bush that the P.A. had satisfied a requirement for new leadership by appointing Arafat's chief
lieutenant, a fabulously corrupt, seasoned terrorist with a *nom de guerre*,
as prime minister with limited autonomy from Arafat himself. Predictably, no sooner had Powell given his blessing to the arrangement and
turned over some $50 million in U.S. taxpayer funds, than the Pales-
tinians started up the old dodge again: suicide bombings followed by
official denials, crocodile tears, and demands for more concessions

lest more terrorism follow. For Arafat and friends, the battle of Iraq might as well not have happened. And why not? For their purposes, U.S. policy seemed to agree.

SAUDI ARABIA

It is no exaggeration to say that the problem of international terrorism is an extension of the internal problems of Saudi Arabia's royal family. These are threefold: dependence on the dangerous, radical Wahhabi sect, divisions within the family based on different harem lines, and generalized corrupt, moneyed, impotence. For nearly a half-century, U.S. policy has moved heaven and earth, and overlooked much, to keep the Saudi regime from collapsing. But since September 11, many Americans—though next to none in the State Department—have asked the hard question of whether America would be better off were the Saudi regime allowed to succumb to its congenital ills. Its value had sunk so low that it would be worthwhile to use the leverage of military success in Iraq in order to make upon the Saudi regime demands essential to America's war on terror, regardless of how they might destabilize that regime. But State (and oil interests) easily persuaded Bush to continue betting on Saudi stability.

On May 13, massive bombs exploded in the Saudi capital in compounds inhabited by Westerners working for parts of the Saudi regime, killing eight Americans. Powell arrived in Riyadh that day and repeated U.S. demands that the regime crack down harder on anti-Western activities. Those demands almost certainly neglected the fact that the bombs were principally tools in intra-Saudi disputes that may have marked the beginning of the end of the regime. September 11, the war on terrorism, and fighting in Iraq had inflamed the strife. This may lead to much, soon. In sum, events would likely push against George W. Bush's threshold of embarrassment, forcing consideration of how to apply the leverage of military success to the regimes that spawn terror.

WAR AND REGIME IN AMERICA

In the next section, we will turn to the ways in which the Department of Homeland Security is changing the American regime. This book argues that "homeland security" is defeat itself. Setting conditions for dismantling this boondoggle bureaucracy founded on the premise that you and I are terrorist suspects, and for ending the national circus of friskings and ID checks, is the minimum sign of seriousness about victory.

VICTORY WATCH: ENDS, ENEMIES, AND FRIENDS*

Socrates: [The guardians of the state] ought to be dangerous to their enemies and
    gentle to their friends.
Glaucon: And where do you find them?
Socrates: Our friend the dog is a very good example...perfectly gentle to
    friends and the reverse to strangers...why, a dog whenever he sees
    a friend is happy, and when he sees an enemy is angry, even
    though the one has never done him any good or the other any
    harm....He distinguishes friend and enemy by knowing and not
    knowing. Plato, Republic

"And they began to deal with one another as foreigners." Montesquieu, The Greatness of the Romans and Their Decline

"You can do anything with bayonets, except sit on them." Napoleon

Knowing and not knowing about friends and enemies is the key to using force unto victory rather than being hoisted on one's own bayonets. It is essential to the survival of any organism.

George W. Bush's statement on May 30 that the war "will not be endless" had been the only hint since September 11 that his administration might have thought of ending the War on Terror more or less in accordance with former U.S. Senator Phil Gramm's common sense definition of victory: "I don't want to change the way I live." By summer 2003, however, it seemed that in Iraq, on the diplomatic front, and above all in America itself, the Bush team had deployed massive power without that definition of ends, that discernment between friends and enemies, which alone makes means meaningful.

This essay appeared in the Claremont Review of Books, Fall 2003.

In Iraq, having stepped into the void of a regime that had purposely dissolved itself, the Bush team tried to remake the country while making as little distinction as possible between America's Baathist enemies and *their* enemies. As in Vietnam, American officials touted improvements in socio-economic conditions—except that the "security situation" continued to claim American lives. Any connection between the American governance of Iraq and the destruction of America's enemies was speculative.

In relation to the other matrices of terrorism—Syria, the Palestinian Authority, and Saudi Arabia—the Bush team followed Secretary Powell in continually lowering the criteria for qualifying them as friends and helping them against our friend, Israel. Rewarding these regimes ensured a continuing supply of terror and threats.

Also, two years after September 11, American forces were seriously involved in places like Colombia, Yemen, Liberia, and the Philippines, with no prospect that success in any or all would return the American people to the easier way of life they had enjoyed before the War on Terror. Indeed, the Bush team avoided questions concerning whether it intended ever to rescind the increase in the national government's police functions. Much of the government enjoyed the new powers for their own sake; interest groups including the Democratic Party profited from them and asked for more; the polls said women voters equated more "homeland security" with safety; and conservative commentators by and large treated as unpatriotic any criticism of security measures. Talk of an end to the war, much less of "victory," had become embarrassing.

Victory—the peace *we* want—comes when enemies are identified correctly, then killed or cowed. For this, one must draw a razor sharp, bloody distinction between enemies and friends. The practical definition of friendship regarding foreigners is: their clear and present enmity towards our enemies of the moment. As George W. Bush once put it: "Those who are not with us are against us." The practical definition of "us," is the sentiment that our own fellow citizens are our kin. Victory in war requires—absolutely—the constant pursuit of these distinctions.

For the Bush administration, however, these distinctions proved to be mere rhetoric. It proved more willing to change America than to abandon its own progressive dream of creating a world order in which *the issues of war*, rather than enemies, would disappear. This turned the War on Terror into a waste of power abroad and perpetual "homeland security" at home.

Distinguishing between friends and enemies as well as dogs do is especially important when fighting terrorists, because terrorist warfare aims precisely at confusing the distinction. Here is how Egypt's Gamal Abdel Nasser instructed his senior officers a half-century ago:

> The great advantage of indirect warfare is that our enemies cannot answer back. If we ordered our armies to capture the oil pumping stations...this would unite the entire world against us; but if we sent a commando unit to blow up those pumping stations, we would achieve the same result and the Great Powers would watch us with their hands tied.... Irregular warfare costs us little and costs our enemies dear.

This formula works only to the extent that the victims are willing to play along; to believe the inciters' crocodile tears when they deplore the terrorists' methods while feeling sympathy for their ends; to agree that perhaps if the targets were to make some concessions to the likes of Nasser, or his many successors, they might help with the terrorists. The formula works best of all if the target governments take less interest in doing away with their enemies than in pursuing schemes irrelevant to the war, and may even befoul themselves by confusing enemies and fellow citizens. Let us see how.

IRAQ

The Bush team was never clear why Iraq's Baathist regime was dangerous to America. Who or what was the enemy, the problem, in Iraq? Once before, in 1991, its principals—Powell and Cheney—had judged that the danger had been Saddam's military power. Then, after a decade during which Saddam's regime, shorn of most of its military, had become the palimpsest of anti-Americanism, had supplied at least the documents by which the commanders of the 1993 World Trade Center bombing traveled, and after Iraq's intelligence service (in the person of Mohammed al Ani) had dealt with the commander of the September 11 hijackers, one of those principals, Colin Powell, convinced President Bush to agree that the problem in Iraq was its "weapons of mass destruction." If those were done away with, the regime thereby would change character, posing no threat to America. Cleverly, Bush justified the 2003 invasion of Iraq in terms of disarming it of WMDs. If it turned out that Saddam had indeed disarmed himself, Bush compounded his error, pretending that his judgment had been correct. One cannot blame his political enemies too much for asking malevolently why Bush invaded Iraq.

How indeed did Iraq's regime threaten America? It did so politically because it had successfully defied it, and because Saddam used this success as well as the non-Iraqi Arabs his regime trained at its base at Salman Pak, as well as its many terrorist connections, to terrorize Americans and anyone who would stand with them, encouraging others to do so. The problem was a whole regime's anti-American identity. The deadly political threat that such regimes pose can be done away with only by the frightful demise of their cadres.

The U.S. forces that invaded Iraq carried a cleverish deck of 55 cards with the pictures of some of the regime's most infamous members. Capturing or killing them would go some way toward killing the regime. In the case of Saddam and his two sons, a long way. But American authorities did not know, and did not want to do away with the two thousand or so cadres who embodied the regime's anti-Americanism. Of course, these cadres' Iraqi enemies knew them and wanted to do away with them. Of course, there is no surer way to eliminate our own enemies anywhere than to empower *their* domestic enemies. Indeed, that is really the only way. But the Bush team feared that were the Baath's domestic enemies to take over, they would massacre their former tormentors with perhaps even more fervor than the Lebanese militias who took power after Israel's successful 1982 invasion of Beirut massacred their enemies in the Sabra and Shatila camps. Unwisely, the Bush team decided to treat Iraqis evenhandedly—to disarm the enemies of America's enemies, along with the few enemies of America that they could find by themselves, and to wield power through an American viceroy.

In fact, prompted by the State Department and CIA, the Bush team tried to work with as many of these cadres as possible. Most of all, it did not want to empower the Baath Party's domestic enemies because these agencies had long, friendly relations with the Baath. Inexorably, Iraqis learned that whereas no one would kill them for being anti-American, some people would kill them for *not* being anti-American, and that the Americans could not protect them. American troops went from a springtime combat romp to occupation duty in the desert summer, either as sitting ducks or barging about the country on "search and arrest" missions that parodied Vietnam's "search and destroy" campaigns against insignificant persons in the Mekong swamps and the central highlands. All this amounted to going through the motions of war while avoiding war's essential purpose: the frightful demise of enemies whose deaths would end the war.

Just as in Vietnam, the main thrust of U.S. policy aimed at reforming local society: improving schools and hospitals, and reducing the space for what the Americans judged religious extremism. One could almost hear Lyndon Johnson's definition of the enemy: "ignorance, disease, poverty...." U.S. policy assumed that once the socio-economic situation improved, attacks on Americans and those working with them would diminish. Washington had learned nothing since Vietnam. As in Vietnam, the real war was supposed to be won by the civilian administrators working for the American viceroy. Few if any spoke Arabic, and they had to rule from behind barricades because the "security situation" for Americans and locals working with them was far worse than it had been in Vietnam.

But U.S. policy had only bad guesses about the sources of those attacks. Indeed, four months after the Baathist regime deliberately had dissolved itself, and a dozen years after the Gulf War, U.S. intelligence had no idea what calculations had underlain the enemy's actions. Nevertheless, the Bush team proceeded as if its own ignorance did not matter.

By mid-summer the American viceroy, scrambling to put an Iraqi face on the American occupation, appointed a twenty-five member governing council. But since ultimate authority—above all for dealing with America's enemies and their own—remained with the Americans, it was by no means clear whether its members had done themselves or America a favor by accepting the roles and restrictions (dare we call it friendship?) the Bush team offered. It was all too easy to imagine Ahmed Chalabi's Iraqi National Congress facing the deadly choices of Ngo Dinh Diem in 1963: succumb to the enemies that the Americans refuse to let you kill; or be thrown to the wolves by the Americans for insufficient dedication to their apolitical agenda; or maybe join America's enemies.

The consequences for America's terrorist enemies were mixed. On the one hand, the sight of Saddam Hussein's sons torn apart by American bullets, the fact that American forces proved they could go anywhere and displace any regime, could only give such people pause.

On the other hand, the fact that the Americans spared the cadres of such a horribly brutal regime the massacres at the hands of their domestic enemies that they had richly earned, could only give terrorists the sense that the Americans will never empower *their* enemies, and hence that they are playing with a safety net. As Henry Kissinger once put it, while being America's enemy is sometimes inconvenient, being America's friend is invariably fatal.

OF DODGES AND WASTES

Cultivated obtuseness is needed to wonder who America's terrorist enemies in the rest of the Middle East are, and who their enemies in the region are who might rid us of them with ease and delight. Plato's dog would rightly be satisfied to note who danced in the streets as Americans were burned and crushed on September 11, as well as who had violently supported the causes on behalf of which September 11 was perpetrated: the PLO/PLA, the originator of anti-Western terrorism, murderer of American citizens and officials, bomber of buses and hijacker of airplanes; Saudi Arabia, source of most of the 9/11 hijackers, source of most of the money for the world's terrorists, symbiotic patron of the Wahhabi heresy that justifies it all and spawns anti-American terrorism in U.S. prisons, mosques, and even in the armed forces; and Syria, the jackal state headquarters to most of the world's terrorist groups. That simple dog would know that Syria's fragile regime lives at the mercy of Turkey and Israel, that every cadre of the PLO/PLA lives under Israel's guns, that the Israelis also control that criminal gang's electricity and livelihood, and that only America's patronage prevents the Saudi regime's internal divisions from tearing it apart.

I have already dealt with U.S. policy toward these regimes and the foolishness of restraining Israel's efforts to secure itself, and us, against them. The point here is to make clear that this policy flows from the wish that these regimes were something other than the irredeemable sources of evil that they are, and that this fathers the will to fall for the dodge at the heart of terrorist warfare: to take a terrorist chieftain's word that not he and his entourage, but only "renegade" groups, are responsible for the carnage.

When the Clinton administration in 1993 chose to act as if the terrorist organization PLO were a legitimate regime, it allowed a terrorist group the dodge that the U.S. government had continually granted to terrorist regimes since the days of Nasser. Thenceforth, America would exonerate the PLO's criminals as "mainstream," and blame only "splinter" groups like Hamas.

The Bush policy on Syria, Saudi Arabia, and the Palestinian Authority, after September 11 as before, accepted the dodge. Then, in July 2003, Secretary Powell took the dodge to its ultimate conclusion, offering to consider Hamas mainstream, a neutral if not a friend in the War on Terror, if it performed the same verbal rituals that had already satisfied the Bush team as to the lack of enmity from the PLO/PLA, Syria, and Saudi Arabia. Clearly, there is no end to this confusion about enemies, because there is no end to the will to disregard reality.

Further evidence of the forcefulness of this disregard came in August, when the Bush team refused to release to the American people a list of the main sources of financing for terrorist activities, because all sides agreed that it showed vast involvement by leading personages of the Saudi regime. The Bush team did not want to expose the Saudis to the ire of persons it trusted less than the Saudis: the American people. Nasser's many successors could only congratulate themselves on the accuracy of his insight.

We can mention here only one example of how bad judgment about friends, enemies, and war was vitiating the efforts of U.S. troops in the far corners of the globe. In Colombia, U.S. troops were deeply engaged in a fight against the FARC, an old Soviet-line guerrilla group that had grown rich and powerful by trafficking in cocaine, which the U.S. government had opposed as part of its "war on drugs," and that, after September 11, it had relabeled "narco-terrorists." The Colombia operation was transferred over to the War on Terror. There had never been any doubt that the FARC were bad people, bad for a country to which America wished well. The U.S. government, however, could not show that defeat of the FARC would diminish terrorism in America. Sure, the drug traffic contributed heavily to violence in America. But that could be ended with a stroke of the pen, just as repeal of Prohibition cut off much of the violence of the 1920s and 1930s. More important, calling any given problem "terrorism" was becoming a convenient, bad habit.

Just as important, the U.S. government proved as unserious about fighting the FARC as it was about fighting terrorists in the Middle East, and for the same reasons. The FARC, you see, had plenty of powerful enemies in Colombia. Foremost among these, various "right-wing paramilitaries" had successfully pressured the government to fight the FARC more energetically, and themselves had cut the FARC down to size. The U.S. government's confusion about friends, enemies, and war made a bad situation worse. The Clinton administration had foisted onto willing Colombian politicians a "Peace Process" that strengthened the FARC while suppressing the efforts of those fighting it (just as earlier it had foisted the identical item onto like-minded Israeli politicians). When the Colombians revolted against this and elected a President, Alvaro Uribe, committed to undoing the FARC, the Bush team conditioned its aid on fighting also the FARC's most effective enemies, the "paramilitaries." Not unlike in the Middle East, not unlike in Vietnam, American administrations of both parties fought in Colombia with willful, deadly, apolitical disregard of the distinction between friends and enemies. The consequences of confusion about friends and enemies at home are more serious.

HOMELAND DEFEAT

President Bush's hint on April 30 that the War on Terror "will not be endless" is contrary to his administration's actual policy. The U.S. Department of Homeland Security's statement of its mission, signed by President Bush, states unmistakably that it is not about a war with an end, much less an end in which Americans will be free of the threat of terror. U.S. policy, President Bush says here at length, is all about changing the way Americans live, adapting to the inevitable.

"The terrorist threat to America," says the statement, "is an unavoidable byproduct of the technological, educational, economic, and social progress" that produces the good life. "Terrorism is an inescapable reality of life in the twenty-first century. It is a permanent condition to which America and the entire world must adjust. The need for homeland security, therefore, is not tied to any specific terrorist threat." Any notion that we may rid ourselves of it is unrealistic because terrorism "*takes many forms...is often invisible.*" Homeland Security does not ask politicians and intelligence services to identify enemies. It assumes that enemies are ubiquitous and indistinguishable. Because we can never know them—note well the basic premise of Homeland Security—"[w]e can never be sure that we have defeated all of our terrorist enemies." Hence September 11 was not the beginning of a war that must end, but rather "a wake-up call," even a welcome one, about a reality that many are too happy to accept. The document does not attempt to argue any of this. It just states the government's position, and its plans for changing America.

Those plans are all about giving the U.S. government powers and discretion, without any substantive direction regarding how those powers are to be exercised. Homeland security is to be aimed, like de Gaulle's *Force de Frappe*, at everybody and nobody, *"tous azimuts."* Of course, de Gaulle's profession of ignorance about friends and enemies was not dangerous because he was kidding. He knew perfectly well at whom his missiles were aimed, who France's enemies were, how little and how much France could count on her friends. Alas, the U.S. government's profession of ignorance on this matter, its preference for power without direction, is for real, and has a long history.

From the onset of terrorism in the 1960s, the government's approach has been to mistrust the American people; to assume that only law enforcement, preferably federal and massively armed, could provide security. Although in the 1960s more hijacking attempts were foiled by passengers (often with guns) than by law enforcement, the government in 1972 decided to disarm all passengers. Thus it made sure that only hijackers would be armed. In 1975 it went further, making it a violation of federal regulations for private individuals to resist aircraft hijackers. Beginning in the same year, the Texas University shootings, as well as the Israeli military's heroic hostage rescue at Entebbe, Uganda, prompted American law enforcement agencies, federal, state, and local, to set up Special Weapons and Tactics Teams (SWAT).

Prior to expansion under the War on Terror, massive funding for the War on Drugs had provided every significant federal agency, as well as some 500 localities, with paramilitary capabilities. Tanks, armored personnel carriers, artillery of various kinds, machine guns, laser listening devices, body armor, masks, goggles, and sexy black uniforms that conceal the wearer's identity had become the marks of elite units around the country. For their members, SWAT teams were more thrilling than paintball wars, and safer than the armed forces, since they involved manhandling and shooting at people with only a remote possibility of being shot at themselves. *Washington Post* critic Stephen Hunter put it well:

> You might have policy differences with the SWAT concept, as I do, and feel it's not necessarily a good thing to turn police units into highly militarized, heavily armed commando squads, and therefore it's not necessarily a good thing to glamorize that phenomenon. Put young men in black jumpsuits and Kevlar body armor and festoon them with every cool gun known to man, and

pretty soon they'll see themselves not as police officers but as gunfighters and they'll *want* to pull the trigger.

The militarization of police went hand in hand with what might be called the securitization of America, and the near-outlawing of guns in the hands of private individuals. People younger than forty have no memory of an America in which anyone could enter and roam public buildings at will, where security codes and badges were unknown, and no distinction was made between government employees and the general public. In the last quarter of the twentieth century, America's public places were redesigned to eliminate places unobserved by security cameras. The nightly news and the movies inured a generation of Americans to squads of fatigue-clad masked-men sporting the word "Police" or "Federal Agent" on their backs, shouting "go, go, go!" to one another as they rushed into "situations." It has become routine, and almost acceptable, for such people to shoot unarmed citizens because "I thought he might have a gun." Being in the way of "security" became, effectively, a crime punishable summarily.

None of this had made America safer. In some televised cases, notably the deadly 1999 rampage by two Colorado students against their classmates, the SWAT team huddled safely behind its barricades for two hours, preventing anyone from helping bleeding victims, and then roughly handling the survivors. And why not? The SWATs did not know who was who, and would not expose themselves to danger. They would treat any parent who rushed into the school to help his child as a terrorist, and they treated the victims as potential terrorists. After all, *how did they know?* Indeed, the federal instructions to passengers in hijacked airliners say "expect to be handled roughly" by the legal authorities. The same instructions, not to our knowledge rescinded after September 11, still require passengers to follow the orders of hijackers. Security is the business of "security."

The Bush team's response to September 11 was not to question the trends of the previous quarter-century, but to accentuate them. Some 8,000 national guardsmen with automatic weapons were put into airports, as if terrorists were about to rush the gates. (Actually, if they did, they would don jackets identifying them as Federal Agents, would shout "go, go, go!" and the guardsmen would help get people out of their way.) The government hired 50,000 screeners to make sure that Grandma's shoes were not packed with plastic explosives. How could *anyone* know whether Grandma was or was not a terrorist? President

Bush's Homeland Security budget simply granted the Securitycrats' requests for *more*. The biggest chunk, $ 4.6 billion, went to the physical security of...government employees. Border patrols were increased, and the growth industries of computer security and "bioterrorism preparedness" were doubled or tripled in size.

Homeland Security, however, is congenitally dumb, in principle unable to distinguish between the citizens it is supposed to protect, and the terrorists it is to protect them against. Whereas at the time of World Wars I and II American society, with the government's help, required the German American community to cleanse itself of sympathizers with Germany, *a fortiori* to be inhospitable to German agents, the Bush team has gone out of its way to make sure that no pressures are placed on Muslims, and especially Arabs, in America to distance themselves from terrorist causes. Focusing on such people is politically incorrect. What is the worth of adding some 430 FBI agents and doubling the budget to fight biological terrorism when, in 2001, the government confined its vast, utterly fruitless effort to find the source of weapons-grade anthrax in the postal system to a hypothetical American "mad right-wing scientist"? At the time, evidence that the September 11 hijackers, and ultimately Iraq, were the source was politically incorrect. What was the good of the government's vast 2002 search for the Washington-area sniper when political correctness dictated that he be an anti-government white man, and not the Black Muslim who was stopped and released several times during the search? Again, more harm than good.

The most awesome aspect of Homeland Security is the discretion, untrammeled by fact or reason, with which it wields its vast, permanent powers. President Bush's statement underlines that the Patriot Act of 2001 penalizes giving aid and comfort to terrorist organizations, but it does not mention that the law also empowers the U.S. government to designate any organization or association as "terrorist." The law gives no guidelines, and the government does not have to justify its designation to anyone.

The U.S. government has never had a firm grip on the concept of terrorism. For years, the reigning definition was CIA's: "one man's terrorist is another's freedom fighter." After September 11, the working definition got looser and now approaches something like "anything we say it is, or that gets in the way of what we call anti- terrorism." The temptation arbitrarily to "round up the usual suspects," to convict inconvenient persons by somehow labeling them as terrorists,

Angelo M. Codevilla

to manage the distinction between friend and enemy for one's own short-term convenience, must prove easier than making war on real terrorists—especially when one believes that one is managing a permanent condition rather than fighting a war with an end.

The Bush team is composed of the best and brightest of its generation. Perhaps, then, anything like victory must await a time when America is governed by simpler creatures.

⋘⟡⋙

VICTORY WATCH: NO VICTORY, NO PEACE*

"I fear that we shall crawl out on a limb to reap the odium and practical disadvantages of our course, from which all countries will then hasten to profit. Such is internationalism today. Why, oh why do we disregard the experience and facts of history which stare us in the face?" Joseph C. Grew, U.S. Ambassador to Japan, 1937

In October 2003, having occupied Afghanistan and Iraq, imprisoned some 2,000 foreigners, refocused U.S. law enforcement, reorganized the U.S. government, and made "security specialist" the biggest new endeavor in America, President Bush claimed that "the world is more peaceful and more free under my leadership and America more secure."

In 1966, Daniel Boorstin's *The Image, A Guide to the Pseudo Event in America*, showed that advertising by government as well as business aims to counter reality. If the toilet tissue really were "soft," there would be no need for an ad campaign to persuade us that it is. Russians knew when their government trumpeted good harvests that they had better hoard potatoes. By the same token, if contemporary Americans felt victorious and at peace, claiming credit for that feeling would be superfluous. Since reality tells us otherwise, such claims recall Groucho Marx's story of the husband caught *in flagrante*: "Who you gonna believe, me or your own eyes?" In short, as 2004 loomed, there was no peace from terror, and no prospect of any, because there was no victory.

*This article appeared in the Claremont Review of Books, Winter 2003.

On October 16, Defense Secretary Donald Rumsfeld secretly asked his top lieutenants to think about why. The questions were not well thought out. The most specific, how America could cause Islamic schools to turn out more moderates and fewer extremists, recalled the foolishness of the CIA's corrupt, counterproductive, covert cultural activities of the 1950s. No one could imagine why any Muslim should accept American atheists as arbiters of what is and is not properly Islamic. Rumsfeld's main request, for better "metrics" of success, was reminiscent of Robert McNamara's effort quantitatively to define victory in Vietnam in terms of operations successfully carried out. Nevertheless, Rumsfeld's questions properly pointed to the heart of the matter: Why have all our massive efforts not produced better results? What else can we do?

WHY ISN'T IT WORKING?

The root of Rumsfeld's frustration was that the Bush team—though pulled in different directions by its principals' conflicting priorities— had ended up doing pretty much all the things that all its members had wanted.

The Doves, Secretary of State Colin Powell and CIA Director George Tenet, plus Tom Ridge and the FBI, had argued for waging "the war" with a combination of foreign diplomacy and domestic security. They got their way. Bush put his heart and soul not only into wooing the UN and "the Europeans" but also into securing help from Arab states such as Syria and Saudi Arabia. Bush even incurred serious political costs at home by publicly hiding information detrimental to the Saudis. He angered his own supporters by financing Yasser Arafat and the Palestinian Authority, while shielding it from Israel's wrath. Yet none of this brought solidarity with America. Syria mocked us, and ostentatiously helped Iraqi fellow-Baathists kill Americans. Saudi Arabia continued to be the mainstay of Arab anti-Americanism. The P.A. showed that all of Bush's words and money were unable to shake its status as the focus of anti-Western *jihad*. As for the UN and "the Europeans," nothing dispelled the impression that they were circling the Bush team like vultures eager for it to stumble. Nor did the billions of dollars, the legislation and regulations devoted to "homeland security," the captives "brought to justice" for association with terrorists, bring any more solace. The Bush team knew that for every captive, many more enemies of America were laughing proudly at the fact that they were the reason why every day at airports, a million Americans were taking off their shoes and being frisked.

At the same time, Paul Wolfowitz and Donald Rumsfeld himself, the advocates of offense, of "regime change," also had gotten their way. They had thought that rolling into Kabul and setting up command posts in Saddam Hussein's palaces would ignite a democratic revolution in the Middle East, which would make terrorism impossible. They turned out to be mistaken as well.

The reason why operations, each arguably successful in itself and all together covering much of the spectrum of the possible, had brought America no closer to peace is that war does not consist of operations any more than love consists of intercourse. In both cases, all depends on your intentions and on having the proper object. Always, the proper question is what ends do the means serve, and how appropriately do they serve them? What do your operations actually do? In war, the question that gives meaning to all operations is who is the enemy whose death gives us peace? Never, ever, had the Bush team dealt with this question. Here was the root of the Bush team's problems, the reason why it had done a lot, done it wrong, and wound up worse off than before.

Doing "the war" right would have meant not bothering much with al-Qaeda. Evidence of its central role in anti-American terror was always weak, and came from Arab sources that do not wish America well. Most of all, because neither it nor any other organization is the source of hate and contempt for America, wiping it out does America little good. What then is the source of anti-American terror, what leads people to think that fighting America is profitable and has a future? The answer, as New York Times columnist Thomas Friedman learned from my essays, and as the Bush team had yet to grasp fully, is that 98 percent of terrorism is what regimes want to happen or let happen.

IT'S THE REGIME, STUPID!

Regimes, as serious people know, are a lot more than governments. They are the priorities, standards, ways of life, embodied by the most prominent persons in the land, and very much by their henchmen. For our purposes, the question is: who makes anti-American violence the standard for others; who are the people whose deaths would diminish it?

By that standard, the Taliban regime was of scarce relevance. The Taliban, like other Afghans, know little and care less about what happens on the other side of the mountain, much less the ocean. Yet the Taliban had developed a symbiotic relationship with a group of Arabs who, with Saudi money, had partially financed them and helped them against their domestic enemies. In return, the Taliban provided these "Afghan Arabs" a base for intrigues they carried on *with the regimes and intelligence services of their homelands.* Only in this third-hand way were the Taliban part of America's terrorist problem. Once America *helped other Afghans* sweep the Taliban away, the Afghan tribes realigned with little bloodshed and virtually annihilated the "Afghan Arabs." Al-Qaeda then became scattered individuals, whose importance depended exclusively on the Arab regimes that continued to use them, and others.

These Arab regimes, and nothing else, are the entities that gave and give people the means and above all the hope of success that make anti-American terrorists.

That is why invading Iraq was, potentially, so very useful in convincing those inclined to fight America that there is no future in doing so. But what, in the way that the Bush team fought this battle, convinced America's enemies of the opposite? What did the Bush team do that made these regimes less afraid of us than before, that tilted the balance of fear against us more than ever?

In a nutshell, the Bush team mistook Saddam Hussein's top echelon for the regime itself. Second, it proved *unwilling to help Iraqi enemies of the regime pull it up by the roots, or even to allow them to do it.* Third, unpardonably, it placed the U.S. armed forces and America's Iraqi collaborators in the deadly position of static defense—sitting on bayonets pondering the Marine "Small Wars Manual" while being shot at. All this, combined with dovish diplomacy vis-à-vis the rest of the Arab world, told enemy regimes that, once again, America would let a battle won turn into a war lost.

As previously explained in these pages, the dictatorial regimes of the Arab world consist of some 2,000 men, while the Saudi regime is perhaps twice that size. In such places, where regimes exist by brutalizing opponents, changes in regime necessarily involve the bloody settling of bloody scores. Unless and until the "outs" brutalize at least this number of "ins," the regime has not really changed. In such places, "who rules" really means who brutalizes whom unto death or submission. Vengeance, a human drive everywhere, is especially compelling in the Arab world. *The Eumenides* is not part of Arab literature. Hence the dream of many Americans—Norman Podhoretz expressed it in Chapter V of this book—that there could be a gentle imperialism that would hold Iraq together, spreading liberal democracy from it to the rest of the Middle East, is impossible. Most impossible was it in Iraq because its unusual racial and religious divisions further complicate the previous regime's unusual brutalities.

In sum, around the world, as in Iraq, being pro-American was likelier to get you killed than was being part of an anti-American network. Hence, in the third year of the War on Terrorism, America found itself on the short end of the balance of fear. Turning that balance to the enemy's disfavor is the primordial task of our war.

OUR WAR

No one should declare war without being clear against whom it is being declared: who the enemy is whose demise will give us peace.

In October 2003, mortar shells fell into the Baghdad compound of the Coalition Provisional Authority, giving U.S. bureaucrats an epiphany. Reversing a decade's worth of CIA judgments, they concluded that elements of Saddam's regime were working together with religious extremists. That was equivalent in perspicacity to cruise ship passengers noticing humidity in the ocean. Saddam's political victory in the Gulf War had consisted precisely of using enmity to America to transcend the many divisions among Arabs, indeed Muslims, and of putting himself at the head of that enmity. Hence his regime, which lived by quotidian, bloody persecution of Islam, became the vanguard of what Saddam effectively defined as the new defining element of Islam: anti-American action.

The spreading sense throughout the Islamic world that anti-American action was good and safe, and that opposing it was bad and dangerous, became a mortal threat to America. This deadly phenomenon took on a life of its own. Like any disease not countered in its early stages, countering it would require ever more radical exertions.

Beginning right after the Gulf War, Saddam's intelligence service put him at the head of otherwise disparate elements. The Soviet Union had left behind a network of mostly secular, nationalist terrorist groups. Iraq's and Syria's Baath parties were parts of that network, as were the P.A. and its various offshoots, e.g., the Popular Front for the Liberation of Palestine. These were headquartered either in Damascus or

Baghdad. But Third World nationalism made sympathy with all the above politically significant from Morocco to Pakistan. In most cases these elements were well-connected with the secular governments of the Islamic world. They had pressured those governments to support Saddam against America. On the religious side of the Islamic world's greatest divide were the Islamists—everywhere except in Iran (and for other reasons in Jordan and Morocco) enemies of their governments as well as of the West. The number of Islamist organizations was legion, including both Sunni and Shia. Then there was the divide between the groups that were sponsored by well-financed Saudi Wahhabis and the rest of Islam.

The great event of the 1990s was that violence against Israel and America—correctly perceived as successful—went a long way toward effacing the differences amongst the Islamic world's activists. Daily veneration of the Palestinian struggle, daily rituals of hate against the West, Jews, Israel (and the American devils behind it), brightened millions of miserable lives. Images of Israel being bloodied, and of America being bloodied, and of Muslim potentates safely offering their observations on the carnage, became a paradigm for a generation of Muslims. Any regime that, assuming it had been inclined to do so, put restrictions on anti-American, or anti-Israeli speech or action did so at its own peril.

America's war would have to consist of reversing that paradigm. Victory for America would be on the way when Muslims around the world would see every evening on the news those to whom they had looked up being tried, discredited, and executed by Muslims for crimes against Muslims, when television audiences would gasp at crowds of Iraqis and Syrians physically dismembering the Baathist thugs who had slaughtered the party's political enemies, when Arab news magazines would detail the corrupt, un-Islamic lives of the entire Saudi royal family, when good Muslims, victims of the Wahhabi heresy, would detail how the heretics had defiled Islam. What a paradigm-shift it would be were Palestinian members of families victimized by Arab thugs publicly to take vengeance on their tormentors. Such events would change the Muslim world's agenda and place regimes that advocated or allowed anti-American propaganda, the organizations or "charities" that have produced anti-American terrorism, at peril.

To produce such results, America's operations of war would have to destroy regimes—not build nations nor export democracy. Whereas doing away with Saddam Hussein in 1991 might well have convinced the Muslim world that anti-Americanism had no future, by 2003 evidence that worldwide Muslim elements were helping an Iraqi "resistance" to bleed America, even as the supposedly united efforts of Islam were bleeding Israel, was energizing terrorists. By this time, nothing less than the bloody demise of the most egregious anti-American regimes would convince the others not to foster or allow terrorism. Only this would give us peace.

What Is to Be Done?

In short, the regimes whose death would give us peace have enemies who are eager to kill them. U.S. forces cannot possibly police foreign lands, much less force gentler, kinder ways upon them. Experience in Iraq should have made this plain. Only locals, not foreigners, can do that. Their methods are unlikely to be kind and gentle. Democracy may not be part of their agenda, and liberalism surely will not be. That is their business. It is enough for our peace that there be people who have their own reasons for destroying the people and culture— the regimes—that are the effective causes of violence against us. U.S. military operations should make it possible for them to do it.

In Iraq, the U.S. government should do in 2003–2004 what it should have done in earlier years. Having destroyed Saddam's main armies, Americans should arm the 80 percent Shiite and Kurdish parts of the population, and wish them well. Most surely, *they* would destroy the remnants of the Baathist regime. Though they have more detailed knowledge than we possibly could have of who is who, they would be far less careful than we of killing only the strictly guilty.

It is no business of America's whether the people who live between the Persian Gulf and the Black Sea decide that there shall be an Iraq or not. We should have learned from experience in Bosnia that crafting the fiction of a state that does not exist in the hearts and minds of its supposed members—who think themselves not Bosnians but rather Muslims, Croats, and Serbs—is an expensive way of gratifying folks in the State Department who should know better. Nor should Americans care that the Saudi royal family and Sunni Arabs in the Gulf would not like an independent or semi-independent group of 15 million Shiites near the head of the Gulf because they might ally with Shiite Iran. Being Arabs, they probably would not. But whether or not they did would be no problem of America's.

America's interest would be secured by the fact that the regime's anti-American priorities would die with its members. The foreign Islamic fighters would die in ways even more discouraging to anyone inclined to follow in their footsteps.

All too hazily, in 2003 the Bush team perceived that Yasser Arafat's P.A. somehow energized all Muslim terrorism. But Bush sought to remove this regime as a negative factor by negotiating some kind of accord between it and Israel. Wrong. The P.A. regime's interest is entirely incompatible with peace, because the regime lives not by serving its people but—on the contrary—by serving as a part of a broader Arab and Muslim anti-Westernism. The only way to remove it as a major energizer of that movement is to do away with it, as a way of crushing that movement.

Destroying the P.A. is easier done than said. The regime lives physically by daily infusions of cash from American and European sources that can be cut off in an instant, as well as by communications, electricity, and other utilities that Israel can cut off almost as quickly. Moreover, its leaders are mostly marked men under Israeli surveillance. Perhaps more important, they have lots of Arab enemies who have saved up much vengeance for them. If Americans and Israelis decide to eliminate the regime's main force, to make clear that death and destruction is to be the lot of anyone who even looks like he might follow the old regime, its enemies are more than likely to finish the job. This is not to say that a generation of Palestinian young people schooled in a culture of death would learn new ways instantly. But regimes are all about a complex of incentives—moral, social, and material. Surely, though liberal democracy would likely not reign among Palestinians any more than love for Jews, undoing the regime that waged the Arab-Israeli conflict would remove the drug that has done so much to stimulate a generation of anti-American terrorism.

The Saudi regime is the nursery of the Wahhabi heresy that for two centuries has vied for leadership of Islam. It is also the source of the billions of dollars by which, since the 1970s, the Wahhabis have spread their influence further than ever before. Anti-American terror would hardly be conceivable without widespread Wahhabi influence. The Bush team's belief that the Saudi regime is anything other than an enemy (indeed the reason why Bush excluded the Saudis from the list of those to whom he proposed freedom in lieu of stability) is based on the supposition that the regime can control Wahhabism. But the regime is Wahhabism's enabler and full partner. There is no way to stop anti-Western terror so long as Wahhabism is prestigious, secure in its base, and wealthy. There is no way to make it otherwise except to undo the Saudi regime.

At the end of 2003, some kind of insurgency was under way in Saudi Arabia. The only certain things about it were that it involved some members of the regime against others, and that it involved Wahhabism. It was also certain that there were countless Muslims, in and outside the Arabian Peninsula, who wished that at the end of the day the Saudi oil fields would no longer be providing the means by which the Wahhabis had troubled the life of Islam, even more than that of America. All this is to say that the necessary undoing of the Saudi regime would not be difficult, and that there was no shortage of Muslims who would approach with alacrity cleansing the peninsula of the peculiarly Saudi combination of heresy and fraud. This cleansing was likely to happen without American involvement. Indeed, only the Bush team's illusion that it may be possible to save the regime as a vehicle for democracy was likely to stand in the way of this healthy development.

OUR PEACE

Americans, no less than foreigners, are the only ones who can determine the character of their regime, the way they live. Only we can determine what kind of peace will be ours—what we will put up with and what not.

The titles of America's first post-September 11 operation, "Enduring Freedom," as well as of its first major piece of legislation, the "Patriot Act," suggest Boorstin's *The Image* as well as any of George Bush's speeches. As I've argued previously, attacking Afghanistan was not calculated to preserve any of America's freedoms, while the Patriot Act's criminalization of association with any entity declared "terrorist" by executive action seems, on its face, not patriotism but rather a double-violation of the United States Constitution. Since the Act did not bite and the invasion of Afghanistan produced exciting TV images, and "the war" was at its beginning, the public found no reason to question the reality behind the titles.

That is, until after the invasion of Iraq. Then Americans there began dying in noticeable numbers without any prospect that the dying would stop. The ease with which irregulars carried out their attacks on Americans and their collaborators in Iraq reminded Americans of how easily terrorists could cause havoc on American streets, and of the fact that neither the Bush team's homeland security nor any number of "patriot acts" could stop it. Once again, it became clear that there is no such thing as a phony war, a war with limited liability. Once blood is spilled, the previously existing order, the previous peace, is broken forever. What peace will prevail in the end depends on who, by killing and willingness to be killed, can force the other to accept his version. And so, after the invasion of Iraq had raised the stakes, the American people were closer to realizing that what they wanted out of the war was a certain kind of peace, and that to get it they needed a certain kind of victory. This would involve identifying their enemies and doing away with them. Otherwise, there would never be peace.

Beginning just after September 11, I have sought to show that America's peace depends on America's victory, and to show that the path to victory is the destruction of the main regimes without which terrorism would not exist, *pour encourager les autres*. The obstacles to our peace, our victory, flow not from the strength or cleverness of our enemies, but rather from the tendency of America's leaders to deal with images rather than with reality.

VIII: War, and the Ultimate Elections

THE REAL WAR*

"Six American tanks were lined up at a busy intersection, their turrets swinging languidly from side to side as cars and trucks honked ... American soldiers crouched behind concrete blocks, their weapons trained on a huge crowd of Iraqi onlookers who stood across the street and stared." New York Times, April 6, 2004

"Among critics of the United States ... there was satisfaction that chances are growing more remote by the day that Iraq will serve as a model that would eventually reshape the region. There is a sense that Syria and Iran are off the hook, while on a broader scale the violence is further undermining Washington's credibility and making Americans ever more unpopular." New York Times, April 9, 2004

"What you are fighting against is ... also loss of empire and danger from the animosities incurred in its exercise. Besides, to recede is no longer possible ... For what you hold is, to speak somewhat plainly, a tyranny; to take it perhaps was wrong, but to let it go is unsafe." Thucydides' Pericles

"It is better to be feared than to be loved." Machiavelli

"In war there is no substitute for victory." Douglas MacArthur

Once the U.S. government had set its basic approach to Iraq—disarm and pacify, rebuild, unify, and prepare the country for democratic elections that would make it a model for the region—it was stuck

Part of this essay appeared in the Claremont Review of Books, *Fall 2004.*

between impossible ends and inadequate means. By 2004 armed opposition had foreclosed the option of a glorious, even a gracious, withdrawal from Iraq. The resulting stalemate stems to a large extent from the felt necessities of American domestic politics. Much as the Left yearned to disavow involvement in Iraq, it found that it could not advocate anything that smelled like defeat. John Kerry, Democratic candidate to replace George W. Bush, pledged that he would keep U.S. troops in Iraq as long as needed to ensure that it would not become "a failed state." He did not suggest what those troops could or should do to avoid failure.

The Bush administration, for its part, shies away from energetic policies that might actually produce victory, fearing that the public might oppose them as too harsh. And so U.S. troops will stay and die in Iraq indefinitely on behalf of a mission—pacification, democratization, and nation building—that is the lowest common denominator among domestic American political forces, but concerning the accomplishment of which there is little knowledge and less agreement.

Not even the capture of Saddam Hussein himself alleviated America's predicament. The billions of dollars spent on civil affairs and nation building bought not hearts and minds but contempt and resources for the opposition.

By spring of 2004 the Bush team had decided to turn Iraq over to its favorite Iraqis *du jour*. To what extent would the U.S. government make war against some in Iraq to secure the power and dreams of others when it had proved unwilling to do it for its own cause? Above all, what would the victory of any Iraqi faction other than the Baath contribute to or detract from America's war on terror? At any rate, by 2004 no one argued that the "battle of Iraq" had struck a decisive blow against terrorism. The Iraq war now consisted of fighting mostly people who fought Americans because they were in their country. Whereas at its outset the war targeted one of the world's main causes of terrorism, it had become distinct from the war on terror—except in the Bush formulation that the cause of democracy was identical with that of anti-terrorism.

The Bush team's concentration on a foredoomed attempt to build a new Iraqi regime left no room for concern with existing regimes that it might be in its interest to destroy, or for thinking about its strategy in the war on terror. For their part, America's enemies were waging the terrorism war with greater gusto than ever. America would have to fight and win a bigger, lonelier, more dangerous war. To defeat foreign enemies, Americans would have to change attitudes and assumptions deeply rooted in its own elites.

TILTING AT WINDMILLS, 2004

Since the Bush administration reflected contradictions and compromises, it could neither take advantage of favorable events nor manage adverse developments.

The capture of Saddam Hussein himself, on December 12, 2003, offered a unique opportunity for the U.S. occupation, already deeply unpopular, to unite with the vast majority of Iraqis around common hatred of their former tyrant. How easy and instructive it would have been merely to subject the tyrant to daily televised confrontations (across prison bars) with representatives of people he had victimized. Countless Iraqis would have been more preoccupied with settling old scores and less receptive to the call to kill Americans. An early public trial might have had the same result. As the attention of Iraqis focused on the evils of the regime, the Americans would have found it easier to dismantle its remnants. But while some on the Bush team wanted to do that, others did not. And so, the team made no use of the ace of spades it held in its hands. And if the U.S. would not even try to exploit this "gift from heaven" (as Ho Chi Minh would have called it) what would it do for itself?

During the three months following Saddam's capture one could still believe that perhaps the "security situation" could be improved by gathering more intelligence on the perpetrators of anti-American violence, and hunting them down. The countless Iraqis who were getting jobs, goods, and training from the Americans might be a network that would gradually remake the country. American officials looked forward to June 30, when, to cap off a successful viceroyalty, they would turn nominal sovereignty over to some kind of generally recognized Iraqi provisional government. But not having eliminated or cowed their enemies in a wholesale manner, U.S. troops' efforts to deal with them on a retail basis proved counterproductive, and undermined everything the Americans tried to do.

Meanwhile, thousands of Sunni Arabs in central Iraq, the body and beneficiaries of Saddam's regime, did not believe they had been defeated for the simple reason that they had not been decimated. They had every intention of reestablishing themselves in something like the old regime. All they had to do was to cause America to leave Iraq without arming their enemies. And so Iraq's main oil export line to Turkey was sabotaged. In August, attacks on southern oil fields cut oil deliveries in half. As a result of these unabated attacks on its main source of wealth, the country was poorer than during Saddam's time. Electrical lines were cut, towers toppled, stations damaged or destroyed. A total of 111 sabotages in the year following the invasion prevented the Americans from turning the lights back on. Between April and July insurgents had captured some eighty foreign workers and threatened to kill them unless their countries and companies stopped doing business with the U.S. armed forces and the reconstruction effort. In the face of the Americans' inability either to protect their citizens or intimidate the kidnappers several countries gave in. By slaughtering some five Iraqi policemen or other officials per day, the insurgents made clear that no official of any government of which they did not approve would be safe.

Nor would Americans be safe. By November, the toll on Americans from roadside bombs and suicide bombs reached some four per day from half that number a half-year earlier. These mostly Sunni, Baathist insurgents, joined by foreign Islamist fighters, had learned that the Americans would respond to attacks by searching out the individuals responsible—answering war with policing, rather than by making war. Above all, everyone knew that American troops had no offensive mission. Their job was to sit and safeguard—aggressively. The presence of foreign Islamist fighters also gave the lie to the CIA dogma that secular and religious radicals don't work together.

President Bush and his advisers had told the troops that the violent insurgents were merely "dead-enders." This was another version of the notion that terrorism was the work of hopeless individuals. But from the very beginning, U.S. troops had learned the hard way that these "dead-enders" were well financed, represented concrete political causes, and believed in victory. The combination of American troops' power and ignorance eventually led them to behave in the classic manner of occupation forces—that is, they responded counterproductively.

American troops relied a little on directives from Washington that reflected the Bush team's shifting judgments on enemies or friends. They relied more on "intelligence" from other Iraqis who the Coalition Provisional Authority or CIA sources designated as friends on any given day. The troops, however, had direct contact with Iraqis. So, as time went on, they developed their own informants and contacts. Just about all intelligence, however, was second or third-hand, through interpreters, and as often as not pointed to persons who the informants wanted to get in trouble. These were enemies of their accusers more than of America. Worse, a large and increasing amount of "intelligence" would come from persons the military picked up near the scene of bloody incidents on the chance they might know something about who had done what.

And so, since the summer of 2003, U.S. troops had been barging about Iraq, surrounding blocks of houses, combing through people, and taking away some 250 per week. Already by the summer of 2003 an inspection by the Army's Provost Marshal had noted that any number of Iraqis had been imprisoned for nothing more than "displeasure or ill will" toward Americans, and that they were being kept in violation of Army regulations. The International Committee of the Red Cross also inspected American prisons for Iraqis and reported that military intelligence officers believed that between 70 and 90 percent of the inmates "had been arrested by mistake." One study by military intelligence said that fifty-five out of fifty-seven inmates had no intelligence value. Nevertheless, the officer in charge of military intelligence in Iraq, Brig. Gen. Barbara Fast, usually overruled decisions to release prisoners. Most would be confined in what had been Saddam's house of horrors, the Abu Ghraib prison, run by Brig. Gen. Janet Karpinski. No higher officer overruled them.

The attempt to gather reliable intelligence from persons arrested as the U.S. military was arresting them was nonsense. To ask a meaningful question, an interrogator must have good reason to believe that his prisoner knows the answer. Moreover, the interrogator must know enough about the subject matter to judge whether the answers he is getting make sense. He must conceal his prejudices, lest the prisoner simply confirm them. Usually, the interrogator's demonstration of his own knowledge of the subject is the strongest factor in convincing the prisoner that he might as well answer. Trying to compensate for the lack of these basics by applying physical or psychological pressure makes things worse.

Experience in the U.S. prison in Guantanamo Bay, Cuba, had taught that lesson again. The prisoners had been handed over to the Americans by the Northern Alliance Afghans who had captured them. American intelligence officers noted that few of the prisoners had any intelligence value. Indeed, after nearly three years the military was able to make military tribunal cases only on 15 out of some 1000 prisoners.

Nevertheless, poor sources as these prisoners were, they were just about the only ones in American hands. Top Pentagon officials justified keeping them in exemplary confinement by describing them as "the worst of the worst," people who would chew on the hydraulic lines of the airplane transporting them to bring it down. After two years of interrogation using countless ploys and pressures, interrogators discovered that they had largely wasted their time. Most prisoners would be released. But if they had not been involved in anti-Americanism in the past, their experience with America made it likely they would be in the future.

Americans interrogating Iraqis captured mostly for being at the wrong place at the wrong time had even worse outcomes. By the autumn of 2003 when it became clear that interrogation of captured Iraqis was yielding little intelligence, Stephen Cambone, Undersecretary of Defense for Intelligence, decided that the military police in charge of Iraqi prisons should dispose the prisoners to talk by applying stress in various ways. This determination showed a complete failure to grasp the obvious practical reason why military forces are not supposed to mistreat prisoners—to do so only encourages our enemies to mistreat our own citizens and allies when they are captive. This decision had the all too predictable consequences.

First of all, intelligence thus gathered led to wilder goose chases. Second, it confirmed the age-old truth that the surest way to corrupt any army is to assign it to occupation duty. Corruption from top to bottom showed in images of American guards sexually humiliating helpless prisoners, in reports of senior officials who had known of the problems (U.S. viceroy Paul Bremer is said to have discussed them with Secretary of State Colin Powell in the fall of 2003) as well as of senior Generals who had known of two female subordinates' superintendence of abuses but lacked the manhood to override them until publicity forced their hand. The Americans' slight mistreatment of Iraqi prisoners gave a gloss of legitimacy to the insurgents' beheadings and burnings of Americans and of those who worked with them. All this amounted to a betrayal of troops who had to suffer enemy violence heightened by the well-publicized prison exposé.

In March, April, and May 2004 publicity about prisoner abuse helped fuel an insurrection that overcame what remained of American officials' resolve to carry through their plans for Iraq. The crisis began when Sunni insurgents in Fallujah, a city of 250,000 west of Baghdad, lured four American private security guards into an ambush. After dismembering and burning them, they hung their remains from a bridge for the world's TV cameras to see, and to dare the U.S. Marines to do something about it. The Marines moved into the city with bombers, AC 130 gunships, and artillery to search for the killers. Meanwhile, to give Sunnis the impression that he was even-handed, U.S. viceroy Paul Bremer announced that he had issued a warrant for the arrest of Moktada al Sadr, a young Shiite cleric who had gathered a passionate, armed following, and was agitating against the American occupation. Not coincidentally, Sadr was an enemy of some of the Iraqis who the shifting forces within the Bush team had made into favorites of the Coalition Provisional Authority. The announcement led to riots by Shiites in the Baghdad suburb of Sadr City, which left eight American soldiers dead. The Army attacked the Sadr militias in the south-central Shiite cities of Karbala, Kufa and the holy Shiite city of Najaf.

Meanwhile, mostly in the Sunni areas, Iraqis who had enrolled as policemen, hired on as workers, and to whom Americans had distributed equipment and largess, simply switched sides. Indeed it appeared that the four security guards who had been burned in Fallujah had been led to their deaths by their employees or by Iraqi police. The Iraqi security forces so elaborately trained melted in the face of the insurgency. No Iraqi would fight another Iraqi on behalf of the Americans. There is never a way of knowing who, if anybody, is on the side perceived to be losing.

Now fighting Sunnis and Shiites at the same time, Bush took a tough line: "If they think that we're not sincere about staying the course, many people will not continue to take the risk toward freedom and democracy." But military action would fail precisely because Bush saw no contradiction between staying the course and calling off the military effort to choke off what had become a full blown insurgency.

The Bush team's Plan A had failed. As casualties mounted (ten Marines in Fallujah, twenty-four Army soldiers in fights against Shiites during the first week of April), officials became acutely aware that vast elements of two communities that were usually at odds, people who they had come to liberate, had united against them. The entire American design of benevolent tutelage over Iraqis eager to learn, grateful for help, and preparing to take over the policing of their country in cooperation with America, had turned out to be an illusion. There was no Plan B. So the Bush team pretended that the original plan was working, while in fact abandoning it. There were no attractive choices— the Bush team made perhaps the worst.

Taking military control of downtown Fallujah, Najaf, etc. and killing a few dozen fighters while arresting some more, surely would not
have shut off the insurgency. On the other hand, not doing so would
mean acknowledging defeat, creating secure bases from which insurgents could kill Americans, and discouraging whatever friends remained. During the second week in April, the *al Jazeera* and *al Arabya*
television networks told the world that U.S. troops had already killed
600 civilians in Fallujah and Najaf. No independent reporter had access to those places. Nevertheless the Bush team, afraid of fueling an
anti-American conflagration in the Arab world and under pressure
from the Arab regimes as well as at the suggestion of some of its
favorite Iraqis, chose to stop the Army and Marines.

THE DEAL

On the surface, it was magic. American forces accepted the offer of
Mohammed Saleh, a former General of Saddam's Republican Guard
and high ranking Baathist who, in exchange for the cessation of U.S.
military action in Fallujah, agreed to command a brigade of moderate
"former" insurgents to police the city. Bush and his aides also had
decided to make a similar deal with the militia of the Shiite Moktada al
Sadr. So long as the militia stayed off the streets of Najaf, the Americans would not enter the city. Thus, having found Iraqis who promised to search for terrorists and keep order, the U.S. had achieved its
objectives without further bloodshed. Analgesic nonsense. The opposite would happen.

From privates to Generals, the armed forces feared having to pay in
blood for this show of weakness, and did not want to write off their
dead to a losing cause, never mind to deal with enemy "sanctuaries."
For its part the Iraqi provisional government, consisting of anti-Baath
politicians and balanced between Sunni, Shia, and Kurds, blanched at
America's reversal of de-Baathification. The empowerment of the very
people who had oppressed Shiites, Kurds, and anti-Baathists portended
future civil war.

The official view, reported to Congress in May, was all about benefits: in the short term there would be a cease fire, and in the long
term the Americans and the Iraqis to whom they would turn over
nominal sovereignty would negotiate an agreement to fold all militias
into a national army and police. This agreement was signed on June
7. By then, the cease fire was ancient history, and dealing with enemy

sovereignties in both Sunni and Shiite strongholds (Fallujah was said to have become the base for al Zarqawi, and Sadr would seize a police station in Najaf three days later) had become the order of the day. The Kurds made it clear that while they might change their army's name, under no circumstances would they give it up. On June 28, 2004, the U.S. government replaced the *Provisional* government which it had established the previous year and which it had begun to disregard almost immediately, with the *Interim* government, on which it now placed its hopes.

THE INDIRECT APPROACH

The composition of this group resulted from struggles not between Shiites, Kurds and Sunnis, but rather between State, Defense, and CIA.

State's position was simple: the Arab world and the stability of its relationship with Iran, is best served by an Iraq dominated by its Sunni minority—just as the British had set it up when they broke up the Ottoman Empire. Whether Sunni rule was exercised by a Hashemite king, a Nasserite progressive, or a Baathist thug mattered less—but it had to be at least somewhat brutal to keep Shiites from excessive friendliness with Iran, and to keep the Kurds from making their own state and thereby alienating Turkey. The CIA's position shared State's concerns. But the CIA has always been in the business of progressive coups. In 1958, the CIA sponsored the Nasserite coup against the Hashemite king, and in 1963 and 1968 the Baathist coups against the Nasserites. Since 1991 its stock in trade had been "covert action" to encourage lesser Baathists to replace Saddam. Though the Clinton administration and a majority of Congress legislated a policy of re-placing Saddam with "democracy"—meaning in practice the anti-Baathist exiles of Ahmed Chalabi's Iraqi National Congress—State and CIA continued to rely on (presumed) dissident Baathists both inside and outside Iraq. George W. Bush's Defense Department, however, made the cause of democracy in Iraq a lively policy option for the first time. Defense Department civilians had favored invading Iraq. More-over, Defense wanted to constitute an Iraqi government in exile com-plete with a small army, transfer it to safe Kurdish territory, recognize it, help it overthrow the Baath regime, and then withdraw U.S. troops. State and CIA had tried to prevent the invasion. After the decision for invasion had been made, the two agencies succeeded in cutting down the role that anti-Baath exiles would play in the new Iraq.

Between fall 2003 and spring 2004, increasing discontent with the muddled Iraqi invasion shifted the balance of power within the Bush team away from the Pentagon and toward State/CIA. Bush made a major policy shift about Iraq's future at meetings of the National Security Council in January and April 2004. The U.S. viceroyalty in Baghdad gradually excluded the interim government (in which Defense's favorite civilians were heavily represented) from any decisionmaking, and dealt as much as it could with the people to whom it would eventually pass "sovereignty."

The Bush team covered its change of policy by charging Chalabi with security violations, and would repeat the CIA's charges that much of the false information on which it had based its "slam dunk" judgment that Iraq possessed WMDs had come from a fabricator codenamed "curveball," provided by the Iraqi National Congress (in July CIA was forced to recant its association of "curveball" with the INC. But at the same time it charged Chalabi with financial crimes, in a futile attempt to ban him from Baghdad). In short, the shift had nothing to do with security or intelligence sources—much less with the war on terror. It was all about choosing sides in Iraqi domestic quarrels. George Bush's protestations about democracy notwithstanding, the U.S. government—effectively accepting the State/CIA definition of "regime change"—would hand power mainly to "former" Baathist officials. The Prime Minister would be Iyad Allawi, the CIA's paladin of several unsuccessful coups to establish "Saddamism without Saddam."

It was no surprise that right after taking over "sovereignty" the Allawi government let it be known that its solution to the problem of Fallujah was to entice its Baathist elements away from their Islamist partners and into closer relations with the government. As well, the Allawi government planned to recommission Republican Guard officers as the core of a new army and to reconstitute the old regime's intelligence services. This, along with its assignment of emergency powers to itself raised further suspicions among Kurds and Shiites. In mid-August, Moktada al Sadr led a new insurrection from Najaf, fueled by the Shiite majority's fear that the Americans were helping the Sunnis to reestablish their tyranny. And in fact, in August U.S. Marines came perilously close to invading Shia Islam's holy of holies at the behest of the new "sovereign" government. Of course a government dominated by Sunni Baathists could work its will on the rest of the country only if the U.S. armed forces were to help it win a civil war.

FORCEFUL MICROMANAGEMENT

In the summer of 2004 the Bush team's tactical objective in Iraq prior to the November U.S. elections—quiet preparations for a post-election military campaign to "enable" the Iraqi elections scheduled for January 30, 2005—were as clear as its strategic objectives afterward were almost beyond speculation.

The tactical objective was the city of Fallujah, which had become the center of ever expanding "no go" zones—Sunni areas where the Iraqi government could go only with the permission of the insurgents and the Americans could not go at all. The point of the offensive would be for the Americans physically and psychologically to reverse the effective grant of sovereignty it had made to the insurgents in April. In the process, the American forces hoped to kill or capture the insurrection's leadership and radically reduce the number of its fighters. Fallujah, nearby Ramadi, and similar places would return to government control, and elections could take place there—and if there, then they could be held anywhere in the country.

The well-advertised November attack well-nigh leveled Fallujah. Some 1000 Iraqis (mostly Sunni, many of whom were Baathists, with a roughly 5 percent admixture of foreigners) died resisting the Americans, and another 600 were captured—at the cost of 40 Americans killed in action. But of course the insurgency's leadership had long since escaped with the bulk of its forces. As the attack began, the insurgents implemented a new military strategy: instead of taking and holding small cities, they would melt into large ones and wage guerrilla warfare from a variety of neighborhoods. Thus the insurgents struck at police stations in Mosul and Baghdad itself, as well as continuing to hit Americans along the roads. Its tactical objective, as always, was to cause casualties and restrict U.S. movements. By mid-November, Americans gave up traveling to and from the airport except by helicopter—and even that was becoming more perilous. The insurgents' widespread, untrammeled killing of Iraqis also spread a sense of inevitability. The U.S. military was attempting to keep the insurgents on the run, and the insurgents in their turn were trying to keep the Americans on the run.

By now, the Americans' strategy had boiled down to enabling the elections. To that end, 1200 more troops were to garrison the country by January. But U.S. officials realized that the insurgents' offensive against the elections was even more political than military. Since the

Sunnis knew in advance that the ballot box would reflect the other groups' distaste for them, the insurgents were persuading the Sunnis that their real leverage lay not in their cooperation with the other groups but in their capacity to make the country unlivable. The strategy of U.S. officials and of the ex-Baathists they had appointed to the Interim government for countering this was to lure the Sunni population into cooperation. This of course angered the Shiites and Kurds. More important, these tactical political maneuvers obscured the question of what election outcomes would be acceptable to America, or unacceptable and, above all, why? By the end of 2004 the Bush team declared the elections themselves, which it equated with the establishment of democracy, to be the objective of its entire venture in Iraq.

If President Bush had asked the Congress for authority to spend some $400 billion—roughly the amount spent on Iraq between 2003 and 2005—and some 1500 lives for the purpose of establishing democracy there in the hope that this form of government would spread throughout the region and thus somehow end terrorism, he would have been rebuffed. Nevertheless, by 2005 the Bush administration's sole hope for victory in the war on terror had come down to democracy, and hope for the spread of democracy rested on the hope that out of the elections would come one Iraq, in which all major groups are represented fairly and treat each other equitably.

The problem is, that the peoples who live in Iraq have no intention of treating one another equitably, and none expect that the others will treat them equitably. Hence none want a fair distribution of power and all regard democracy as a weapon in the settling of scores. The elections would prove to be another stage in the civil war that began with Saddam's ouster, a war by, of, and for Iraqis. The Shiites longed for relief from oppression, and for vengeance. The Kurds longed to be free of Arab rule. The Sunnis fought for their privileges as sacred rights. Hence the Shia saw elections as the possible fulfillment of their dreams, the Kurds welcomed them warily, and the Sunnis fought them as their worst nightmare.

The U.S. government dreamed that the three groups would compete peacefully, peacefully accept the results of the elections, and share power peacefully. But the Sunnis judged that they were likelier to get a bigger share of power through bullets than through ballots. It is essential to note that the Sunnis fought the elections not because they were rigged, but precisely because they were not rigged. One of the reasons why the Sunnis thought that not participating in the elections was an effective strategy, is that the U.S. government put such a high value on the unity of Iraq. For the sake of that value, the Sunni leaders reasoned, the U.S. government would end up support-ing their demands. And it seems that they were correct.

The elections gave political power to many Shia, a fair number of Kurds, and very few Sunnis. The majority of Iraqis, especially the Shiites, were unwilling to compromise any further with the Sunni in-surgents. Unsurprisingly they viewed the elections as a warrant for pursuing their civil war, tearing out the roots of the old regime with ruthlessness typical of that region. The logic of democracy would seem to encourage them to do just that. But the U.S. government was not about to stop playing sorcerer's apprentice in Iraqi politics and let nature take its bloody course. Not yet. Even before the elections, it set about setting aside the results by adding to the new Constitutional Committee and the new government a number of its favorite unelected Sunnis. A "national round table," they and their democracy experts called it.

Yet, inevitably, any Iraqi government would surely act against the core interests of one or more of the other Iraqi groups. Any such gov-ernment would surely ask the U.S. to help enforce its writ on its oppo-nents or impose its will on the rest of the country and by doing so the U.S. armed forces would have to help it win a civil war. What justifi-cation could allow the Bush team to take part in such a war? On whose side, if any, would America's own interest lie? How could one support the claim that, absent American suppression, those who felt aggrieved or cheated by the new Iraqi government would somehow terrorize Americans at home? How far would Americans be willing to stretch their commitment to fighting terrorism to cover nation build-ing? For better or worse, sooner rather than later, will the U.S. be forced to acknowledge that it is in the middle of other peoples' quar-rels, and perhaps Iraq should be on its own?

Meanwhile, after three years in which America's power had been misdirected, America's predicament vis-à-vis the world's terrorists had worsened. America would have to rethink and restart the war on terror from a position less advantageous than on September 11, 2001.

DOING IT THE HARD WAY

When in a hole, the beginning of wisdom is: stop digging. The pros-pect of terrorist violence that the U.S. government could not stop haunted the months prior to the 2004 elections. A 2005 presidential inaugural so armored that it made the spectacles of totalitarian countries look like festivals of freedom made it painfully obvious that America had not won its peace. This lack of peace should have been enough to convince anyone to look skeptically at the policies, and their premises, that had gotten us in the present hole. How have we lost sight of the path to victory, the only sure path to peace? I have chronicled why and how the U.S. government thought of myriad things other than victory. The point, however, is that victory is not the main thing in war. Victory is the only thing that makes sense of it. Let us think through the path to victory in the current war.

ABANDON PREJUDICES

Worthy as it may be, the notion that we must somehow limit the war, to reduce the number of enemies, to include as many allies as possible, to seek as much public support as possible, or to think of democracy as a *condition* of victory amounts to putting the cart before the horse.

Sometimes, democracy is the *fruit* of democrats' victories. Always, allies are available in inverse proportion to the need for them. Though the notion "you can't fight the world" makes superficial sense, the fact is that who and where we fight is not entirely up to us. Our enemies have much to say about such things. Once blood is drawn, the prospects for victory and defeat largely determine who gets allies and support and from whom. Success begets support, and shrinks the ranks of one's enemies as well as the war's scope. Though in the eyes of God might does not make right, in human eyes losing is wrong and contemptible.

In the fall of 2001, because so many assumed that the U.S. government would do whatever necessary to rid the world of terrorists, no one dared suggest publicly that the scope of U.S. operations be limited. Expecting the worst, Arab regimes cowered, friendless—until our government let them off the hook. By contrast, in 2004 the U.S. government's demonstrated incapacity to do away with its enemies—to figure out at whom it should point its many guns—led many to oppose whatever America did to defend itself. What prejudices led the U.S. government to put the cart of favor before the horse of victory? How should these prejudices be reversed?

HATE AND CONTEMPT

I have noted that the Arab world's hate and contempt for America are recent phenomena. I have dwelt at some length on the fact that Americans alone are responsible for the contempt in which they are held, and thus that Americans can do away with contempt easily enough by targeting their enemies correctly and doing away with *them* in an exemplary manner.

But what about the hate? No doubt, as Bernard Lewis writes, the Arab world's hate for America in part is a reflection of its own feelings of inferiority. These are well founded—the GDP of 300 million Arabs is less than half that of 30 million Californians. Americans can do nothing about that, nor about the Arab habit of blaming their troubles on others—other than to refrain from lending legitimacy to it.

Part of the hate is due to America's support of Israel. But the Arab world's dysfunctions do not derive in the least from the existence of Israel. No one argues that were Israel to disappear the Arabs' work habits and educational standards would improve, their culture of hate would abate, their governments' corruption would cease, and they would like Americans. Hence giving in to Arab demands regarding Israel only generates more demands, and turns hate into contempt. At least this has been the experience of U.S. administrations since that of Richard Nixon. This source of hate will ebb, though not disappear, only when the Palestinian-Israeli conflict is no longer a rallying cry in the Arab world. And that can happen only after either the Jews are pushed into the sea, or Palestinian regimes cease to live by that conflict. Hence, *pace* the counterproductive efforts of so many distinguished statesmen, the only productive way to lessen the hatred that radiates from the Palestinian-Israeli conflict is to encourage, and if need be to help, Israel win it definitively.

Americans can do more to abate the hate that comes from political contact with the Arab world. Since mid-twentieth century, regimes that ape Western ways and are somehow supported by Western powers, especially by the U.S., have worsened the Arabs' miseries. The rise of political Islam against these regimes has prompted Westerners, and especially Americans, to increase that support—and that misery. Good intentions don't count. Attempts to export democracy and women's rights add insult to injury. The way to reduce hate is to practice arms' length diplomacy—on condition that, on pain of war, Arab regimes not permit either by word, deed, or act of omission, any harm to come from their house to ours.

Holding regimes responsible for their products, we must attack them rather than those products.

CAUSES AND REGIMES

Regimes cause terror by embodying causes. I have noted that people make war to advance causes, and that the most effective way to stop them is to kill not thousands of individuals, but the few causes they serve. Of course killing causes usually involves killing those who embody them. (The Communist cause was an exception because its leaders killed it themselves.)

The tools for killing causes are well known: sword, sermon, and example. Nothing quite so deflates a cause as the sight of its promoters humiliated and killed along with anyone who stood with them, their crimes exposed, their hopes in vain. Explanation is the intellectual counterpart of physical destruction. Nazism became a dirty word for most Germans after 1945 because it had brought dire consequences on all Germans, but also because the Allies rubbed the Germans' noses in the Nazis' misdeeds. Preaching about the Nazis' evils was effective for the Western Allies also because they behaved as practical examples of the opposite. By contrast, in the East, the Soviets' Nazi-like behavior negated their preaching.

How then to kill the causes for which terrorists fight? We have already alluded to the need to put an end to the hopes of many that Israel's Jews will be driven into the sea—hopes that feed anti-Americanism far beyond "the river and the sea." That can be undone only by the physical, political, and moral destruction of the murderous kleptocracy that has ruled the Palestinian people. As in all cases in which killing a regime is essential to killing what it represents, the most effective way to do it is to empower the regime's local enemies— provided they meet the minimum conditions of neither doing nor permitting harm to ourselves, and that they proceed to expose fully our common enemies' faults. Our enemies' demise is always the prerequisite for having our words listened to, and our example heeded.

WAR ON WORDS

The causes for which terrorists fight exist substantially in thin air—literally in the media of Arab regimes. Causes, after all, consist of perceptions and interpretations. The Arab world's habit of blaming foreigners' conspiracies for its ills extends even to terrorism. Saudi regent Abdullah, for example, told his TV audience that his intelligence service was confident that terrorism is the work of Zionist agents. The *al Jazeera* television network tells the Arab world that the U.S. government masterminded September 11 to give itself a pretext for attacking the Arab world.

Even in the staid world of a quarter-century ago, the most moderate of Saudi newspapers—the English version, yet—featured cartoons that made the worst Nazi propaganda look mild. In short, the fact that millions of Arabs cheer when American blood is drawn, and that drawing it has become a pastime for thousands, is conceivable only because of the cheerleaders. These causes live and die by words. Logically, these words, these manufactured images, perceptions, interpretations, are the ultimate causes of terrorism.

In a vain attempt to dispel them in the Arab media, the U.S. government has done everything from buying advertisements to tempering high policy. The U.S. media is generally silent about how, by contrast, their Arab counterparts go out of their way to disparage America. This disparity feeds the Arabs' contempt, and ensures the continued recruitment of terrorists.

A serious war on terror would ensure that nothing broadcast or printed in the Arab world incited to terrorism. The Arab media simply reflect the will of the regimes in which they operate. The U.S. government classifies Saudi Arabia, and Qatar, home to *al Jazeera*, as friendly. Yet to sponsor deadly incitement is the greatest enmity. Regardless of what else the U.S. government does, so long as the Arab media remain as they have been since the 1970s, the supply of recruits for terror will continue. Every terrorist act will be celebrated, every terrorist killed will be a martyr to inspire others.

Making war to shut TV stations and newspapers may sound extraordinary. But what is proper in war depends on what the problem is that the war addresses. To pretend either that incitement is not key to terrorism, or that the police regimes from which it emanates are not responsible for their media, is self-deception that invites defeat. International law and common sense justify war to enforce the cessation of incitement. Any regime is capable of deciding whether or not to encourage its media to encourage killing us. We have to decide whether to suffer the consequences of incitement, or to kill those who encourage killing us.

WAR ON CHIEFS

The role of regimes in terrorism is nowhere more evident than in the relationship between terrorism's most fearsome instruments, the suicide bombers, and the inciters. Note well that no "radical" cleric, nor any member of his family, neither any "radical" politician nor any member of his family, has been known to sacrifice his life in an act of terror. The same goes for any and every family that is part of an Arab regime. No Arab journalist who celebrates suicide bombing has taken his own advice and done it.

Yet those clerics, politicians, and regime stalwarts are the *sine qua non* of suicide bombings, the ones who pay for, glorify, and arrange the sacrifices. Typically, these "effective causes" of terrorism enjoy their lives and protect their enjoyment. It follows that suicide bombings and similar acts will continue so long as their effective causes are alive, and act without fear for their lives. Factor *them* out, and few if any terrorist acts would happen.

Such prominent persons do not wear uniforms, or confront us with arms in hand. Their weapon of mass destruction is political. Their strength and safety lies in blending and confusing themselves with ordinary civilians. Their success in doing so depends in no small part on the (thus far accurate) perception on the part of ordinary civilians that being close to these chiefs carries benefits and no dangers.

War, as opposed to police action, has a rough Roman justice about it: those who stand with the enemy will suffer with him. Hence a serious war on terror that aimed to kill these "effective causes" would demand that the societies ruled by these chiefs sort themselves out. Perhaps the major reason why Iraq's Sunni population caused the U.S. so much trouble after April 2003 is that the U.S. government's admirable commitment to spare innocent civilians inadvertently created a safety zone for would-be enemies. The point here, quite simply, is that war against a regime must be fearsomely indiscriminate enough to cause even its committed members, never mind hangers-on, to run away from it.

WAR ON MONEY

Does anyone contend that the onset of Arab terrorism and the increase of disposable cash in the hands of Arab regimes circa 1970 are coincidental? Can anyone imagine terrorism were Arab regimes not awash in oil money? Conversely, can anyone imagine that Arab terrorism will cease so long as they are? The U.S. government's approach to the fact that terrorism runs in part on money from Arab regimes has been akin to old style American police work: assume that everyone is innocent until proven guilty. Hence the U.S. government's war on terrorist financing has investigated suspect Arab "charities," and has stopped the flow of a few million dollars from a dozen sources. It has not confronted the fact that the regimes themselves—entities far more vast than governments—support terrorism financially in uncountable ways. More important, the U.S. government and American elites have not begun to face the hard fact that they themselves have made it possible for Arab regimes to dispose of unearned billions.

A serious commitment against terrorism would reverse not only the direct financing that the U.S. government and the European Union provide to the Palestinian Authority, but also the indirect financing that they have given to Arab (and Iranian) regimes by granting them property rights in the oil beneath the countries they rule. This reversal would require rethinking many shibboleths of twentieth century thought. But the alternative is to suffer no end of well-financed terror.

THE PRICE OF VICTORY

Were the U.S. government to wage war as suggested above, it would produce a world as different from today's as the turn of the twenty-first century was from that of the twentieth. Since the roots of terrorism are inherent in the international system of the last century, tearing up those roots necessarily shatters that system. Managing the consequences would be the price of victory.

Prior to World War I, British and American progressives conceived a world in which all peoples would have their own state, and each state would deal with others in sovereign equality through international law. War would be *passé*, as would any people's rule over another. Already, the Best and Brightest had turned their backs on colonialism. Already, they had the embryonic notion of what was to become the League of Nations and later the United Nations. Of course, these hopes depended on the twin suppositions that all the world's peoples shared the same hopes, dreams, and values, and that the extent to which values and habits differed did not matter anyway. The expectation was that the science of peace, of international relations, would overcome the jumble of the world's unscientific values, equally true and equally false because of their inherent subjectivity.

After World War II, American statesmen spurred their European counterparts to turn their colonies into over a hundred sovereign governments headed by native progressives—the "Third World." Some fulfilled their sponsors' hopes. Many others became what historian Paul Johnson called "Caliban's kingdoms," sewers of man-made misery, corruption, and oppression. Values, it turned out, were unequal, and the differences mattered a lot. But while Third World regimes in Africa troubled the world mainly with pitiable images, Third World regimes in the Middle East began to choke the world by restricting the flow of petroleum, and to terrorize it by exporting their quarrels.

The slaughters of September 11, 2001, in America; of March 11, 2004, in Spain; the everyday carnage in Israel and elsewhere; the growing boldness of terrorist movements; their role as the double-edged swords of regimes; the increasing inability of Arab regimes to play any constructive role in the world—all lead Americans and the rest of the civilized world to the brink of thinking what they would rather not think: how can we ensure our safety and the supply of oil *despite* Arab regimes in particular and Third World regimes in general?

Were Americans (and sooner or later Europeans) really to enforce their undoubted right under international law to eliminate incitement to violence against themselves from Arab regimes, were they to make war against the "efficient causes" of terrorism and anyone who stands with them, were they to revoke their grant of property rights over oil to regimes that misuse them, they would have to make war on many states that are fellow members of the United Nations, decapitate them and enforce standards of international behavior for successor regimes. Were Saudi Arabia and the Gulf states to descend to the chaos and insecurity characteristic of Iraq today, how could the civilized world ensure its supply of oil? It would have to isolate the oil fields from the chaos as much as possible, perhaps doing so under some sort of international mandate.

To do any of this, Americans would have to abjure a century's conventional wisdom. Understandably, the U.S. government—*a fortiori*

European ones—would prefer not to. Today, rhetoric aside, Americans as well as Europeans have resigned themselves to tolerating the current level of terror.

Neither the U.S. nor anyone else has done anything serious to stop the incitement to terror, to cut off the money that fuels it, or to eliminate its organizers. But the hope that we may limit the enemy's war by limiting our own is unreasonable. Hence, Arab terrorists, not Americans, are setting the level of terror. Because terror is proving more effective than ever, no one should be surprised if more Arabs find fulfillment in it, and the level of terror rises. At some level, that increase will compel Americans to face Archidamus' question: "What will be our war?"

THE ELECTION AND THE WAR

By general agreement, The War on Terror was the chief issue in the U.S. election of 2004. But so uncomfortable were both political parties (each for their own reasons) with the meaning of victory, the kind of peace to be sought, and how to bring it about that the only meaningful question in any war, "What is to be our war?" was no part of the political debate.

Nevertheless, underneath the Democrats' charges that George W. Bush read too much into intelligence linking Iraq with terrorism, and the Republicans' charges that the Democrats would wait too long to act against a looming threat, there were differences that touched the essence of the American regime.

In my primer on war I wrote:

> War is always both the violent negation of the enemy and the violent affirmation of what one's own side is all about....So, from society's humblest soldier to its biggest pillar, war forces men to choose the causes to which they will or will not lend themselves.... one does not have to resort to treason if one does not fully espouse the aims of one's own side or dislikes its leaders. Apathy is usually quite enough to ensure that the other side will prevail. Domestic factions are usually ready to exploit the discontent that always accompany wars. Furthermore regimes are seldom as open to change, for better or worse, as they are during life and death struggles.... [B]ecause wars require the active, enthusiastic participation of large numbers of people to resolve the most important issues with which men deal, they are the ultimate form of

election. And wars offer unusually effective ways of registering one's vote.[1]

Every war, then, is an election settled less by the kinds of ballots that Americans typically cast in November than by the loves and hates, the support, the alienation and the sabotage that war brings forth from people. It shows what peoples are all about.

In 2004 the Democrats charged President Bush with invading Iraq on the basis of CIA intelligence affirming that Iraq had Weapons of Mass Destruction. The president should have known better than to start a military campaign on such thin and ultimately wrong information, they argued. He should be defeated for agreeing with the CIA. On the other hand, they also claimed that Bush should be defeated for acting contrary to the CIA's judgment that all the evidence of relationships between Iraq and the terrorists of 9/11 did not amount to "conclusive evidence" of a "collaborative relationship." Though the CIA's intelligence on terrorism was grossly inadequate, the Democrats still claimed that President Bush should have abided by its judgments. Clearly the Democrats valued the contents of intelligence only so far as these supported condemning Bush's inclusion of Iraq as a target of the war on terror.

The Democrats claimed that operations in Iraq distract us from our operations against al-Qaeda. This complaint—despite the fact that al-Qaeda no longer had a base, its contingent of soldiers had been captured, killed, or scattered to the winds, and its principal figures were out of action, *while at the same time terrorism had increased*— suggests that the Democrats were less interested in fighting terrorism than in fighting against the invasion of Iraq.

Finally, Senator Kerry and his party contended that going into Iraq had weakened America by alienating it from "the international community." Yet they knew that while some governments opposed invading Iraq, others supported doing so. They did not explain why Americans should care more for the former than for the latter. Again, the Democrats' accusation meant to deflect the electorate from the real question: why were they so *adamant* against fighting Iraq?

The party's vehemence shows that it was not merely taking sides in the details of disputes within the U.S. intelligence community. Was the fact that Ramzi Yousef's back-up identity papers as Abdul Basit

1. *Angelo M. Codevilla and Paul Seabury,* War: Ends and Means *(New York: Basic Books, 1988).*

Karim were doctored, complete with switched fingerprint cards, during Iraq's 1990 occupation of Kuwait sufficient or not to show that
Yousef was an Iraqi agent? What is the meaning of the fact that substantially the same non-Islamist terrorists ran the 1993 and 2001 attacks on the World Trade Center, and managed to put an Islamist
label on both operations? The party's base does not know and its
leaders do not care about the answers to such questions. Nor is this a
dispute, really, over policy. "Wonkmanship" is not the name of this
game. Rather, I am forced to conclude that the party's animus against
the Iraq War reflects its tendency, much increased since the 1960s, to
identify with any and all things anti-American.

In this respect, the most revealing phenomenon is the millions of
Americans who have paid to see Michael Moore's *Fahrenheit 9/11*, a
filmed cartoon ridiculing President Bush and suggesting his criminal-
ity. By no stretch of the imagination could the film be called an argument. Persuading one another through bona fide arguments is as much
at the heart of the American regime as is love of country. Hence the
important question is to what extent the American people will be persuaded to accept anti-American caricatures in lieu of arguments about
facts and policies. To the extent they do, the American regime will
become something else.

Yet the success of Michael Moore's cartoon and of the Democrats'
self-contradictory arguments concerning intelligence was possible only
because America was losing the war. Had we been winning, the Democrats' charges would have been implausible on their face, and self-
defeating.

The other side was not much more serious. The Bush team did not
try to explain why it agreed with the CIA that Iraq threatened America
with weapons of mass destruction, but disagreed with its exoneration
of Iraq regarding terrorism. No more than the Democrats did the Republicans deal with the details of the relationship between the 1993
attack on the World Trade Center and September 11. For Republicans,
too, image seems more important than facts. While Democrats often
think that their worldly social superiority dispenses them from having
to think about victory, Republicans think that loud patriotism is a
sufficient substitute for concrete plans for achieving it.

Both Democrats and Republicans, however, vie vigorously to support increasing the size and scope of "homeland security," as if that
could safeguard America. When pressed, few argue that defensive
measures have much of a defensive effect. Yet all can see that they

change the way we live. They change our regime. Still, for both parties, Homeland Security became a convenient way to avoid the question: How do you propose to win? That question is equivalent to: How do you propose to preserve our way of life?

In this war, as in all others, the regime itself is at stake. Victory itself is the most powerful argument that any regime can make for its own survival. By eschewing victory the Bush team made possible, indeed invited, caricatures of America. In the 2004 elections the American people instinctively shied away from the Democrats because they were too obviously uninterested in preserving our way of life. The voters gave the Republicans the chance to show seriousness, deadly seriousness, about winning the war. The American people, it seems, are serious about preserving their way of life. Whether any of our leaders share that seriousness, remains for them to prove. Showing seriousness, deadly seriousness, about winning the war on terror would be the most effective argument that the Bush team could make for the American regime, as well as for themselves.

Appendix A

Clashing United States government agencies have made Iraq into a workshop for the sorcerer's apprentices.

Today's Iraq, the biblical Land of Ur, interested Americans of all but our time only as history and exotica—the Marsh Arabs at the mouth of the Tigris and Euphrates, north of that, the supposed fabled location of the Garden of Eden, above that Baghdad and Mesopotamia, the land of Abraham, of Babylon, of Israel's Babylonian captivity, and of the Arabian Nights. There, in the third century BC, Xenophon's Ten Thousand Athenians fought the *anabasis* up the Euphrates valley, through the Kurds, and over to the Black Sea. After the Islamic conquest and the great Mongol invasion, the area was a sleepy part of the Ottoman Empire until Woodrow Wilson broke that up. Iraq was born of the Versailles settlement of 1919 that brought forth so many other botches.

Iraq was not a good idea in the first place. American and British Wilsonians decided to recreate something like the Babylonian empire: Sunni Mesopotamian Arabs from the Baghdad area would rule over vastly more numerous southern Shiia Arabs, and Arabophobe Kurds. Why the ruled should accept such an arrangement was never clear. But before a local Mesopotamian ruler could be found, the British made matters worse by "parachuting" in a foreign imperial client. During the War, Britain had fought the Turks in the Middle East largely through Lawrence of Arabia's alliance with the Hashemites—descendants of the Prophet and traditional rulers of the Hejaz area of

A version of this essay appeared in the American Spectator, November 2003.

southwestern Arabia, including Mecca. But the British had also allied with their rivals, the house of Saud, rulers of the east central region of Nejd which, joined to the Wahhabi sect, aspired to control the whole peninsula, especially Mecca. In their war for Arabia and Islam, the Saudis promptly showed how impotent were the post-war British to protect their clients. And so it happened that on the floor of the U.S. Senate, Henry Cabot Lodge spoke as follows:

> The following dispatch appeared recently in the newspapers: "HEDJAZ AGAINST BEDOUINS. The forces of emir Abdullah recently suffered a grave defeat, the Wahabis attacking and capturing Kurma, East of Mecca. Ibn Savond is believed to be working in harmony with the Wahabis. A squadron of the Royal Air Force was ordered recently to go to the assistance of the king." Under Article 10 [of the Treaty proposed for ratification] if King Hussein appealed to us for aid and protection *we should be obliged* to send American soldiers to Arabia...in order to protect his independence against the assaults of the Wahabis.

Lodge scorned Britain's "fair creations" in Arabia by comparing them to "the Mosquito king" that it had set up in Central America. He argued that there is no logical end to such games. The British proved him right. Having failed to protect the Hashemites in Arabia they set them up as alien rulers elsewhere—Abdullah the lesser in Palestine and Hussein the greater (and his son Faisal) in his consolation prize, Iraq. This added to the Iraqi regime's unpopularity. If America had helped Britain to defeat the Wahhabis, Iraq might have been a tad less frail with a native ruler. But the Americans who most supported the Versailles Treaty were least eager to help Britain maintain its empire. Still no one could have wiped away the problems that required Britain to use 100,000 troops to keep Iraq together in the interwar period.

From the beginning, while what one might call the right wing of American policymakers hoped to see the British empire continue but was unwilling to help it do so, the left wing pushed for the British empire to fade away, believing it would leave behind rulers even more orderly and open to fruitful relations with America. They imagined reaping the benefits of empire without bearing its burdens. And so the pattern of American policy was set for Iraq as well as for the other cripples that came forth from the wreckage of empires in the twentieth century: some Americans wanted nothing to do with them, others wanted to impose their will, while others yet thought that the locals would adopt democracy and become equal members of the world community. Few American policymakers have measured the ends they sought against the means they were willing to commit. All seemed more interested in getting discrete actions approved despite their domestic opponents. If policy is a complex of measures reasonably conceived and brought to term, there has been no policy. Instead, clashing priorities have produced results that none wanted.

Today's problems in the Persian Gulf began in 1953 with the joint British-American sponsorship of the military coup that overthrew Iran's leftist Prime Minister Mossadegh and placed power in the hands of the young Shah. Some Americans believed that Iran's Shah, plus Iraq's and Jordan's British-sponsored monarchs, would be enough to lead their region to every kind of progress while fighting Communism. Other Americans in the State Department, and even more in the CIA, were less concerned with stability and fighting Communism but more committed to fostering what they thought was progress in the region. They sought to act as the world's truest revolutionaries. In Egypt, the CIA sponsored a set of young army officers led by Colonel Nasser and allied with the Muslim Brotherhoods that overthrew the compliant but too conservative King Faruk. Americans sponsored Egyptian-type movements throughout the region because they thought that Western-sponsored kings were not nationalistic or socialistic enough. Among the fortunes these Americans advanced were those of the Baath, a national socialist movement founded in Syria in 1943 under Nazi influence.

Not surprisingly, even as the two strands of American policy fought one another with words and budgets in Washington, their proxies in the Middle East fought one another with knives and guns. After Nasser's American-aided success against Britain, France and Israel for control of the Suez Canal in 1956, the CIA-supported Baath party took power in Syria, and the Nasserite Abdul Karim Kassem took over in Iraq. Almost immediately, he wrecked the structure that Americans had built in the region. Nasser had merely received Soviet aid. But Abdul Karim Kassem, immediately after taking power in Baghdad in 1958, aided the Soviet Union by killing the American-sponsored Central Treaty Organization (CENTO), which had joined Turkey, Iraq, Iran, and Pakistan (then consisting of western and eastern regions). Iraq's membership in CENTO had made containment a geographic reality by anchoring NATO in the West to the Southeast Asian Treaty Organization (SEATO) in the East. Iraq's withdrawal left a gap that frightened those at State and CIA who cared most about anti-Communism and embarrassed those who created and supported Arab national socialism.

The latter group, however, believed that the problem had just been that the wrong revolutionaries had come to power. They would fix that. So out of their magic bag, they picked six contacts, including a twenty-two year-old Baathist thug named Saddam Hussein, and sent them to assassinate Abdul Karim Kassem in October 1959. They botched it. The CIA then set up Saddam in luxurious exile in Cairo, where he continued to be handled both through Egyptian intelligence and directly from the U.S. Embassy.

By 1963, Kassem had made enough enemies in Iraq that CIA needed only join a mixed native coup against him. Success for the Baath faction had to wait until 1968. The CIA's gunman, Saddam, contributed enough to that faction's success that he became the head of its secret police. As such, he headed the Baath's murder of some 4,000 people, described to gullible Americans as "Communists." The CIA congratulated itself on a success that seemed to show the efficacy of its subtle covert action and to justify its dealing with people like Saddam. But their assumption that the likes of Saddam would follow CIA's agenda and be subordinate to CIA's authority rather than serve themselves was hallucinogenic smoke. Disappointing Americans who fancied themselves his handlers, Saddam never exhumed CENTO. Instead, Iraq and Syria's Baathist regimes became close military and political allies of the Soviet Union. By 1970 they had isolated Iran's Shah, now America's only surrogate. Iraq had become the Shah's chief challenger.

American statesmen were of many minds about this. Some thought that Baathist Iraq posed less danger to the Shah and to the American order in the Persian Gulf than it presented opportunity to improve relations with progressive Arabs. They voiced Sunni Arab desires for the need for some substantial Arab power to exist in the region to shield fragile Saudi Arabia and the weak Gulf states against Shiite Iran. And they argued that supporting Iraq was necessary to quiet Turkish worries about the Kurds. Nevertheless these Arabists at State and CIA compromised with those who feared that the rise of pro-Soviet forces in the region would sweep away the Shah, and agreed to a plan of moderate pressure: the CIA would arm Iraq's Kurds, actualize their latent threat to the Baghdad regime, and thus force it to cease bothering Iran. By 1975 this plan to straddle Sunni and Shia, the conservative Shah and the progressive Baath, seemed to have worked to perfection. Iraq sent Khomeini off to Paris. In exchange, the Americans left the Kurds to their fate. Saddam gassed and otherwise slaughtered them by the thousands. Henry Kissinger's reaction to this, that foreign policy was not to be confused with humanitarianism, amounted to retail Machiavellianism and wholesale naiveté. Too clever statecraft reaped the worst of both worlds.

By 1978, Saddam's secret services were contributing logistics, cash, and Shiite agents to the coalition that destroyed the Shah. Although the Ayatollah Khomeini was indispensable to it, so were Soviet-line organizations. Notably, Yasser Arafat's Palestine Liberation Organization provided the bulk of the street fighters. The radio of the Islamic revolution was run by the KGB out of Soviet Baku. Indeed, overthrowing the American order in the Gulf had become so dear to progressives around the world (including those in State and CIA) that President Carter himself was persuaded to help ease the Shah out of office in the hope that his doing so would ingratiate America with Khomeini and with progressive Arabs. Hopes for this rose in 1979 when Saddam took power directly in Iraq. But his attitude toward America turned harder than ever. Then Iranian revolutionaries took American embassy personnel hostage. Paris' *Le Figaro* wrote: "Open Season On Americans!" U.S. policy was reduced to nothing more than a shamble of self-inflicted wounds.

Saddam's invasion of Iran on September 22, 1980, gave American factions more opportunities to make thing worse. Though those who had championed the Shah hated Khomeini, they continued to see Iran as something of a bulwark against Soviet and Arab expansion. Among them were Secretary of State Al Haig and NSC staffers Howard Teicher and Oliver North. They did not object to Israel selling Iran parts for its American weapons. With these munitions, Iran was able to turn back Saddam's unprovoked attack.

But when, in 1981, Israel used American-supplied aircraft and intelligence to destroy Iraq's Osirak nuclear reactor, the pro-Arab progressive elements at State and CIA, led by Assistant Secretary of State Richard Murphy, enlisted CIA deputy director Bobby Ray Inman and Defense Secretary Caspar Weinberger to tilt U.S. policy toward Saddam. To Congress they argued that Israel had recklessly fouled a sophisticated effort, already showing success, to bring Iraq out of the Soviet orbit into the "family of nations" and to make of it America's point of reliance in the oil-rich region for the post-Shah era. To prevent Israel from doing such a terrible thing again, CIA cut Israel's access to U.S. intelligence and began instead to supply Iraq with satellite photos. To muted congressional guffaws, State took Iraq off the list of states that abet terrorism.

In 1982, with the help of George Shultz, Haig's replacement as Secretary of State, this group turned President Reagan to its view. In December 1983, Reagan's special ambassador, Donald Rumsfeld, told Saddam that his defeat would be against U.S. interests. Vice President George Bush made calls to smooth the flow of U.S. weapons, credits, and intelligence to Iraq. The U.S. even tried to help Saddam build an oil pipeline along the Israeli border. And so the tide of battle turned again—not because of any Machiavellian design to exhaust two bad regimes, but because of contradictory U.S. policies.

There was to be yet another round of contradictory policies. By late 1985 the administration's cold warriors convinced Reagan that, from the perspective of what he valued most, the U.S.–Soviet conflict, the real disaster for America would be Iran's defeat by Iraq's Soviet-backed force. With renewed U.S. help, Iran advanced. At the same time, National Security Adviser Robert MacFarlane pressed Reagan to trade U.S. arms to Iran in exchange for the release of U.S. hostages in Lebanon and for the chance at reestablishing something like the old geopolitical relationship between America and Iran. But as some hostages were released, others were taken—a supply-side hostage policy. But the tilt toward Iran had not undone the pipeline of weapons flowing from the U.S. to Iraq. And after the 1986 revelation that revenues from arms sales to Iran had financed the Nicaraguan war in violation of law forced the departure of the pro-Iranians (MacFarlane, John Poindexter, and North) from the National Security Council, the tilt toward Iraq went further yet. Vice President Bush even advised Saddam to bomb with increased vigor.

When Bush became president, he felt that since America had helped Iran, it now had to compensate Saddam. Hence in 1989 Bush ignored Pentagon warnings that Iraq was building nuclear weapons. In October, Secretary of State James Baker met with his Iraqi counterpart Tariq Aziz and excluded specific concerns about Iraq's development of weapons of mass destruction. Until the very eve of Saddam's invasion of Kuwait in August 1990, the CIA continued to share intelligence with Saddam and opposed congressional efforts to limit the resources flowing to him. All told, U.S. taxpayers guaranteed five billion dollars in never-repaid loans to Saddam. When U.S. Ambassador April Glaspie met with Saddam on the eve of the 1990 invasion of Kuwait and expressed no U.S. objection to it on the supposition that he would not take "all" of Kuwait, she was faithfully implementing Bush's expressed hope to "bring him into the family of nations." That hope was not backed by means reasonably calculated to effectuate it, chiefly because it is impossible to imagine what might have accomplished such a thing.

II

Neither were the hopes that the Bush team attached to the Gulf War of 1990-1991 so calculated. A half-million American troops, and a battle won so spectacularly that, as a consequence, America could do whatever it wished, did not make up for a vision that was both unrealistic and self-contradictory. Bush wanted Saddam defeated, humbled, and possibly even removed from power. But, following State and CIA, he also wanted Iraq to remain a unified nation under control of the Baath party. The problem was that thoroughly defeating Saddam would also deprive the Baath party of power, and without Baath power (there was no other) the Iraqi empire's components would go their own unpredictable ways. And so, after a military campaign that consisted of killing untold thousands of Iraqis who did not matter while sparing the few who did, the Bush team faced the choice it should have faced before making war: to accept either the uncertain costs of undoing the Iraqi regime, or the certain problems of merely reducing its military force. Since State and CIA had soured only on Saddam, without questioning their commitment to the regime, to Iraq itself, or even to the cavalier way in which they related ends and means, and since Bush accepted uncritically their judgment as well as the priorities of Saudis, Turks, Jordanians, et al. in favor of Sunni power, he saved Saddam and called it "victory."

Victory gives the winner his version of peace, turns the page, and lets him go on to other matters. But Saddam did not treat America as if it had won. The Gulf War had made Iraq a continuing test of America's competence in the world. Saddam did not make that test easy for America's leaders. To neighboring states and peoples he presented the fact that he had fought and survived a mighty onslaught as proof of his potency, and of his leadership in a common cause: opposition to America—foreign, envied, apparently mighty, but ultimately impotent. American elites in the 1990s for once were united—in missing the magnitude of Saddam Hussein's political achievement. Thanks to their forbearance, this ex-CIA agent, this atheist, this bloody persecutor of Muslims, this tyrant, glutton of the finest Western food, drink, and whores that billions can buy, managed to convince millions of poor, hungry, powerless, devout people that he represented their fondest hopes, that America stood between them and those hopes, that America was beatable, and that they should war against America.

This politics, not any military power, was Saddam's weapon of mass destruction—all the more effective because America demonstrated that what it was willing to do would have no consequences for the things that the Iraqi regime held dearest. Saddam's ends could be achieved by coercive diplomacy; America's ends were achievable only by war— and perhaps not even by war. Indispensable to Saddam's success was the U.S. government's ignorance of his mind, due in part to the CIA's habit of relying on sources controlled by Iraqi intelligence. A decade after the Gulf War, never mind after the 2003 war we still speculate, but do not know, what he thought he was doing.

Two Bushes and one Clinton spent the decade after the Gulf War trying to bring Israelis and Arabs together, protect Saudi Arabia, and sanction Iraq economically lest it produce certain weapons. Saddam turned all these efforts to his credit and America's detriment, while at the same time fostering acts of terror. In Palestine, his money, propaganda, and henchmen made sure that no local Arab could afford to be less demanding of Israel or less damning of America than he. Quickly, he made the Saudis realize that relying on Americans for protection against another Arab was a deadly self-indictment. At this writing we do not know how thoroughly Iraqi secret services backed up Iraqi foreign policy of fostering Islamic resentment amongst Saudis. But appeasing Saddam—trying to prove in countless ways how truly Arab, meaning by now anti-American, the royal family really was—became a political necessity that overshadowed Saudi relations with America. Saddam used economic sanctions to strengthen his grip on his people, by shifting privations to peoples who opposed him while giving his supporters even greater relative advantages. Because the sanctions centralized Iraq's foreign trade, it let Saddam impose on those who dealt with him kickbacks that enriched them and him at the expense of the Iraqi people.

Textbooks teach that because economic resources are fungible, those who are subject to sanctions (other than total blockades on small countries) are forced only to pay higher prices for whatever they want. But neither Bushes nor Clinton were much on reading. Secretary of State Colin Powell even proposed "smart sanctions"—as conceivable as sharp balloons. By the late 1990s, Saddam was more important than he had been before the Gulf War.

Hundreds of years from now, textbooks will still cite U.S. Iraq policy to define divorce between ends and means. All means of coercion—diplomacy, economic pressure, subversion, and military action itself—are effective to the extent that the plan of which they are part exerts force upon the target greater than the sacrifices demanded of it. In the decade after the Gulf War, Bushes and Clinton had hopes about Iraq, and discrete actions. But there were no coherent, success-oriented plans. How could there have been any? On one hand they wanted the Baathist regime to remain. On the other, they wanted Iraq to change the role it was playing—successfully—in world politics. And their means were half-measures advertised as such.

U.S. diplomacy, consisting of demands that Iraq grant more access to UN weapons inspectors, resembled a Kabuki show. Iraqis would delay and complicate. Americans said darkly that all means of enforcement were under consideration. But the end of the Gulf War had made plain to Saddam the internal contradictions of American policy and the limits they imposed. And so the inspection ritual would limp forward, with economic sanctions as the only American hammer. As more time passed, however, these became more trouble for America than for Saddam. The subversion consisted on the one hand of helping disaffected Kurds, but not enough to give them a chance to establish independence, never mind threatening the regime. When, in 1996, Saddam's army invaded the Kurdish enclave, America advertised its impotence by sending five cruise missiles against air defense sites hundreds of miles away. On the other hand, subversion consisted of placing hopes and money on the CIA's favorite Baathist henchmen, who were really working for Saddam. There was an independent set of Iraqi opponents of the regime, the Iraqi National Congress, supported by the U.S. Congress. But State and CIA conducted covert actions against it.

One of many examples of U.S. military action should suffice to show that it was the clearest proof of fecklessness. In 1993, after discovering an Iraqi plot to kill former President Bush, President Clinton sent some twenty-three cruise missiles to destroy the headquarters of Iraq's intelligence service—at night, killing mostly cleaning women. Clinton intended "to send a message to those who engage in state-sponsored terrorism, to deter further violence against our people...our intent was to target Iraq's capacity to support violence against the United States and other nations and to deter Saddam Hussein from supporting such outlawed behavior in the future." Thus did the chasm between words and reality send the real message: America would not threaten Saddam's core interests. With his liability so limited, he could safely spread hate and contempt of America.

Laurie Mylroie, who was once Clinton's adviser on Iraq, describes Iraq's complicity in anti-American terrorism.[1] Such descriptions are necessarily incomplete and suggestive because terrorism, like all forms of indirect warfare, depends for its success on hiding the state's role as much as possible. While there is room to dispute Iraq's responsibility for any given act of international terror, no one denies that dealing death was Saddam Hussein's indispensable tool in international as in domestic relations, nor that Iraqi intelligence ran camps for training foreign Arab terrorists, nor that Saddam publicly supported the PLO and other longtime allies in the anti-Western cause. The point here is that surely the most effective aid that he received in concealing his hand in this business came from disputes amongst Americans about what ought to be done about Iraq.

September 11 inflamed those disputes to the point of allowing the dispute itself to overshadow America's interest, never mind that of the Iraqi people. Nothing that happened on September 11 had changed the Bush team's primary objective in the Middle East—maintaining the status quo—or its evaluation of what the status quo required, namely, the good graces of Saudi Arabia and Egypt. That meant not touching Iraq, for that would suggest that Bush was somehow dissatisfied with their regimes as well. Indeed, Secretary of State Powell convinced him that the clever way to obtain popular support for regime change was to pretend that the objective was something else: disarming Iraq of Weapons of Mass Destruction. Contradictory premises mixed with the tangled web of dissimulation to produce a mess.

That Saddam Hussein possessed or was trying to possess such weapons was conventional wisdom. That is why the emphasis seemed clever. For example, Senator John Kerry, palimpsest of the Democratic Left, was saying, as late as January, 2003: "Without question, we need to disarm Saddam Hussein. He is a brutal, murderous dictator, leading an oppressive regime...He presents a particularly grievous threat

---

1. Ms. Mylroie is the author of two books on Saddam Hussein. One in particular, Study of Revenge, argues that Hussein was behind the 1993 attack on the World Trade Center. (Washington D.C.: American Institute, 2000).

because he is so consistently prone to miscalculation...And now he is miscalculating America's response to continued deceit and his consistent grasp for weapons of mass destruction...So the threat of Saddam Hussein with weapons of mass destruction is real." By the same token, President Clinton had often talked about using force to disarm Saddam, e.g. in February 1998: "One way or the other, we are determined to deny Iraq the capacity to develop weapons of mass destruction and the missiles to deliver them. That is our bottom line." "If Saddam rejects peace and we have to use force, our purpose is clear. We want to seriously diminish the threat posed by Iraq's weapons of mass destruction program."

Bush thought that merely matching the expressed views of the factions whose support he was seeking would let him make war and get "regime change." This proved too clever by half. Whereas in the summer of 2002, polls had been running heavily in favor of overthrowing Saddam, by January 2003 opposition to attacking Iraq, and to President Bush, had risen sharply. What would the actual purpose of U.S. military operations be? What would replace Saddam? One group in the Pentagon wanted to arm Iraqi exiles and Kurds, recognize them as a provisional government, and run a military operation to put them in power. At the other end of the spectrum, State and CIA having long argued that weapons were the problem and not the regime, were less concerned with eliminating America's enemies. Because they wanted to change Baathist Iraq as little as possible, they wanted no anti-regime locals in the fight at all. Afterward, they wanted to pick and choose among Saddam's entourage while making sure to suppress any separatist tendencies among southern Shiites and northern Kurds. This required an extensive, long-term U.S. occupation force.

President Bush, typically, chose both and added idealism for good measure. True democracy would require elections not prejudiced by the power of Iraqi political personages chosen by— well, by fights between State, CIA, and Pentagon. Despite freedom and impartiality, the occupation and elections would have to guarantee the territorial integrity of the country, prohibit religious fundamentalism, establish the rights of women, etc. How, no one could explain.

Failure to focus on killing America's enemies, as well as on the desire of most Iraqis to be rid of the kind of American expertise that foisted Saddam on them in the first place, is precisely the result of the dysfunctional interplay of overblown personalities and domestic agendas that passes for foreign policy in today's Washington.

Appendix B

HERESY AND US*

When certain deviations from religious orthodoxy mate with political power, they shake the world.

American elites have perceived only hazily that modern terrorism has something to do with the Wahhabi sect of the Arabian Peninsula. But they lump that sect with "radical" or "fundamentalist" Islam, and throw up their hands over whether terrorism is a natural consequence of Muslim fervor or not. In fact, anti-Western terrorism results from a war within Islam that is more serious for Muslims than for the rest of us, because the Wahhabis' *ideas* imply irreconcilable enmity against other Muslims first, and then against others. Western elites, religiously challenged as they are, don't understand the mixture of threat and temptation that the Wahhabis pose to the Muslim world because they do not know how analogous Christian heresies have roiled Western civilization.[1]

Between the eleventh and the seventeenth centuries, Europe suffered arguably more from heresies than from plagues. The intellectual and moral features of these heresies, as well as the pattern of their relationship with political power, are also at the heart of the pseudo religions of Nazism and Marxism that cost perhaps a hundred

* *A version of this essay appeared in the* American Spectator, *May 2004.*
1. *This article refers to three books. Dore Gold's* Hatred's Kingdom *(Regnery, 2003) which describes Wahhabism's doctrine and early history; Stephen Schwartz's* Intellectuals and Assassins *(Anthem, 2002) deals with the threat that Wahhabism poses to Muslim regimes; Norman Cohn's* Pursuit of the Millennium *(Harper, 1963) is an excellent history of medieval Christian heresies.*

million lives in the twentieth century. In Islam as well, heresy has
arisen out of moral outrage and matured into murderous political enterprises. The history of Christian and Muslim heresies teaches the
combination of sword and sermon that is necessary to defeat them.

DANGEROUS DIFFERENCES

In the debates surrounding the great religions, charges and counter-
charges of heresy are motivated as often by secular motives as by
religious differences. However, violence tends to follow only when these
religious differences become the basis of political quarrels. The wars
in the sixteenth and seventeenth centuries between what came to be
known as Catholics and Protestants, were ostensibly over theological
points that had coexisted peaceably until they were taken up by rivals
for power. The wars between what became known as Sunni and Shia
Muslims in the eighteenth century were strictly about power. The theological differences came later. Some religious differences however, necessarily imply political violence. These are the ones that concern us.

Some ideas are necessarily political, and necessarily matrices of
mass murder. Hence, statements such as Thomas Jefferson's that
whether my neighbor believes that there is one God, many gods, or no
god at all neither picks my pocket nor breaks my leg, are applicable
only to Jefferson's peculiar circumstances. If one's neighbor were a
Thuggee, an adept of the Hindu sect that worships *Kali*, the goddess of
death, by killing as many people as possible, one might work for his
conversion to Unitarianism. Even those Americans most virulent
against the Ten Commandments would be compelled to guard their
pockets, legs, and more from neighbors whose commandments obli-
gated them to reverse the Ten Commandments into "Thou shall kill,
steal, swear falsely, take thy neighbor's wife, etc."

Murderous heresies arise as revolutionary movements. They take
one or more of the faith's central tenets and twist it into a warrant for
overthrowing the norms and practices first of the ordinary faithful,
then of mankind. This kind of heresy sets itself apart by the fact that
the heretics entitle themselves with the right to do whatever they want.
The premise of the University of Chicago's 1988 "Fundamentalism"
project, that there is danger in the tendency of many people around
the world to adhere to the fundamentals of their faiths, does not apply.
What drives "fundamentalists," is the tendency to affirm orthodoxy. Fundamentalism binds the fundamentalist. By contrast, the heretics we

are concerned with slip the bonds of orthodoxy and endow themselves with boundless, revolutionary discretion. For them, indulging their wrath, or indeed any of their passions, is the path to holiness.

Such heresies tend to strike Faustian bargains with rulers or would-be rulers. By these bargains, the politicians (who are as likely to use the heresy only as a tool as to believe in it) gain the heretics' support, the claim to absolute moral legitimacy vis-à-vis their other followers, plus leverage against their neighbors—all in exchange for providing the heresy a base for war with the rest of the world. Sooner or later however, the heresy makes more enemies than the host regime can handle, and the war ends with the destruction of both the heresy and the regime.

THE WESTERN EXPERIENCE

"Be ye perfect, as my father in heaven is perfect." "Blessed are the poor in spirit, for theirs is the kingdom of heaven." Ye are not of this world." "[The early Christians] had all things in common." Teachings such as these, as well as the struggle between good and evil, are part of the bedrock of Christianity. The Book of Daniel is a legitimate part of the Old Testament, and the Book of Revelation a legitimate part of the New. Yet all these have been points of departure for horrid heresies. Why? The poverty of some is always a ready pretext for indicting others. Always it is possible for one to claim that his alienation from the world, his enmity to it, is the authoritative sign of a divine call to a death struggle to transform earth into heaven. And in fact, the Western world never lacks people who, in the name of God, point to the imperfections of others as warrant for their own claims to perfection, power, privilege, and the undoing of their enemies.

The movements had names such as Cathars, Free Spirits, Bogomils, Albigensians, Anabaptists, Ranters, Joachites. They arose in varied circumstances. But their ideas and practices followed a pattern: Denunciation of obvious inequities, proclamation of a unique divine message that absolute purity and purification would bring absolute remedy, establishment of a totalitarian regime within the movement. Then the movement's alliance with some regime, or its capture of power somewhere, led to terror against internal dissent, war with outsiders, and eventually the destruction of the movement.

Here is a brief sampler. In the eleventh century, after Pope Gregory VII fought worldliness in the Church, and Pope Urban II proclaimed the Crusade to conquer the Holy Land, countless self-appointed *Propheta* preached a gospel of redemption: The poor, because of their purity, were to take the lead in the destruction of God's enemies. Those who followed these calls set about destroying Jews in Europe as well as bishops and clergy who got in their way, before streaming eastward to fall upon eastern Christians. Only a small minority ever got to fight the Muslims. This was not lost on nobles, some of whom harnessed this frenzy, and one of whom made himself its king, living in luxury and feared by all.

The subsequent would-be Crusaders, fewer and fewer of whom expended less and less effort actually to get to the Holy Land, slaughtered Europe's rich because they were rich, expecting thereafter to live in plenty. In 1251 an eloquent Hungarian preached a crusade exclusively of the pure and poor. He surrounded himself with an armed guard, lived in luxury, and wreaked destruction on Northern French and German towns—the clergy, the rich, the Jews. Other *Propheta* preached the same gospel unconnected to the Crusades, and followed the same pattern: having purified themselves by their opposition to the impure, they would then partake freely of their spoils. The leader would be revered, even to the extent that his disciples would drink his bathwater.

The popular side of these movements was summed up in a German book at the beginning of the sixteenth century. God had sent a message to a corrupt world: only the elect would escape his harsh judgment, on condition that they purify the earth. The Jews, the rich, the clergy, must be slaughtered for their sins. "Only the [former] victims will be spared." There would be "one shepherd, one sheepfold, one faith." But this ends up not being Christianity at all, because the god is the Germanic Thor. Not only is this book and the behavior of its followers reminiscent of Nazis. Nazism's chief ideologist, Alfred Rosenberg, devoted a chapter of his *Myth of the Twentieth Century* to it. Nazi historians celebrated the kinship. Hitler almost certainly never read the book, which makes his own adherence to its arguments all the more impressive.

The pattern repeated itself on more sophisticated levels. The flagellant movement involved *Propheta* who led masses of people on processions in which they would purify themselves and the world by whipping their bodies. But of course, once pure, most of these flagellants would start purifying the world by murdering the usual suspects—Jews, clergy, the rich—while themselves enjoying the spoils. Their leaders became the terrorist chieftains of their day. "Everything is pure to the pure," became the motto.

At a higher level yet, the movement was characterized by the Free Spirits—educated people who believed that two principles vied for control of the world, that by their own efforts or intellectual insight, and that their oneness in substance with God combined with the fact that most people did not understand that oneness, made them incapable of sin. To prove that they had really purified themselves, they must do what is forbidden to the run of mankind. Hence for example, their promiscuity was grim business. Such thoughts filtered down to the masses through clergy and nobles who were willing to use them to cement a following in revolutionary situations. Typically the major slaughters associated with events such as the Parisian Jacquerie of 1358, the Flanders revolt of 1323, and the English peasants' revolt of 1381 involved one kind or another of free spirits. The 1208-1229 war between the southern French nobility and much of the rest of Christendom was about little else.

While the bloodthirsty preaching of Thomas Muntzer did not bring about the German Peasants' war of 1525 all by itself, Muntzer was its only leader. The core of his "party" were intellectuals like himself. "Now at them, at them, and at them!" Muntzer urged the peasants as they happily ravaged the land. Muntzer's heresy united orthodox Christians of all persuasions against him. He and his army of 3000 were crushed. But Karl Marx, Friedrich Engels, and Marxist textbooks around the world celebrated him even centuries later. The only book Benito Mussolini ever wrote praised the burnt heretic, Jan Hus, as a precursor of secular, nationalistic socialism. Hus was more than that, but Mussolini was only interested in his revolutionary element.

In 1533-1535 the Anabaptist sect took over the German city of Munster. Its leaders, including a Dutchman, Jan Bockelson, proclaimed the usual message of purification, knowledge that this was the last of three ages that would end in the destruction of a sinful world, with the exception of the elect. They filled the city with people drawn by the twin promises of loot and salvation, cleansed the churches of books and ornaments, despoiled the rich, enforced polygamy on the women who could not flee, established a reign of terror, and made war on the outside—only to be crushed by it.

Only when the princes of the affected areas realized that they too would be involved in the heresy's endless wars did they decide to become defenders of orthodoxy and join to destroy the heresy's host regime. That destruction however had to be accomplished in a manner that discredited regime and ideas. This always involved humiliating as well as killing the leaders. The princes who captured Munster's Bockelson exhibited him as a dancing bear, tortured him, and hauled his body in a cage to the top of the cathedral. The cage remained there for centuries. Just as important, orthodox preachers explained the heretics' errors far and wide. Thus the destruction of the Albigensians was due as much to St. Dominic's preaching as to the armies of Christendom. Finally, for such preaching to be effective, it had to be accompanied by efforts on the part of church and nobility to address some of the legitimate accusations made against them. Hence the end of the age of religious heresies in Europe came when the Reformed churches—followed by the Catholic Church after the Council of Trent, emphasized austere living.

Norman Cohn concludes: "The ideologies of Communism and Nazism, dissimilar though they are in many respects, are both heavily indebted to that very ancient body of belief which constituted the popular apocalyptic lore of Europe....This did not disappear with the fall of the New Jerusalem at Munster....what had once been demanded by the will of God was now demanded by the purposes of history. But the demand itself remained unchanged: to purify the world by destroying the agents of corruption. What is more, the agents of corruption were still identified with the social groups which had been so regarded already in the Middle Ages...Such was the tradition of apocalyptic fanaticism which—secularized and revivified—was inherited by Lenin and Hitler.

THE ISLAMIC EXPERIENCE

"There is no god but God." This is the core of Islam, and its glory. Affirming the oneness of God has been Islam's gift to regions of the world where it displaced polytheism, while raising its converts to a higher plane of life. The Koran is adamant about monotheism: "Kill those who ascribe partners to God, wheresoever you find them." But affirming monotheism is also the core of the Wahhabi heresy.

Ibn Abdul Wahhab born around 1700 in a remote village in a remote region of Arabia, was early impressed with the central tenet of Islam, as well as with the deviations from it both of the Ottoman Empire's sophisticates, who, in his view, had adopted Christian ways, and of village simpletons who idolized shrines and trees. He wrote that Islam is: "above all a rejection of all gods except God, a refusal to allow others to share in that worship that is due to God alone (*Shirk*). *Shirk* is evil, no matter what the object, whether it be king or prophet or saint or tree or tomb." Wahhab destroyed the tombs of the Prophet's earliest disciples because they had become the object of veneration. Wahhab declared ancient Islamic scholars "unbelievers" and "polytheists," not only Shia Islam, but also the Sufi spiritual tradition and Islamic law, and burned their books. His quest for purity alienated his village's authorities, including his father.

One of the region's tribes, however, found him useful against the others, and gave him shelter. That was the house of Saud. Wahhab's version of Islam became the official creed wherever the Saudi family ruled. The bargain was sealed by Wahhab's marriage to Ibn Saud's daughter. Dore Gold writes that "tribal raiding could now be carried on as a religious cause. What had once been taken as tribal booty was now demanded as *Zakat* (the charitable payments required as one of the five pillars of Islam). Significantly, Wahhab legitimized Jihad against fellow Muslims for the first time." Killing those who would not accept his version of the faith (and Saudi sovereignty), as well as taking their possessions, was now a religious obligation.

Wahhab's teaching about Jews and Christians was of the same sort. Rather than respecting them as "people of the book," as misguided followers of the One God, Wahhab called them polytheists, "devil worshipers," and sorcerers, to whom the Biblical punishment of death is applicable. Hence Wahhabism assured its combatants of the manifold blessings of Muslim martyrdom and set them to war with the entire world.

By the time Wahhab died in 1791, the Saudi/Wahhabi influence had reached the Persian Gulf. Oman and Bahrain paid tribute. By 1803 Mecca itself fell to the Wahhabis, and parts of present day Iraq a few years later. The Wahhabis' warfare involved exterminating men, women, and children. The Wahhabis inflicted a historic massacre on the Iraqi city of Kerbala. Between 1811 and 1818, however, the Ottoman Empire struck back. To Istanbul, Wahhabism and the Saudi state were identical. The Ottomans, using French military equipment and greater manpower defeated the Saudis, leveled their capital, and took the Saudi leader, Abdullah, prisoner. They humiliated him, tortured him, beheaded him, and threw his body to the dogs.

The Ottomans however failed to discredit Wahhabism doctrinally. They did not teach orthodox Islam and insist that it be taught, much less did they live it. Nor were they vigilant when the heirs of Abdullah came back to reestablish the family's power base, which of course included Wahhabism. So it was that by the 1830s Wahhabi *Jihads* were taking place even in the Indian sub-continent. By 1912 Wahhabi cells existed as far as central Asia.

The contemporary Saudi state arose from Ibn Saud's alliance with the British against the Ottoman Empire during World War I. Ignorantly, the British believed the Saudis' protestations that their hatred of the Ottomans for their Islamic impurity did not also imply enmity to Christians. Besides, thought the British, what power could these or any Arabs wield against the mighty British Empire? The British began to find out when, after the War, their weakened will watched impotently as the Saudi/Wahhabi combination swept Britain's other Arab clients, the Hashemites, from the Arabian Peninsula. Unlike the Ottomans, the British were unable to mount even the military dimension much less the political and religious dimensions of the offense needed to defeat a heresy such as Wahhabism.

The American policymakers who took over stewardship of the region from Britain never understood the problem. The Intelligence office of the oil company ARAMCO is said to have explained Wahhabism as the Muslim equivalent of Unitarianism. Insofar as the U.S. government understood Wahhabism, it expected the power of the Saudi family to restrain its extremism. That the Saudi family could mount a theological campaign against Wahhabism is as inconceivable as its adoption of the Spartan lifestyle that Wahhabism preaches. Without the Wahhabis, the Saudi royal family would not be lords of the peninsula, or of anything. No orthodox Muslim would accredit their lifestyles as Muslim. But somehow the otherwise ultra strict Wahhabis do. The notion that the Saudi royals could earn non-Islamic legitimacy as democratizers is fantasy. The Saudis are bonded to the tiger they ride.

Whereas in London, in France, or in America's streets and prisons, Wahhabism is an irritant, in the Islamic world it is one of the two main challenges to ordinary life (the other being the corrupt, Western-imported, secular, nationalistic socialism, against which Wahhabism rages.) From the northern edges of Africa, to Bosnia, Pakistan, Indonesia and the eastern islands of the Philippines, estimates of the percentage of the new mosques and schools financed to Wahhabi specifications vary from a third to three-fourths. No other form of Islam enjoys anything like the flood of money that comes from Saudi sources, and almost none have developed a violent cadre to back up its demands. For any Sunni Muslim, life has to look richer, safer, more purposeful, on the Wahhabi side. Stephen Schwartz writes: " Bin Laden is a Wahhabi. So are the suicide bombers in Israel. So are his Egyptian allies who exulted as they stabbed foreign tourists to death at Luxor not many years ago, bathing in blood up to their elbows and emitting blasphemous cries of ecstasy. So are the Algerian Islamists terrorists whose contribution to the purification of the world consisted of murdering people for such sins as running a movie projector or reading secular newspapers. So are the Taliban-style guerrillas in Kashmir who murder Hindus. The Iranians are not Wahhabis, which partially explains their slow movement toward moderation and normality."

WHOSE FIGHT? WHOSE FAITH?

Any faith's heresies are first of all problems for that faith, and only then for others. Co-religionists are the heresy's first targets, and the only ones with the combination of knowledge, incentive, and legitimacy to deal with it. Only Christians can understand enough about what is and is not proper to Christianity. If they fail to define what it means, the heretics will do the defining. The same goes for Muslims. It would have been impossible for the Ottoman Empire—at the height of its power in the early sixteenth century—to play a role in defeating the Anabaptist heresies that roiled Germany. By the same token, today the notion that secularist Americans might teach Muslims right and wrong about Islam is silly and utterly irresponsible.

Nevertheless, just as the Muslim world was not entirely irrelevant to the struggles of medieval Christianity, today's West willy-nilly has some influence on intramural Muslim struggles. Medieval Muslims, after all, gave orthodox Christianity a big, indirect hand by defeating the Crusades. If medieval Muslims had let the Christian heretics succeed against them, the heretics would have used their new-found prestige perhaps to defeat their main enemy in Europe. In our time, however, Judeo Christian civilization has not given that kind of indirect support to Muslim orthodoxy against the Wahhabi heresy. On the contrary: rather than giving the Wahhabis defeats, the West has given them victories that have strengthened the movement's hand immeasurably in its decisive intramural battles. In sum, the West has let the Wahhabis set up bases outside the reach of their Muslim enemies, has let its terrorism run rampant, and has safeguarded its main base, Saudi Arabia, from the natural consequences of its rulers' Faustian bargain.

More than shielding the Saudi regime, Americans enabled it to spread Wahhabism to a heretofore unimaginable extent when, in 1973, they agreed to give Saudi Arabia the power to set the world price of oil. The Saudi royals' money, we must not forget, is theirs only because America's best and brightest think it proper to assign property rights to persons who contribute nothing to the product. So in the end, the Wahhabi heresy intimidates Muslims around the world only because it is fueled by U.S. money directed to them through Saudi Arabia. The validity of American judgment underlying this policy is not self-evident.

The Wahhabis attract other Muslims as well as threaten them. Successful anti-Western terrorism has been perhaps the main instrument of that attraction. Weak governments cannot possibly take sides against a sect whose exploits excite their peoples' atavistic pride more than they do. Indeed, in our time, some orthodox Muslims have forgotten how deep the Wahhabis' hatred for them is and rather take pride every time a Wahhabi inspired terrorist act humiliates and cows the West on behalf of Muslim causes. When Westerners react to Wahhabi terrorist acts by indicting ordinary, traditional Muslim practices—veils, sexual customs—they make it even more difficult for orthodox Muslims to go after the heretics.

Also, the Wahhabis attract all rulers of Muslim peoples who live un-Muslim lives because, just as medieval Christian heretics supported their hierarchs' outrageous lives, they buy secular support by selling religious legitimacy. Hence Wahhabi support for outrageously corrupt Saudi elites. The limit case is that of Iraq's Saddam Hussein—an atheist, theologically speaking the personification of everything Wahhabism lives to destroy—who persecuted Islam to the limit of his power, but who nevertheless managed to make himself the leader of an Islam increasingly redefined as violent anti-Westernism. The Wahhabis held their nose and supported him too.

Wahhabism can be defeated only after the destruction of Saudi rule—preferably by other Muslims. The Saudis' Wahhabism makes them the natural enemies of all the world's orthodox Muslims, especially Shiites. Iran, the great power of Shia Islam, is Wahhabism's main enemy. America's best and brightest, however, have supported the Saudis against the Iranians because they understand only the categories of "moderate vs. fundamentalist" and see neither Shiites nor Wahhabis, neither orthodoxy nor heresy.

In short, the heretics are winning their war with Islamic orthodoxy. Islam is being redefined—indeed hijacked. That is due in part to the support the heretics enjoy, none the less powerful for being indirect, from the West in general and America in particular. The point of all this is that even the best and brightest of officials need to know what they are about and, knowing that, to do no harm.

About the Author

A U.S. citizen since 1962, Angelo Codevilla married Ann Blaesser in 1966. They raised five children, and now live in Wyoming's Dunoir Valley, California's Sierra wine country, and on Boston's Bay State Road. Since 1995 Codevilla has been a professor of international relations at Boston University. Between 1985 and 1995 he was a senior research fellow of the Hoover Institution, Stanford University.

Between 1977 and 1985 Codevilla served as a senior staff member of the U.S. Senate Select Committee on Intelligence, supervising the U.S. intelligence budget. He was instrumental in developing space based missile defense. During the same period he served on Ronald Reagan's Presidential Transition teams for the State Department and the CIA. Prior to that, he served as a U.S. Foreign Service Officer and as a U.S. naval officer.

Codevilla's books range from comparative government to political thought, to the theory and practice of conflict, especially intelligence and missile warfare. They include *Informing Statecraft: Intelligence for a New Century*, *War: Ends and Means* (with Paul Seabury), *The Character of Nations*, and a translation of *Machiavelli's Prince*. He is the principal author of the seven volume series *Intelligence Requirements for the 1980s*. He is at work on the intellectual history of U.S. foreign relations.

Angelo Codevilla's articles and op eds have appeared in *Commentary, Foreign Affairs, The National Interest, New York Times* and *Wall Street Journal*, as well as in comparable publications abroad.